GW00336208

WINE
BUYER'S
GUIDE

DORLING KINDERSLEY
London•New York•Stuttgart•Moscow

A DORLING KINDERSLEY BOOK

First published in Great Britain in 1995
by Dorling Kindersley Limited,
9 Henrietta Street, London WC2E 8PS
Copyright © 1995 Dorling Kindersley Ltd, London
Text and illustration copyright © 1995,
WINE Magazine,

A CIP catalogue record for this book is available
from the British Library.

ISBN 0 7513 0246 5

Printed and bound in Great Britain
by BPC Hazell Books Ltd

CONTENTS

INTRODUCTION

From the 1982 Château Petrus which sells at auction for over £1000 per bottle, to the murky contents of the European wine lake, the word 'wine' covers a multitude of sins - and delights. Today, one has only to glance at the shelves of any British off licence or supermarket to feel at once fascinated and confused by the extraordinary array of bottles and labels on offer.

With each merchant setting out selections of 500 or more wines, from countries as diverse as Argentina and Zimbabwe, made from grape varieties ranging from the Spanish Airèn to the Austrian Zweigelt, it was perhaps inevitable that, sooner or later, someone would devise a method of sorting the vinous wheat from the chaff.

A GUIDE TO VALUE

That method is *WINE* Magazine's International WINE Challenge, the annual competition which sets thousands of wines of every style and provenance before several hundred of the world's most finely tuned palates. In the following pages, listed by nationality and price, are the 1700 medal winners from the 1995 International WINE Challenge. Whether you are looking for the cheapest drinkable Australian Chardonnay on the market, a great bottle of claret to lay down, or the best value in Rioja, you will find a selection of wines, complete with tasting notes and guidance on where they can be bought and for what price.

THE CHALLENGE

The *WINE* Magazine International WINE Challenge began life remarkably humbly in 1984 as the basis of a feature which sought to discover how well English winemakers were doing when compared with, their counterparts in other countries. When setting up that tasting, *WINE*'s editor Robert Joseph and associate editor Charles Metcalfe had no idea that they were laying the foundations for what would become the world's biggest, most comprehensive and, increasingly, most respected wine competition.

That first year, there were just 38 wines and 20 tasters; a little over a decade later, the figures were 6,500 and 560 respectively. So, why has this competition grown so successful so quickly? There are several answers, but the simplest is probably the most valid; the International WINE Challenge filled a growing need for information and informed opinion about wine.

A taster deep in thought

By the mid 1980s, London had developed from being the centre of the fine wine world - through its auction houses and merchants - to the centre of the world of wine *per se*.

From the remotest corner of Tasmania to the heart of Tuscany, wine producers have acknowledged that, however successful they might be in their own markets, to earn international prestige

All wines are tasted blind before being rigorously tested

for their products they had to convince the most sophisticated palates in the world in the shape of the British wine trade and critics.

--------- THE LEVEL PLAYING FIELD ---------

As supermarkets took wine increasingly seriously, and traditional merchants fought off competition from mail order clubs, wine warehouses and high street chains, and as New World Cabernets and Chardonnays nudged Bordeaux and Burgundies from the shelves, it was generally recognised that there was a need for a level playing field on which wines and merchants could compete, irrespective of marketing hype and historic reputation.

From the outset, the International WINE Challenge has not been run in the same way as other competitions. First and most crucially, it differs in having as judges for the most part professional wine buyers rather than the winemakers who taste at competitions else-

7

where. These highly trained men and women - including no fewer than 35 Masters of Wine, holders of the most sought-after vinous qualification in the world - judge wines as severely as they would in their own tasting rooms. So, of 6500 entries this year, 3000 received no award, 1900 were given a Commendation and a mere 1600 won medals.

The entries themselves differ too in being mostly submitted by distributors and retailers rather than by the producers. This helps to explain how wines come to be tasted from prestigious French estates which never deign to enter competitions themselves. This is the only contest in which Classed Growth clarets compete in the same arena as bag-in-box wines from Eastern Europe and big-name boutique wines from California and Autralia. Sense is made of this diversity by matching wines against others of the same style and price. In other words, a Challenge award indicates good value for money.

The international tasting team in full flow

Mindful of the way in which opinionated judges can influence their fellow tasters to give a higher or lower mark than they might, there is at the Challenge a unique safe-guard procedure to ensure that every wine is as fairly judged as possible. All wines reckoned to be medalworthy are tasted

The team of more than 40 sort and select

twice – as are any wines on which panels cannot agree. This year, for the first time, there were introduced 'Super-Jurors', senior Masters of Wine and respected members of the trade whose job it was to taste (albeit briefly) and, if appropriate to send for re-judging, wines which had been rejected by the initial panel.

Challenge staff then busily pump results into the computers, creating a unique database to which subsequently are added the details of where and at what price each successful wine is sold. Accuracy is paramount and we have learned a great deal since 1984.

Whilst it would be impossible to claim that no good wine is ever denied the award it deserves – just as no one could say that fine players are never knocked out in the first rounds of tennis tournaments – there is no question that every medal winner from Château Mouton Rothschild to the humblest Bulgarian Cabernet or red Vin de Pays from southern France has had to prove itself against extremely tough competition.

All of which helps to explain why, when you buy the winners listed in this book you will find yourself drinking some of the tastiest, most interesting and best value wines in the world.

THE TROPHIES

Having tasted the 6500 entries and chosen the 120 or so Gold medals, the final task was the tricky one of deciding which wines in each category were the supreme champions, the Trophy winners. At this stage, price and provenance were disregarded; the wines had to compete against each other with neither advantage nor handicap.

The judges who were invited to take part in the Trophy tasting were, for the most part, the Super-Jurors who had done such sterling service during the Challenge. Among them were Derek Smedley MW, David Peppercorn MW, wine writers Tom Stevenson, Stuart Walton and Oz Clarke, Dr Caroline Gilbey MW, John Boyes MW, Willie Lebus of Bibendum, Hew Blair of Justerini & Brooks, Claire Gordon Brown MW and Ian Bamford MW.

Unlike many such events, the judges were not constrained by the obligation to award a single Trophy in every category. From the outset, they were told to make awards only where they thought they were deserved.

The first Trophy to be decided was for the best CHARDONNAY. Would it be a Burgundy or a contender from the New World? In the event, the winner was the subtle **1993 Private Reserve** made by the Swiss-owned firm of Beringer.

Next came the SAUVIGNONS - and a battle between New Zealanders which was won by the **1994 Nautilus** from Marlborough. The AROMATIC TROPHY went to an even-money favourite in the shape of Zind Humbrecht's **1990 Clos Windsbuhl Gewürztraminer,** while, on the other side of the Rhine, the winning German wine came from another top producer, Reichsgraf von Kesselstatt, which won the GERMAN TROPHY with its **1990 Piesporter Goldtropfchen Riesling.**

The RHONE-STYLE category brought a tussle between two very different wines, both of which were made from the Syrah. At last, it was decided to give the Trophy jointly to the **1992 Mount Edelstone** from Henschke in South Australia and the **1990 Côte Rôtie Côtes Brune et Blonde** from Guigal.

Having decided to make no award for an Iberian red, the tasters moved on to give the TROPHY for best ITALIAN Wine to a

1990 Brunello di Montalcino from Argiano which interestingly beat competition from some Bordeaux-style 'new wave' wines.

Leaving the reds for a moment, the judges paused to use their prerogative by creating a SPECIAL SEMILLON TROPHY for the **1993 Willows Vineyard Semillon** from the Barossa Valley in Australia before tackling the vexed matter of the best BURGUNDY-STYLE RED. Making what was undoubtedly the toughest decision so far, they made the award jointly to the classic **1992 Chambertin** from Rossignol Trapet and, to the tasters astonishment a **1992 Frauenkirchen St Laurent** from the Umathum winery in Austria.

The tasting for the BORDEAUX-STYLE TROPHY was, inevitably, a battle of the giants, and it was won by a giant wine - the **1990 Château Mouton Rothschild** which put its fellow clarets and New World contenders firmly in their place.

After the tannic reds, the tasters made another award to an Austrian wine, giving the LATE HARVEST TROPHY to the luscious **1993 Feiler-Artinger Ruster Ausbruch**.. The sheer hedonism of that wine put them in the mood for the FORTIFIED TROPHIES. Here, again, it was a trio of past winners who carried off the prizes, the astonishingly youthful **1976 Fonseca Guimaraens** taking the PORT TROPHY, the **Gonzalez Byass Matusalem Oloroso Dulce** winning the SHERRY TROPHY and the **Yalumba Museum Show Reserve Liqueur Muscat** securing the MUSCAT TROPHY. Choosing between these three very different wines for the overall FORTIFIED TROPHY was hard; in the event, it was the **Gonzalez Byass** which once again scored the highest points.

The F Bonnet **Carte Blanche Champagne** then won the SPARKLING WINE TROPHY against an array of top class fizz, ranging from Victoria Wine's own label Vintage Champagne to Dom Perignon.

Finally and most trickily of all, the judges had to choose their top red and white. The former proved to be a relatively easy race; only two tasters failed to place the **1990 Mouton Rothschild** at or near the head of their list for RED WINE TROPHY. The choice of WHITE WINE TROPHY was far more vexed; indeed the votes were so close that everything hung on the marks given by the last taster - who finally nudged the trophy into the hands of the **1993 Feiler-Artinger Ruster Ausbruch.**

WINES OF THE YEAR

From the outset, the Wine Challenge has aimed to help introduce as many people as possible to the best and most interesting *affordable* and *widely available* wines – the WINES OF THE YEAR.

So, having assigned the Trophies, the judges were asked to taste the most highly marked wines which fitted two crucial criteria: price - under £5 and £8 for table wines and under £12 for fizz - and widespread availability.

THE WHITES

The **Viña Casablanca 1994 Sauvignon Blanc** comes from the new region of Casablanca whose cool climate really suits grapes like the Sauvignon.

The success of the **Ninth Island Chardonnay**, an unoaked wine, confirms Aussie Chardonnay is not always big, ripe and oaky. The third award goes to the **Dom. Mandeville Viognier** from the Languedoc Roussillon.

── THE REDS ──

All three Red Wines of the Year were made from similar grape varieties but in different continents. The **1994 Duboeuf, Côtes du Rhône Domaine des Moulins** is principally made from Grenache in the Rhône, while the **1992 Penfolds Bin 28 Shiraz** - in its second vintage as winner of this award - comes from Kalimna in South Australia, while the **L.A. Cetto Petite Sirah** was made from an unrelated grape in Baja California in Mexico.

── THE FIZZ ──

This year, there were no fewer than three sparkling wines, all made by the Champagne method but outside the region of that name.

Scharffenberger is, however, related to Champagne; its producer in California is a subsidiary of Pommery. **Nautilus**, the New Zealand winner, like the winner of the Sauvignon trophy, comes from the Marlborough region. As for the **Simonsig**, it scores a hat trick for South Africa which produced last year's Pongrasz and the Boschendal Grand Pavilion wines of 1993.

HOW TO USE
THIS BOOK

Every wine in this guide has been awarded a medal at the **1995 International WINE Challenge**. We have listed the winning wines by country, region and then: red, white, sweet white, rosé, fortified and sparkling. In the New World regions of Australia, New Zealand and North America the wines are sorted by grape variety, a method increasingly used to differentiate wines.

Under each of these headings the wines are then listed in price order, from the least to the most expensive. Every wine carries the same range of information; the wine name (and vintage where applicable), the tasting note, the average retail price, the code for stockists (see page 242), and the medal the wine was awarded. All gold medal wines have been highlighted, and wines of the year have been identified by the Wine of the Year badge.

There is also an alphabetical index starting on page 251 and price listings of red and white wines, sparkling wines and champagnes starting on page 233.

Below is an example of how the wines are listed.

The wine name, vintage and region	*The average retail price*		*The Medals; G Gold, S Silver, B Bronze*
CASSEGRAIN FIVE MILE HOLLOW RED 1993 New South Wales	*Minty Cabernet, pastille aromas. Intense, locked-in cassis with cherry tannins.*	£6.00	GRB	(G)

The Challenge tasting note   *Stockist codes*

THE
WINES

AUSTRALIA

Fast overtaking California as the most reliable source of New World wines, Australia is now surprising observers with its readiness to develop new regions and create new styles which stand alongside the ultra-fruity blockbusters with which it first made its name internationally. Clear regional styles do exist, but there is an increasingly wide range of wines being produced throughout the continent.

CABERNET SAUVIGNON

CO-OP AUSTRALIAN CABERNET SAUVIGNON, ANGOVES 1992 South Australia	*Stylish, smooth wine. Good attack of sweet fruits, softening towards finish. Rich, pure, impressive claret.*	**£4.40**	CWS	B
PENFOLDS RAWSONS RETREAT RUBY CABERNET/CABERNET SAUVIGNON/SHIRAZ 1993 South Australia	*Predominantly spice and oak bouquet a little restrained. Well-made, simple wine. Juicy fruit.*	**£4.50**	Widely available	B
LINDEMANS BIN 45 CABERNET SAUVIGNON, LINDEMANS 1993 South Australia	*Minty, eucalyptus nose, with touches of strong blackcurrant perfume. Good, ripe fruit and soft tannins.*	**£4.90**	Widely available	S
ANGOVES NANYA CREEK CABERNET SAUVIGNON, ANGOVES 1993 Nanya Creek	*Chocolate, mocha and attractive fruit on nose. Light on palate with sweet strawberry flavour. Velvety.*	**£5.00**	NUR	S
ANGOVES RIDGEMOUNT ESTATE CABERNET SAUVIGNON, ANGOVES 1992 South Australia	*Creamy vanilla oak on nose. Softly mature with ripe tannins and gentle acidity. Satiny finish.*	**£5.00**	BES	B

AUSTRALIA • RED

TOLLANA BLACK LABEL CABERNET SAUVIGNON, TOLLANA/PENFOLDS 1992 South Australia	*Layers of ripe blackcurrants, blackberries and sweet vanilla. Mouthfilling, persistent. Immense appeal.*	£5.00	WR BU TH	(S)
GEOFF MERRILL CABERNET SAUVIGNON 1990 South Australia	*Deep purple. Lively mint nose. Full fruit on palate balanced by fresh, youthful oak.*	£5.00	PLE OD	(S)
HARDY'S BAROSSA VALLEY CABERNET SAUVIGNON, BRL HARDY WINE CO 1993 South Australia	*Savoury, crisp style. The nose suggests freshly sawn wood and mint. Rich, brambly berry fruits.*	£5.50	HBR DBY	(S)
DE BORTOLI WINDY PEAK CABERNET SAUVIGNON / MERLOT 1991 Victoria	*Dark chocolate nose reveals Cabernet flavours; chewy, meaty, rich fruit. Old-fashioned, with austere tannins.*	£5.80	SAF	(B)
HARDY'S COONAWARRA CABERNET SAUVIGNON, BRL HARDY WINE CO 1992 South Australia	*Ripe fruit on nose. Mouthfuls of soft, Australian Shiraz-style fruit. Jammy strawberries and cream.*	£5.90	HBR VDV	(B)
BLEASDALES LANGHORNE CREEK CABERNET SAUVIGNON 1993 South Australia	*Rich, plummy, oak palate. Intense berry fruits and vanilla oak. Strong finish.*	£6.00	M&S	(B)
CASSEGRAIN FIVE MILE HOLLOW RED 1993 New South Wales	*Minty Cabernet and pastille aromas. Intense, locked-in cassis with ripe cherry tannins. Vanilla finish.*	£6.00	GRB	(G)

Pinpoint who sells the wine you wish to buy by turning to the stockist codes. If you know the name of the wine you want to buy, use the alphabetical index. If the price is your motivation, refer to the invaluable price guide index; red and white wines under £5, sparkling wines under £10 and champagne under £15. Happy hunting!

TESCO BAROSSA MERLOT, GRANT BURGE 1992 South Australia	*Lightish bouquet of fresh fruits and wood. Vibrant, intense blackcurrant. Quaffable fruit.*	**£6.00**	TO	(S)
LEASINGHAM DOMAINE CABERNET MALBEC, BRL HARDY WINE CO 1993 South Australia	*Unusual nose of smoky embers and dying fires. Rich, ripe, chunky style. Generous, warm fruit.*	**£6.00**	HBR VDV OD R	(S)
LEASINGHAM DOMAINE CABERNET SAUVIGNON MALBEC, BRL HARDY WINE CO 1992 South Australia	*Blackcurrant and mint aromas. Tasty plum and chocolaty, wood flavours. Superb fruit, blended tannins and vanilla oak.*	**£6.10**	HBR DBY CWS VDV OD R	(G)
ROSEMOUNT ESTATE CABERNET SAUVIGNON, ROSEMOUNT 1993 New South Wales	*Tasty, chewy, chocolatey licorice flavours. Ripe, fat, rounded fruit. Toasty oak. Good stalky tannins.*	**£6.30**	Widely available	(S)
GOUNDREY MOUNT BARKER CABERNET SAUVIGNON/MERLOT, GOUNDREY 1992 Mount Barker	*Powerful wine. Massive, minty style with ripe, rich, oakey character. Lovely balance.*	**£6.40**	Widely available	(B)
MONTROSE WINES MUDGEE CABERNET SAUVIGNON, MONTROSE WINES 1989 New South Wales	*Deep, rich and velvety in glass with perfect spice and blackcurrant on nose. Good, fruity and clean.*	**£6.50**	CAX AMY	(G)
BASEDOW CABERNET SAUVIGNON, BASEDOW 1992 South Australia	*Minty cassis aromas. Cooked, jammy fruit. Powerful wine, with delightful, dried date flavours.*	**£6.50**	BI VWC VDV	(B)
YALDARA RESERVE CABERNET SAUVIGNON/MERLOT, YALDARA 1991 South Australia	*Rich and juicy. Wonderful blackcurrant cabernet, blending well with plummy, pleasing merlot.*	**£6.50**	SWS VDV DIR AV HVW MRF WOI	(B)

TIM KNAPPSTEIN CABERNET SAUVIGNON/ MERLOT 1992 South Australia	*Fine, strong cedar nose, with nice, sweet fruit. Quite tannic with a rich texture.*	**£6.50**	GRA JS	(B)
MAGLIERI MCLAREN VALE CABERNET SAUVIGNON 1993 South Australia	*Medium weight wine with excellent cinnamon spiciness and blackcurrant smoothness. Clean, luscious finish.*	**£6.50**	PLB	(S)
SIMON HACKETT CABERNET SAUVIGNON, SIMON HACKETT 1993 South Australia	*Powerful, earthy, rich cassis flavours. Sultanas on palate. Good weight and obvious vanilla oak.*	**£6.60**	Widely available	(B)
TIM KNAPPSTEIN CABERNET SAUVIGNON/MERLOT 1993 South Australia	*Good depth of minty, blackcurrant fruit, a light touch of oak, soft tannins and good length.*	**£6.70**	GRA DBY JS OD WIN	(B)
CHATEAU REYNELLA BASKET PRESS CABERNET SAUVIGNON, BRL HARDY WINE CO 1992 South Australia	*Purple/black colour. Concentration of blackcurrants on nose with sweet berry flavours and new oak.*	**£6.70**	HBR VDV OD	(B)
CHATEAU REYNELLA CABERNET MERLOT, BRL HARDY WINE CO 1993 South Australia	*Spicy, strong Cabernet nose with toasty, vanilla new oak. Deep, rich palate.*	**£6.80**	HBR DBY CWS VDV FUL	(B)
HARDY'S COONAWARRA CABERNET SAUVIGNON, BRL HARDY WINE CO 1993 South Australia	*Fabulous nose of spicy oak and chocolate with tarry overtones. Concentrated blackcurrant.*	**£6.80**	HBR MTL DBY VDV FUL	(G)
WOLF BLASS YELLOW LABEL CABERNET SAUVIGNON, WOLF BLASS 1993 South Australia	*Chocolate Cabernet nose. Intense berry fruit with touches of coconut and vanilla pod. Delicious!*	**£6.90**	Widely available	(G)

CHAPEL HILL CABERNET SAUVIGNON, CHAPEL HILL WINERY 1992 South Australia	*A brooding monster. Excellent concentration of deep berry. Creamy and full. Plenty of tannin.*	£6.90	AUC BOO TO HOU	**G**
SIMON HACKETT THE DIRECTORS RESERVE CABERNET SHIRAZ 1992 South Australia	*Glorious blend of eastern spice, coconut and berry fruit. Slightly leathery nose with charismatic finish.*	£7.00	VAU	**B**
SHAREFARMERS RED, PETALUMA 1990 South Australia	*Vanilla, oak and black-currant nose with a full berry fruit flavour. Stylish and light.*	£7.00	GRA WIN SHB	**B**
RIDDOCH CABERNET SHIRAZ, KATNOOK ESTATE 1992 South Australia	*Peppery, rich nose. Blackcurrants, raspberries and dash of eucalyptus on nose. Lovely wine.*	£7.00	Widely available	**S**
DELATITE DEVILS RIVER CABERNET SAUVIGNON / MERLOT 1992 Victoria	*Fresh, strong oak and a fine, tight, fruit body with hints of rhubarb. Lovely, sweet fruits and firm tannins.*	£7.00	AUC TO	**B**
ROBERTSON'S WELL, MILDARA 1993 South Australia	*Powerful, hot, concentrated. Spicy and Shiraz-like. Intense cassis flavours. Ripe cherry tannins.*	£7.10	WFB OD AMY	**G**
MITCHELTON RESERVE CABERNET SAUVIGNON, MITCHELTON WINES 1992 Victoria	*Deep colour. Cassis/raspberry flavours; creamy and fine. Good length and clean finish.*	£7.10	WCR MTL VDV VIL COK	**B**
SEPPELT HARPERS RANGE CABERNET SAUVIGNON, SEPPELT & SONS 1992 South Australia	*Fresh oak on the nose with glorious, soft berry fruit on the palate. Well balanced tannins and fruit.*	£7.40	WSG DBY HOU DIR CUM NY COK	**B**

ST HALLETT CABERNET SAUVIGNON/CABERNET FRANC/MERLOT, ST HALLETT 1992 South Australia	*Friendly, juicy wine with heaps of plum and blackcurrant. Merlot balances the more tannic Cabernet.*	£7.50	Widely available	(B)
THE MENZIES COONAWARRA CABERNET SAUVIGNON, YALUMBA 1991 South Australia	*Black/red colour. Cigar box and chocolate nose. Strong flavours of cherry and blackcurrant.*	£7.50	GRA OD	(B)
MITCHELL CABERNET SAUVIGNON, MITCHELL 1992 South Australia	*Notes of eucalyptus and mulberries. Stewed fruit, rhubarb and soft, slushy fruits. Sweet oak.*	£7.70	MVN ADN L&W G&M TAN AV	(B)
WYNNS COONAWARRA ESTATE CABERNET SAUVIGNON, WYNNS 1991 South Australia	*Rich, spicy nose. Oaky sweet fruit with a hint of coffee. Concentrated and elegant.*	£7.70	Widely available	(B)
YARRA RIDGE CABERNET SAUVIGNON, YARRA RIDGE 1993 Yarra Valley	*Forthcoming, developed aroma. Wonderful nose with a touch of mint and eucalyptus. Maturing well.*	£7.70	WFB JS	(S)
LONG GULLY CABERNET SAUVIGNON, LONG GULLY ESTATE 1991 Yarra Valley	*Soft, creamy, oak nose. Superb cassis and rich blackcurrant aromas. Rich, ripe plums. Subtle acidity.*	£7.90	REN DBY AMY NY	(G)
PETER DENNIS CABERNET SAUVIGNON, PETER DENNIS WINES 1994 South Australia	*Wonderful, deep red colour. Fine nose with complex coffee and vanilla aromas. Full and ripe in the mouth.*	£8.00	THP	(G)
PENFOLDS BIN 407 CABERNET SAUVIGNON, PENFOLDS 1991 South Australia	*Brambly nose. Rich, luscious fruit with good tannins. Well-balanced, deep, interesting wine.*	£8.10	Widely available	(B)

PENFOLDS BIN 407 CABERNET SAUVIGNON 1992 South Australia	*Deep colour with wide, complex nose; berry fruit, coconut and leather. Lots of spicy fruit and tannin.*	**£8.10**	Widely available	(S)
LENTON BRAE MARGARET RIVER CABERNET SAUVIGNON 1992 Western Australia	*Notes of mushrooms and delicate fruitiness. Delightful character of hot, slightly cooked fruits.*	**£8.20**	CVR OXB VDV	(B)
HOLLICK CABERNET SAUVIGNON 1991 South Australia	*Lush berries with just a hint of truffles and marzipan. Firm, balanced tannins and long, penetrating finish.*	**£8.30**	BOO OXB L&W VDV OD R	(S)
TALTARNI MERLOT, TALTARNI 1992 Victoria	*Cassis nose in minty style. Spice and oak influence over concentrated, ripe, merlot sweetness.*	**£8.40**	Widely available	(S)
PENFOLDS BIN 389 CABERNET SHIRAZ 1992 South Australia	*Hot fruit and American oak. Tempting sweetness and resin, with juicy fruit.*	**£8.50**	Widely available	(S)
SALISBURY ESTATE SHOW RESERVE CABERNET SAUVIGNON 1992 Victoria	*Purple ruby. Lovely vanilla nose. Complex, iodine flavours, revealing warm, ripe, chewy fruits.*	**£8.50**	EWC ENO COK	(B)
MCGUIGAN BROS SHAREHOLDERS RESERVE CABERNET/MERLOT 1993 South Australia	*Juicy and welcoming. Happy, bubbly, purple merlot fruit. Good leathery nose with long finish.*	**£8.60**	VNO GDS	(B)
PENFOLDS COONAWARRA CABERNET SAUVIGNON 1992 South Australia	*Ripe berry. Heady fruit and opulent cassis. Mint and cedar enhance complexity. Fine tannins.*	**£8.60**	Widely available	(S)

AUSTRALIA • RED

ROSEMOUNT ESTATE SHOW RESERVE CABERNET SAUVIGNON 1992 South Australia	*Inky colour. Rich, choclate, eucalyptus character. Cherry and blackcurrant fruit. Long finish.*	£8.80	ROS DBY TO CUM	(B)
KRONDORF SHOW RESERVE CABERNET SAUVIGNON 1992 South Australia	*Soft, creamy, blackcurrant nose. Charming raspberry and cassis flavours. Well balanced fruit; smoky oak.*	£9.00	WFB	(B)
THE SIGNATURE, YALUMBA 1991 South Australia	*Jammy nose with lush mocha and coconut oak. Fresh, ripe fruit with deep, leathery complexity.*	£9.00	GRA DBY ADN	(G)
MCWILLIAMS BRANDS LAIRA CABERNET SAUVIGNON, MCWILLIAMS 1993 South Australia	*Rich wood aromas and palate. Spicy; notes of soft, vanilla oak and rich fruits.*	£9.00	WAV	(B)
ST MICHAEL ROSEMOUNT ESTATE COONAWARRA CABERNET SAUVIGNON 1992 South Australia	*Cigar box aroma. Sweet fruit. Hard tannins compensated by rich texture of dense fruits.*	£9.00	M&S	(B)
ORLANDO ST HUGO CABERNET SAUVIGNON, ORLANDO WINES 1990 South Australia	*Warm, soft fruits on nose. Ripe, spicy tannins and cooked fruits, balanced by good level of acidity.*	£9.10	DBY CAX	(B)
THOMAS HARDY CABERNET SAUVIGNON, BRL HARDY WINE CO 1989 South Australia	*Bouquet tinged with mint and eucalyptus. Flavours of cedar wood and orange. Integrated tannins.*	£9.20	HBR MTL VDV	(S)
EBENEZER CABERNET SAUVIGNON/MALBEC/MERLOT/FRANC, BRL HARDY WINE CO/VALLEY GROWERS CO-OP 1992 South Australia	*Chunky, generous, meaty, firm flavours. Abundant fruit giving warmth, elegantly balanced against blended tannins.*	£9.20	HBR DBY VW OD R	(G)

AUSTRALIA • RED

ELDERTON BAROSSA CABERNET SAUVIGNON, ELDERTON WINES 1992 Barossa Valley	*Full fruit; cedary new oak. Obvious tannins are well balanced by rich, ripe, concentrated fruit.*	£9.50	ALL	(B)
BEST'S GREAT WESTERN CABERNET SAUVIGNON, BEST'S WINES 1992 Victoria	*Full nose of fruit gums and eucalyptus. Fresh, minty style with currant and American oak.*	£9.50	SWS DBY SHB COK	(G)
PETER LEHMANN CABERNET MALBEC, PETER LEHMANN 1990 South Australia	*Warm, ripe, minty nose. Full, fleshy and long. High acidity and deep, rich finish.*	£9.60	PLE DBY MK VDV CHF	(S)
DALWHINNIE VICTORIA CABERNET SAUVIGNON, DALWHINNIE VINEYARDS 1993 Victoria	*Crimson robe; minty aromas of cassis and brambles. Chewy on palate. Chocolate and woody notes.*	£9.70	WTR SMF	(S)
CULLEN MARGARET RIVER CABERNET SAUVIGNON/MERLOT, CULLEN 1993 Western Australia	*Minty nose softened by vanilla oak and ripe tannins. Good acidic presence. Deep, luscious fruit.*	£9.70	HA DBY ADN CHF DIR	(S)
CLASSIC CLARE CABERNET SAUVIGNON, BRL HARDY WINE CO 1993 South Australia	*Beautiful purple fruit with hints of vanilla and redcurrant on the palate. Spicy, resonant finish.*	£9.90	HBR DBY VDV FUL OD R	(G)
PLANTAGENET MOUNT BARKER CABERNET SAUVIGNON, PLANTAGENET WINES 1992 Western Australia	*Perfumed, sweet Cabernet nose revealing luscious, concentrated blackcurrant. Smooth, silky character and powerful tannins.*	£10.00	SG	(S)
WOLF BLASS PRESIDENT'S SELECTION CABERNET SAUVIGNON, WOLF BLASS 1991 South Australia	*Dry tobacco, oak nose with smoky meats, chocolate and roasted coffee. Cassis on palate.*	£10.20	Widely available	(B)

AUSTRALIA • RED

CHÂTEAU XANADU CABERNET SAUVIGNON, CONOR LAGAN CHÂTEAU XANADU 1992 Western Australia	*Berry aromas, blackberries and violets. Welcomingly heavy on the palate. Well made.*	£10.30	MYS OXB GSH DIR	(S)
PETALUMA COONAWARRA RED, PETALUMA 1990 South Australia	*Mature, plummy nose. Confected, jammy fruit flavours with notes of chocolate on finish. Direct character.*	£10.70	GRA DBY OD WIN	(B)
CULLEN MARGARET RIVER CABERNET SAUVIGNON/MERLOT RESERVE, CULLEN 1992 Western Australia	*Great Bordeaux character but American oak. Concentrated, fat wine with rich plums. Dry finish.*	£10.80	HA DBY ADN CHF DIR	(S)
THE HANGING ROCK VICTORIA CABERNET SAUVIGNON/MERLOT, THE HANGING ROCK WINERY 1992 Victoria	*Juicy, purple, fresh merlot fruit. Tannic, clean cabernet fruit blend deliciously.*	£11.00	THP	(S)
LINDEMANS PYRUS, LINDEMANS 1991 South Australia	*Chocolatey, berried, typical New World style. Delicious, ripe, full blackcurrant fruit, smoothly textured and rounded.*	£11.10	Widely available	(S)
MOUNT BOLD, MAXWELL WINES 1991 McLaren Vale	*Excellent berry on nose. Rich, full, chocolate, peppery middle. Very good balance and some vinosity.*	£11.50	AMD	(S)
LINDEMANS ST GEORGE CABERNET SAUVIGNON, LINDEMANS 1991 South Australia	*Strong blackcurrant perfume. Good, ripe fruit and soft tannins. Lingering finish.*	£11.50	Widely available	(B)
STONIERS RESERVE CABERNET SAUVIGNON, STONIER 1991 Mornington Peninsula	*Rich, plummy wine with tremendous balance and good tannin. Hints of leather and cassis fruit.*	£11.60	DIR WAW OD MRF	(B)

27

AUSTRALIA • RED

WOLF BLASS BLACK LABEL CABERNET SAUVIGNON, WOLF BLASS 1991 South Australia	*Fresh, youthful fruit; scented, sweet oak. Ripe, round, with evident tannins. Boiled sweets on nose.*	£13.00	WFB MTL DBY VDV OD AV	(B)
HENSCHKE ABBOTTS PRAYER MERLOT/CABERNET SAUVIGNON, HENSCHKE 1992 South Australia	*Rich, plummy nose showing terroir. Big, chunky, meaty flavours. Solid, robust style. Opulent and rich.*	£13.00	L&W BOO DBY SEB DIR COK	(S)
MILDARA ALEXANDERS COONAWARRA, MILDARA 1992 South Australia	*Ripe, minty, blackcurrant aromas. Youthful, concentrated, intense fruit, deliciously juicy and luscious. Soft tannins.*	£13.00	WFB	(S)
PASSING CLOUDS ANGELS BLEND, PASSING CLOUDS 1990 Victoria	*Peppery, Bordelais nose of cassis and dried rosemary. Vanilla and confected raspberry, like boiled sweets.*	£13.10	AUE ADN	(B)
IRVINE GRAND MERLOT, JAMES IRVINE 1990 South Australia	*Blackcurrant, oaky nose in elegant, Australian style. Mulberry fruit and sherry sweetness on palate.*	£14.40	VDV AV HVW	(S)
CHÂTEAU XANADU CABERNET SAUVIGNON RESERVE, CONOR LAGAN CHÂTEAU XANADU 1991 Western Australia	*Nose of spearmint and concentrated cassis. Intense, ripe fruit married to soft, vanilla oak tannins.*	£14.20	MYS OXB GSH DIR	(S)
PENLEY ESTATE CABERNET SAUVIGNON, PENLEY ESTATE 1992 South Australia	*Fine nose of mulberry and nutty oak. Firm structure, assertive oak and young, sweet fruit.*	£14.50	L&W BOO DBY NY	(B)
PENLEY ESTATES CABERNET SAUVIGNON, PENLEY ESTATE 1991 South Australia	*Berry, smoky bacon aromas. Toffee, caramel and powerful cassis. Serious American oak on attack.*	£14.90	WTR BOO DBY L&W DIR	(G)

AUSTRALIA • RED

WYNNS COONAWARRA ESTATE JOHN RIDDOCH CABERNET SAUVIGNON, WYNNS 1991 South Australia	*Blood red colour. Gamey, cassis nose with pine wood overtones. Meaty, sweet fruit.*	**£15.60**	Widely available	(S)
PENFOLDS BIN 707 CABERNET SAUVIGNON, PENFOLDS 1992 South Australia	*Good pencil sharpenings. Cedar oak and fresh mint on nose. Delicious, spicy, New World oak.*	**£16.10**	Widely available	(S)
ORLANDO JACARANDA RIDGE CABERNET SAUVIGNON, ORLANDO WINES 1988 South Australia	*Minty, spicy nose; good cassis and blackberry character. A lovely endearing mouthful.*	**£17.70**	CAX OD	(S)
ORLANDO JACARANDA RIDGE CABERNET SAUVIGNON, ORLANDO WINES 1989 South Australia	*Tremendous wine with tons of fresh berry fruit, cassis and caramel chocolate. Ripe spicy finish.*	**£18.00**	CAX	(G)

SHIRAZ

JACOB'S CREEK SHIRAZ/CABERNET, ORLANDO WINES 1993 South East Australia	*Closed leathery fruit aroma; ripe fruit palate with some sharpness.*	**£4.50**	Widely available	(B)
NANYA CREEK SHIRAZ, ANGOVES 1993	*Rich, sweet, plum aroma; white pepper and intense tannin on palate. Good length and complexity.*	**£5.00**	NUR	(B)
ROSEMOUNT SHIRAZ/CABERNET SAUVIGNON, ROSEMOUNT 1994	*Ripe juicy cherries give way to spice and vanilla. Fresh, concentrated flavours. Smooth, round palate.*	**£5.00**	Widely available	(B)

AUSTRALIA • RED

PARROTS HILL SHIRAZ, BRL HARDY WINE 1992 South Australia	*Clean, bright, ruby; clean aromas. Full, rich palate; good, fruit centre. Well-balanced.*	£5.00	HBR MTL DBY VDV	**B**
ROUGE HOMME SHIRAZ CABERNET, ROUGE HOMME 1992 South Australia	*Clean, medium-ruby/purple colour wine; good jammy core of fruit. Well-made.*	£5.20	Widely available	**B**
SALISBURY ESTATE, CABERNET/SHIRAZ, SALISBURY ESTATE 1993 Victoria	*Black cherries, redcurrants and pepper. Medium weight palate with furry tannins.*	£5.20	ENO VD VCW	**B**
ROSEMOUNT ESTATE CABERNET SHIRAZ, ROSEMOUNT 1994 South East	*Cherry red. Cherries, redcurrants, strawberries, damson jam and spice on palate. Clean with oak.*	£5.30	SV ABY JS	**B**
SHIRAZ/CABERNET, MITCHELTON WINES 1993 Victoria	*Clean, ruby; still youthful, roasted/smoky aroma. Raspberry flavour; good length. Excellent.*	£5.50	JEF MTL RAV VDV HW VIL HDL	**S**
ST MICHAEL MCLAREN VALE SHIRAZ, ANDREW GARRETT 1993 McLaren Vale	*Lively aromas of pepper and herbs balanced by ripe plums and damsons. Silky tannins.*	£5.60	M&S WR	**S**
YALDARA RESERVE SHIRAZ, YALDARA 1993 South Australia	*Excellent nose; many wonderful aromas. Densely-packed, lots of flavour. Good length, flavour and fruit.*	£5.70	SWS VDV DIR AV HVW WOI SHB	**S**
PENFOLDS KOONUNGA HILL SHIRAZ CABERNET SAUVIGNON, PENFOLDS 1993 South Australia	*Good depth of colour. Complex, stylish, succulent fruit with well-integrated, though subdued, oak.*	£5.80	Widely available	**S**

AUSTRALIA • RED

WYNNS COONAWARRA ESTATE SHIRAZ, WYNNS 1993 South Australia	*Sweet, jammy fruit; lightly perfumed. Soft fruit in mouth. Simple but pleasant.*	**£5.90**	Widely available	(S)
WYNNS COONAWARRA ESTATE SHIRAZ, SOUTHCORP 1993 South Australia	*Spicy, vanilla nose; pronounced, complex and viscous. Well-oaked, tannic wine; chewy, peppery. Serious.*	**£5.90**	VWC VW VDV HOU OD GSJ	(B)
HARDY'S BANKSIDE SHIRAZ, HARDY'S 1992 South East Australia	*Big, spicy, peppery wine; smoky, minty berry aromas. Long, creamy, structured palate.*	**£5.90**	DBY SPR VDV RT MW	(S)
WYNDHAM ESTATE BIN 555 SHIRAZ, WYNDHAM ESTATE 1993 New South Wales	*Fairly inert fruitful nose; soft, creamy palate. Rich redcurrant, but quite simple wine. Tannic finish.*	**£6.00**	DBY HCK MWW HDL UBC AHW COK	(B)
MILDARA, CHURCH HILL CAB/SHIRAZ MERLOT 1993 South Australia	*Spicy, rich, peppery wine with fresh, exciting oak, sweet fruit and tight tannins.*	**£6.00**	WFB HDL	(B)
RED LABEL SHIRAZ CABERNET, WOLF BLASS 1993 South Australia	*Attractive, fruity bouquet with some complexity. Up-front wine with pleasing palate and impressive finish.*	**£6.00**	WFB MTL D BY HOU OD	(B)
ST MICHAEL SHIRAZ, ROSEMOUNT 1993 South Australia	*Sweet fruit and some perfume; ripe, full palate. Good, up-front fruit flavours.*	**£6.00**	M&S	(S)

Pinpoint who sells the wine you wish to buy by turning to the stockist codes. If you know the name of the wine you want to buy, use the alphabetical index. If price is your motivation, refer to the invaluable price guide index; red and white wines under £5, sparkling wines under £10 and champagne under £15. Happy hunting!

ROSEMOUNT SHIRAZ, ROSEMOUNT 1994 South Australia	*Deep purple; smoky, fruity aromas. Jammy, sweet palate with some residual sugar. Interesting.*	**£6.20**	Widely available	(B)
ROTHBURY ESTATE SHIRAZ, ROTHBURY 1993 South Australia	*Lovely nose; light red fruit, inky palate, quite peppery. Longish tannins and good length.*	**£6.30**	Widely available	(B)
RENMANO SHIRAZ, RENMANO WINES 1993 South Australia	*Rich, red plum bouquet; rounded floral palate, ripe and pliable. Creamy oak and light tannins.*	**£6.30**	HOH MTL DBY SEB VIL NY	(S)
BEST'S VICTORIA SHIRAZ, BEST'S WINES 1994 Victoria	*Soft, sweet, jammy nose; rich, juicy, fruit palate. Good balance with some acidity at end.*	**£6.30**	SWS DBY HLV	(B)
BAILEYS SHIRAZ, BAILEYS 1993 Victoria	*Purple; ripe bouquet. Tannic, fruity palate with long finish.*	**£6.40**	RBW DBY CWS CHF HOU OD	(B)
ROSEMOUNT ESTATE SHIRAZ, ROSEMOUNT 1993 South East	*Up-front, fruity nose following on to palate. Lasting flavours; dry/big style of wine.*	**£6.40**	Widely available	(B)
BASEDOW SHIRAZ, BASEDOW 1992 South Australia	*Lovely oak and fruit nose – clean, fresh, well-integrated. Sweet, chocolate/vanilla palate. Ageing potential.*	**£6.80**	BOO BI VWC VDV CHF COK	(G)
PENFOLDS SHIRAZ 'KALIMNA BIN 28', PENFOLDS 1991 South Australia	*Rich, peppery, elegant wine with velvety smoothness and spicy sophistication. Balanced tannins.*	**£6.80**	Widely available	(G)

PENFOLDS BIN 28 KALIMNA SHIRAZ, PENFOLDS 1992 South Australia	*Ripe, spicy, berry nose; excellent, crunchy fruit flavours; hints of tobacco and chocolate.*	£6.90	Widely available	**G** WINE OF THE YEAR
MAGLIERI MCLAREN VALE SHIRAZ, MAGLIERI 1992 McLaren Vale	*Deep black, cherry; creamy blueberries and redcurrant bouquet; stewed fruits. Excellent, chunky middle palate.*	£7.00	TO	**G**
MAGLIERI MCLAREN VALE SHIRAZ, MAGLIERI 1993 McLaren Vale	*Deep red; concentrated nose; spicy aromas, plenty of new oak following on to palate. Slightly astringent.*	£7.00	TO	**G**
SHIRAZ, EDEN RIDGE 1992 South Australia	*Light, attractive, violet nose; chewy fruit on palate. Low tannins; fresh, simple drinking wine.*	£7.00	HA BOO DBY ADN CHF CWI DIR	**B**
ST HALLETT GAMEKEEPERS RESERVE, ST HALLETT 1993 South Australia	*Juicy; plenty of plum flavours. Peppery, spicy, fruity palate. Very drinkable.*	£7.00	AUC	**S**
SHIRAZ, STEINS WINES, STEINS WINES 1991 Mudgee	*Fiercely licorice, medicinal nose; complex, full-flavoured palate with dry tannins.*	£7.00	ETV	**B**
BASEDOW SHIRAZ, BASEDOW 1993 South Australia	*Lifted nose; spicy palate. Elegant; good length.*	£7.20	BOO BI VWC VDV CHF COK	**G**
CRAIGMOOR SHIRAZ, CRAIGMOOR 1991 New South Wales	*Slightly closed nose; complex palate. Sweet fruit, ripe and full; some astringency in finish.*	£7.40	DBY TAN HDL AHW NY	**B**

AUSTRALIA • RED

SEPPELT CHALAMBAR SHIRAZ, SEPPELT & SONS 1992 South Australia	*Good, deep flavours with straightforward berry juice character. Excellent and vibrant.*	£7.50	WSG BOO HOU COK NY	(B)
THE WILLOWS VINEYARD SHIRAZ 1991 South Australia	*Very creamy vanilla/oak and sweet brambles on nose; slightly jammy, leathery palate. Exhilaratingly ripe.*	£7.60	AUC RD	(B)
MITCHELTON RESERVE SHIRAZ, MITCHELTON WINES 1993 Victoria	*Dark, youthful; rich, plum bouquet. Ripe, juicy wine; good tannins and length. Very satisfying.*	£7.70	JEF MTL VDV VIL	(B)
CHAPEL HILL SHIRAZ, CHAPEL HILL WINERY 1992 McLaren Vale	*Powerful but soft fruit; quite sweet with dry extract and finish.*	£8.00	AUC BOO WR BU TO	(S)
CAPEL VALE SHIRAZ, CAPEL VALE 1993 Western Australia	*Good, fruity aromas following on to palate; dry character, with tannin. Concentrated fruit flavours.*	£8.00	AHW	(B)
CHATSFIELD SHIRAZ, CHATSFIELD 1990 Mount Barker	*Deep, red wine; smoky, leathery nose. Hot, spicy, blackberry, sweet palate.*	£8.10	OXB R	(B)
CORIOLE VINEYARDS SHIRAZ, CORIOLE VINEYARDS 1992 South Australia	*Deep ruby; youthful, oaky, sweet raspberry nose. Confirmed on palate with New World tannins.*	£8.40	WTR VDV TAN	(S)
GRENACHE/SHIRAZ, JAMES HALLIDAY 1994 McLaren Vale	*Warm, ripe, red berries on nose; full acid and rich flavour.*	£8.40	BWC VDV	(S)

ROTHBURY ESTATE RESERVE SHIRAZ, ROTHBURY ESTATE 1993 New South Wales	*Intense, young nose, showing some cedary character. Good aromas, and middle palate. Made to keep.*	**£8.80**	Widely available	(S)
EBENEZER SHIRAZ, BRL HARDY WINE CO/VALLEY GROWERS CO-OP 1992 South Australia	*Deep colour; ripe, spicy character. Medium weight; attractive wine that lasts well.*	**£9.00**	HBR DBY OD	(B)
BEST'S GREAT WESTERN SHIRAZ, BEST'S WINES 1992 Victoria	*Ripe, glossy fruit; scented and confected bouquet. Chewy wine with fresh acidity.*	**£9.20**	SWS DBY VDV SHB	(S)
PRESIDENT'S SELECTION SHIRAZ, WOLF BLASS, WOLF BLASS 1992 South Australia	*Oaky, sweet vanilla bouquet with good flavours in the mouth.*	**£9.40**	Widely available	(B)
BAILEYS 1920's BLOCK SHIRAZ, BAILEYS Victoria	*Deep, young colour; quite closed nose but soft, violet, slightly peppery character. Dry, tannic palate.*	**£9.50**	RBW OD COK	(S)
PATRIARCH SHIRAZ, DAVID WYNN, DAVID WYNN 1993 South Australia	*Minty, New World Shiraz nose. Sweet, young, juicy fruit with good tannins and medium weight.*	**£9.50**	Widely available	(B)
LANGHI SHIRAZ, MOUNT LANGHI GHIRAN 1992 Victoria	*Soft, creamy nose; fruit palate, clean and decent with some heat. Attractive, ripe blackberry palate.*	**£9.50**	EWC DBY ENO CPW SEB CWI DIR	(B)
ST HALLETT OLD BLOCK SHIRAZ, ST HALLETT 1992 South Australia	*Good wine with a sweet vanilla character and pleasing finish.*	**£9.80**	Widely available	(B)

EILEEN HARDY SHIRAZ, BRL HARDY WINE CO 1991 South Australia	*Rich, spicy wine showing maturity; fine and fragrant. Good tarry nose, long and concentrated. Chewy.*	£9.90	HBR DBY ADN OD SAF R	(S)
EILEEN HARDY SHIRAZ, BRL HARDY WINE CO 1992 South Australia	*Oaky nose with sweet vanilla aromas; concentrated flavours. Good acid and fresh structure.*	£9.90	HBR DBY ADN OD SAF R	(S)
CLASSIC CLARE SHIRAZ, BRL HARDY WINE CO 1993 Clare Valley	*Spicy, raspberry palate; Good oak and finish.*	£9.90	HBR DBY VDV FUL OD	(B)
LAWSONS SHIRAZ, ORLANDO WINES 1988 South Australia	*Good, chewy, old-style wine; spicy, mushroom and old oak nose. Fat and sweet palate.*	£10.00	CAX	(S)
LAWSONS SHIRAZ, ORLANDO WINES 1989 South Australia	*Spicy, new vanilla, oak nose; juicy fruit and sweet finish.*	£10.00	CAX	(S)
PLANTAGENET MOUNT BARKER SHIRAZ, PLANTAGENET WINES 1993 Western Australia	*Dark, youthful colour; open nose full of oak and tannin. Will develop.*	£10.00	SG	(S)
MITCHELTON PRINT LABEL SHIRAZ, MITCHELTON WINES 1992 Victoria	*Strong, up-front fruit on nose with good weight and balance. Ripe tannins.*	£10.10	JEF VDV OD	(S)
MCRAE WOOD SHIRAZ, JIM BARRY, JIM BARRY 1992 South Australia	*Good tannins and soft, sweet flavours. Pleasing ripeness and texture; good length.*	£11.20	NEG TAN	(S)

MCRAE WOOD SHIRAZ, JIM BARRY 1993 South Australia	*Ripe, rich nose; good weight of fruit on palate and excellent longevity.*	£11.20	NEG TAN	(B)
LINDEMANS LIMESTONE RIDGE SHIRAZ CABERNET, LINDEMANS 1991 South Australia	*Tar aroma with ripe fruit. Dry, excellent longevity with balanced fruit/acid/tannin.*	£11.70	Widely available	(S)
ABERFELDY, TIM ADAMS WINES, 1993 South Australia	*Hugely elegant; spiced plums and warm, oak nose. Gutsy palate; soft damson and spicy finish.*	£12.00	AUC	(G)
ELDERTON COMMAND SHIRAZ, ELDERTON WINES 1990 Barossa Valley	*Good, full, red wine with nice, sweetish nose. Sweet, slightly spicy with some vanilla.*	£12.50	ALL	(B)
MOUNT EDELSTONE SHIRAZ, HENSCHKE, HENSCHKE 1992 Eden Valley	*Lovely nose of huge plum and talcum powder. Big plum flavours. Reassuringly fleshy; long finish.*	£12.50	Widely available	(G)
ELDERTON 'COMMAND' SHIRAZ, ELDERTON WINES 1988 South Australia	*Front of mouth fruit flavours; ripe, rich and delicious. Fruity wine; excellent balance. Easy drinking.*	£12.50	ALL AV	(S)
E & E BLACK PEPPER SHIRAZ, BRL HARDY WINE 1992 South Australia	*Vibrant, minty nose with marzipan. Lush, rich fruit palate with youthful tannins. White pepper 'twang'.*	£12.60	Widely available	(G)
E & E BLACK PEPPER SHIRAZ, BAROSSA VALLEY ESTATES 1992 South Australia	*Intense, ripe, spicy nose, hints of leather. Complex, developed nose carried onto palate. Concentrated and creamy.*	£13.00	Widely available	(B)

PENFOLDS MAGILL ESTATE SHIRAZ, PENFOLDS 1991 South Australia	*Plum nose; wet wool, farmyard character. Fruit flavour and good tannin; good oak and spice.*	£13.20	Widely available	**B**
JASPER HILL GEORGIA'S PADDOCK, JASPER HILL 1992 Victoria	*Smoky nose with violets, brambles, spice and licorice. Great intensity; hints of new oak influence.*	£13.60	AUE ADN	**G**
DALWHINNIE VICTORIA SHIRAZ, DALWHINNIE VINEYARDS 1993 Victoria	*Intense baked nose; rich, ripe and peppery. Sweet leather, tar and brambles. Sweetish; firm tannins.*	£14.60	WTR UBC	**S**
CHAPEL HILL RESERVE, CHAPEL HILL WINERY 1992 McLaren Vale	*Sweet, gentle, spicy aromas; smoky bacon and sweet plum flavours. Interesting; good use of oak.*	£15.00	AUC	**B**
ROSEMOUNT BALMORAL SYRAH, ROSEMOUNT 1992 South Australia	*Big, tannic wine with rich cassis and damsons and bitter chocolate. Long and meaty.*	£15.10	ROS TO CEB	**B**
WYNNS COONAWARRA ESTATE MICHAEL SHIRAZ, WYNNS 1991 South Australia	*Hints of dark fruits and new wood on nose. Full, soft palate; minty, peppery fruits.*	£15.30	Widely available	**B**
THE HANGING ROCK SHIRAZ, THE HANGING ROCK WINERY 1991 Victoria	*Full, rich, sweaty nose; ripe blackberry and hint of animal! Balanced. Concentration of ripe fruit.*	£16.00	THP	**S**
THE ARMAGH, JIM BARRY, JIM BARRY 1993 Clare Valley	*Essence of blackcurrant aroma; top oak. Lovely texture; good flavours which develop. Strong, acid balance.*	£24.40	NEG TAN OD	**S**

PENFOLDS GRANGE, PENFOLDS 1990 South Australia	*Intense, ripe Shiraz nose; ripe, jammy palate with sweet fruit and quite hard tannins. Impressive.*	**£47.30**	Widely available	**B**

OTHER RED

TESCO MATARO, KINGSTON ESTATE Murray Valley	*Elegant, fruity. Fresh, ripe, spicy style. Juicy fruit and herb aromas. Very approachable.*	**£2.00**	BOO TO	**B**
BUCKLOW HILL DRY RED, SOUTHCORP South Australia	*Lifted, aromatic berry with touch of greasiness and earth. Well balanced with medium length.*	**£3.80**	PEF	**B**
ANGOVES TEA TREE ESTATE MALBEC, ANGOVES 1994 Riverland	*Aromatic, well balanced with rich, smooth, spicy cherries. Ripe fruit, leather adding to complexity.*	**£4.00**	SAF	**B**
BASEDOW BUSH VINE GRENACHE, BASEDOW 1994 South Australia	*Powerful if aromatic. Concentrated cherry and mango fruits. Cream soda and vanilla palate.*	**£6.00**	BI	**B**
CLANCY'S BAROSSA VALLEY RED, PETER LEHMANN 1992 South Australia	*Tobacco nose with cedar and oak traces. Ripe, berry fruit with balanced tannins and deep finish.*	**£7.00**	Widely available	**G**
JAMIESON'S RUN RED COONAWARRA, MILDARA 1993 South Australia	*Aromatic wine of complexity. Spice, cigar-box aromas, smoke and plums on palate.*	**£7.40**	WFB MTL DBY TO HOU OD HDL	**S**

CHATSFIELD CABERNET FRANC, CHATSFIELD 1994 Mount Barker	*Fragrant, spicy cherries on nose. Excellent Cabernet Franc character with currants and slight earthiness.*	£7.60	OXB VDV R NY	(S)
JAMIESON'S RUN RED COONAWARRA, MILDARA 1992 South Australia	*Showing some complexity, but still fruit-driven. Red fruits - plums, cranberries - are intense and juicy.*	£7.70	Widely available	(G)
ORLANDO ST HEWETT PINOT NOIR, ORLANDO WINES 1992 South Australia	*Big, gutsy style of Burgundy displaying warm, spicy raspberry and rich, supple texture. Seductively smooth.*	£8.00	CAX	(S)
TARRAWARRA VINEYARDS TUNNEL HILL PINOT NOIR, TARRAWARRA VINEYARDS 1994 Yarra Valley	*Soft, jammy Pinot Noir. Creamy, raspberry ripple and smooth, velvety texture. Finishes well.*	£8.50	LAW DBY HOU HDL	(B)
YARRA RIDGE PINOT NOIR, YARRA RIDGE 1993 Yarra Valley	*Jammy, New World style of Pinot Noir. Good, smoky, rich fruit with hints of mintiness.*	£8.50	WFB	(B)
STONIERS PINOT NOIR, STONIER, YUILL HAMSON & LIMB 1993 Mornington Peninsula	*Delightful, soft strawberry overlaid with smoky oak. Still young. Will repay further keeping. Well crafted.*	£8.60	HOL DIR WAW OD MRF	(B)
TIM KNAPPSTEIN PINOT NOIR, TIM KNAPPSTEIN 1993 South Australia	*Fresh, balanced style showing supple fruit. Almost too soft, but held together by good acidity.*	£10.00	GRA	(B)
MORRIS OF RUTHERGLEN DURIF, MORRIS WINES 1991 Victoria	*Huge, intense wine with ripe damson fruit. Layers of currants, spice, chocolate and oak. Velvety.*	£10.20	ADN VDV NI CAX AMY NY	(G)

AUSTRALIA • WHITE

MEADOWBANK VINEYARD PINOT NOIR, MEADOWBANK VINEYARD 1994 Tasmania	*Mint and plum aromas. Still youthful. Herbaceous quality. Crisp, fresh raspberry.*	£10.50	HA ADN	(B)
TARRAWARRA PINOT NOIR, TARRAWARRA VINEYARDS 1992 Yarra Valley	*Lovely, ripe, red summer fruit character. Fine texture of melted milk chocolate and creamy vanilla.*	£10.80	LAW DBY TO HDL	(S)
MOUNT BOLD, MAXWELL WINES 1992 McLaren Vale	*Good, spicy berry with eucalyptus twist. Peppery, subtly oaked palate. Good length and crisp finish.*	£11.00	AMD	(B)
STONIERS RESERVE PINOT NOIR, STONIER,YUILL HAMSON & LIMB 1993 Mornington Peninsula	*Deep, rich berry aromas. Clean quality with good concentration and gently warming finish.*	£12.20	HOL DIR OD WAW MRF	(B)
COLDSTREAM HILLS RESERVE PINOT NOIR, COLDSTREAM HILLS 1993 Yarra Valley Victoria	*Generous, clean style. Classic Pinot with delicate perfume and soft, ripe summer fruit flavours. Complex.*	£12.70	BWC VDV CPW OD AV HDL	(S)

CHARDONNAY

ASDA SOUTH AUSTRALIA CHARDONNAY, ANGOVES 1993 South Australia	*Restrained, complex combination of creamy banana. Oily avocado consistency. Good, long finish.*	£4.00	A	(B)
MARIENBERG CHARDONNAY, MARIENBERG 1993 McLaren Vale	*Tropical fruit and coconut. Definite walnut note. Tangy grapefruit middle palate. Vanilla finish.*	£4.50	LHP	(S)

AUSTRALIA • WHITE

TOLLANA BLACK LABEL CHARDONNAY, PENFOLDS 1993 South Australia	*Sharp, lemon yellow with green tints. Creamy, fragrant, vanilla oak on nose. Warm, creamy texture.*	**£5.00**	TH WR BU	**B**
RED CLIFFS ESTATE CHARDONNAY, RED CLIFFS ESTATE PLC 1994 Mildura, Victoria	*Scented pineapple aromas; lifted and yeasty. Dry palate.*	**£5.10**	KAT WR BU TH BI COK	**B**
PENFOLDS KOONUNGA HILL CHARDONNAY, PENFOLDS 1994 South Australia	*Ripe peaches, flesh and vanilla pod aromas. Lean, fresh fruit, good oak, citrus.*	**£5.10**	Widely available	**B**
ROWLANDS BROOK CHARDONNAY, PENFOLDS 1993 South East Australia	*Pleasant vanilla nose. Excellent fruit build of melon and apricot. Easy-drinking summer wine.*	**£5.10**	MVN HHC TAN AV	**B**
ORLANDO CHARDONNAY, ORLANDO WINES 1994 South East Australia	*Well-integrated, creamy, oaky, fruit salad nose. Good acidity and weight. Citrus finish.*	**£5.50**	DBY VW CAX TAN SAF TMW UBC	**B**
LEASINGHAM DOMAINE CHARDONNAY, BRL HARDY WINE CO 1993 South Australia	*Peach, lanolin and vanilla on nose. Peach and lightly toasted oak flavours. Short finish.*	**£5.80**	HBR ODR	**B**
LEASINGHAM DOMAINE CHARDONNAY, BRL HARDY WINE CO 1994 South Australia	*Intense, banana custard nose. Eggy acid on palate. Spritzy lemon and lime finish.*	**£5.80**	HBR DBY OD	**B**
ROTHBURY AUGUSTINE CHARDONNAY, ROTHBURY 1994 Mudgee	*Creamy nose of mangoes and boneyed melon. Limes in middle palate and citrus fizz.*	**£5.90**	RBW MTL DBY HOU COK	**B**

AUSTRALIA • WHITE					
TESCO MCLAREN VALE CHARDONNAY, ROSEMOUNT 1993 McLaren Vale	*Smoky, toasty fruit on nose, chewy fruit on palate. Lively.*	**£6.00**	TO	(B)
TATACHILLA CHARDONNAY, TATACHILLA WINERY 1994 McLaren Vale	*Grapefruit nose; warm, ripe fruit palate with tinges of peanut. Good finish.*	**£6.00**	W	(B)
HARDY'S PADTHAWAY CHARDONNAY, BRL HARDY WINE CO 1994 South Australia	*Creamy, lemon sherbet nose; tangy tropical fruit on palate. Long citrus finish.*	**£6.00**	HBR MTL VDV	(B)
MAGLIERI MCLAREN VALE CHARDONNAY, MAGLIERI 1994 South Australia	*Aromas of French oak and lemongrass. Fruity sweetness, oak and acidity.*	**£6.00**	PLB	(B)
OLD WINERY CHARDONNAY, TYRRELLS VINEYARDS 1993 New South Wales	*Toasty oak, banana and melon come forth. Underlying concentration of fruit and lemony freshness.*	**£6.10**	DBY BU WR TH G&M AV	(B)
RENMANO CHARDONNAY BIN RESERVE 124, RENMANO WINES 1992 South Australia	*Vanilla pod and a touch of lychee and apricot on the nose. Springy citrus fruit on palate coupled with oily emollience.*	**£6.10**	HOH VIL	(S)
COWRA VINEYARD CHARDONNAY, RICHMOND GROVE WINES 1993 Cowra N S W	*Nose of vanilla essence. Sweet custard flavours; wonderful citrus finale.*	**£6.20**	HOU CAX ABY COK	(B)
ROSEMOUNT CHARDONNAY, ROSEMOUNT 1994 New South Wales	*Glorious lemon and lime aroma with hints of melon and pineapple. Sweet fruit flavours.*	**£6.20**	Widely available	(B)

AUSTRALIA • WHITE

SIMON HACKETT CHARDONNAY, SIMON HACKETT 1994 South Australia	*Intense, warm caramelised banana. Sweet and supple palate with tones of vanilla.*	£6.20	AUS DBY HCK HLV CPW HOU	**B**
ARROWFIELD MOUNTAIN LAGOON CHARDONNAY, ARROWFIELD 1993 New South Wales	*Lean with a slightly musty complexity. Broad, full-bodied and mouth filling. Crisp acid.*	£6.30	ALL	**B**
TRENTHAM CHARDONNAY, TRENTHAM 1993 Murray River	*Lemon and lime on nose. Raucously rich palate dappled with pineapple, lemon sherbet and cream.*	£6.30	BOO OXB L&W VDV HVW R NY	**B**
MONTROSE MUDGEE CHARDONNAY, MONTROSE WINES 1994 New South Wales	*Forthcoming fruit; melon and lychee. Unusual rubberiness and rich, tropical sensations. Good length.*	£6.50	CAX AMY	**B**
YALDARA RESERVE CHARDONNAY, YALDARA 1993 South Australia	*Rich, vanilla oak. Intense, sweet pineapple mellowed by buttery smoothness.*	£6.60	SWS DIR HVW	**B**
BASEDOW CHARDONNAY, BASEDOW 1993 South Australia	*Heavy, caramel, oak and tropical fruit. Superb balance of ripe fruit and sweet oak.*	£6.60	VWC BIV WC VDV	**B**
KATNOOK ESTATE RIDDOCH CHARDONNAY, KATNOOK ESTATE 1993 South Australia	*Pineapple and coconut on nose with lanolin smoothness and touches of Crème Anglais. Sherbety finish.*	£6.60	KAT WR BU BI CHF	**S**
BASEDOW CHARDONNAY, BASEDOW 1994 South Australia	*Lovely, creamy, lemon fondant nose. Excellent, muscular Chardonnay; good acidity. Complex flavours.*	£6.70	BI VWC VDV COK	**B**

AUSTRALIA • WHITE				
RIDDOCH CHARDONNAY, KATNOOK ESTATE 1992 South Australia	*Rich, honey colour. Creamy melon with mango. Solid, overt oaki-ness and virile acidity.*	£6.80	Widely available	(B)
INGLEWOOD TWO RIVERS WOODED CHARDONNAY, INGLEWOOD VINEYARDS 1994 New South Wales	*Beautiful, honeyed sweetness on nose with tropical fruit and buttery creaminess on palate.*	£7.00	SV HW	(B)
DENNIS CHARDONNAY, DENNIS WINES 1994 McLaren Vale	*Honey, cream and pineapple aromas. Buttery fruit on palate. Long, lemon soufflé fin-ish.*	£7.00	THP	(B)
REDBANK CHARDONNAY, REDBANK 1994 Victoria	*Sherbety nose with hint of vanilla pod. Coconut, cream, bananas and mango on palate.*	£7.00	GRA	(S)
ROTHBURY ESTATE BARREL FERMENT CHARDONNAY, ROTHBURY 1994 New South Wales	*Magnificent, creamy peach nose. Palate has virile melon, apricots, mango and honey. Touches of kernal.*	£7.10	Widely available	(S)
CHATEAU TAHBILK CHARDONNAY, CHATEAU TAHBILK 1992 Victoria	*Toasty new oak on nose with ripe tropical fruits and apples. Honeyed, peaches and butter.*	£7.40	PLE DBY B TH OD	(G)
LONG GULLY CHARDONNAY, LONG GULLY ESTATE 1992 Yarra Valley	*Subtle, green, lean nose. Good, varietal character.*	£7.40	REN DBY	(B)
ST HALLETT CHARDONNAY, ST HALLETT 1994 South Australia	*Oaky nose. Touches of melon, mango and pineapple. Citrus peel calmed by vanilla, honey and butter.*	£7.50	Widely available	(S)

AUSTRALIA • WHITE				
ST HALLETT CHARDONNAY, ST HALLETT 1993 South Australia	*Melon, pineapple and banana on nose. Big, zesty climax.*	**£7.60**	Widely available	**B**
HILL SMITH ESTATE CHARDONNAY, S SMITH & SONS 1993 Eden Valley	*Heftily oaked pineapple mellowed by touch of kiwi. Warm, spicy; soothed by smooth, friendly oak.*	**£7.70**	GRA WIN	**B**
YARRA RIDGE CHARDONNAY, YARRA RIDGE 1994 Yarra Valley	*Exotic, fruity nose dissipating on palate with coconut and melon. Good acidity and balance.*	**£7.70**	WFB JS	**B**
DRAYTON'S HUNTER VALLEY CHARDONNAY, W DRAYTON & SONS PTY 1994 New South Wales	*Lanolin nose. Concentrated green-gagey, figgish fruit on early palate. Serene finish.*	**£8.00**	OWS	**S**
GEOFF MERRILL CHARDONNAY, GEOFF MERRILL 1993 McLaren Vale	*Exciting oak on nose with herbs and cloves. Vanilla pod on palate. Crème Anglais and mango.*	**£8.00**	PLE JS	**S**
PETER DENNIS CHARDONNAY, PETER DENNIS WINES 1993 McLaren Vale	*Big vanilla oak on the nose with lemon sherbet and custard cream on the palate.*	**£8.00**	THP	**B**
YALUMBA SHOW RESERVE CHARDONNAY, YALUMBA 1993 South Australia	*Delicate, smoky nose; quiet, buttery, with vanilla and sweet lanolin notes. Very toasty and biscuity.*	**£8.20**	GRA WIN	**S**
HOLLICK CHARDONNAY, HOLLICK 1993 South Australia	*Bananas, toffee and caramel aromas. Fresh, toasty oak. Creamy, lanolin character.*	**£8.20**	BOO OXB VDV ODR	**S**

AUSTRALIA • WHITE				
NORMANS CHARDONNAY CHAIS CLARENDON, NORMANS WINES LTD 1994 South Australia	*Vegetal, herbaceous nose; vanilla and raw wood on palate. Mild melon and avocado.*	£8.30	NAD	**(B)**
ST HILARY PADTHAWAY CHARDONNAY, ORLANDO WINES 1993 South Australia	*Beautiful golden/yellow. Pleasant apple, grassy nose. Discreet fruit and toasty oak.*	£8.40	DBY CAX	**(B)**
CASSEGRAIN CHARDONNAY, CASSEGRAIN 1991 New South Wales	*Deep yellow colour. Intense ripe fruit offset by reasonably subtle oak.*	£8.50	L&W	**(B)**
STONIERS CHARDONNAY, STONIER, YUILL HAMSON & LIMB 1993 Mornington Peninsula	*Classic Burgundian features: oak married with ripe, lively fruit. Citrus mid palate with coconut finish.*	£8.50	HOL DIR WAW OD	**(S)**
SALISBURY ESTATE SHOW RESERVE CHARDONNAY, SALISBURY ESTATE 1993 Victoria	*Toasty, smoked, rose-like aroma. Smooth and raunchy; sufficiently oaked and fresh.*	£8.50	EWC ENO	**(B)**
PIPERS BROOK NINTH ISLAND CHARDONNAY, PIPERS BROOK 1994 Tasmania	*Flowery nose with lovely, crisp fruit character on palate. Creamy, buttery finish.*	£8.60	POL DBY W SEB FUL HDL COK	**(S)** WINE OF THE YEAR
TUNNEL HILL CHARDONNAY, TARRAWARRA VINEYARDS 1993 Yarra Valley	*Soft vanilla, oak nose; warm, smooth feel mixed with electric limes.*	£8.60	LAW DBY HDL	**(B)**
ST MICHAEL ROSEMOUNT ORANGE VINEYARD CHARDONNAY, ROSEMOUNT 1993 Orange	*Full nose of vanilla and lemongrass. Neat, zesty balance of lime, pineapple and lemon.*	£9.00	M&S	**(S)**

AUSTRALIA • WHITE

ROSEMOUNT ORANGE VINEYARD CHARDONNAY, ROSEMOUNT 1993 New South Wales	*Toasty, biscuity nose with white truffles. Beautifully citric with lanolin silkiness. Nuts, marshmallow and butter.*	£9.00	ROS W JS	(S)
WOLF BLASS PRESIDENT'S SELECTION CHARDONNAY, WOLF BLASS 1994 South Australia	*Delicious, well-balanced, creamy wine. Traces of peach, mango, Crème Anglais and banana. Luxuriant.*	£9.00	WFB MTL DBY CE B OD EVI	(G)
CHARDONNAY BRANDS LAIRA, MCWILLIAMS 1993 South Australia	*Savoury, oaky nose. Dry, balanced, enhanced by a clean, citrussy finish.*	£9.00	WAV	(S)
HEGGIES CHARDONNAY, S SMITH & SONS 1993 Eden Valley	*Coconut milk and lychees on palate. General creaminess and hints of syrupy ginger.*	£9.10	GRA OD WIN	(B)
COLDSTREAM HILLS CHARDONNAY, JAMES HALLIDAY 1994 Yarra Valley	*Sweet, sherbet, floral nose. Excellent use of fresh, new oak. Strong, aggressive, clean.*	£9.10	DBY BWC OD AV H DL	(S)
DOMAINE CHANDON GREEN POINT CHARDONNAY, DOMAINE CHANDON 1993 Yarra Valley	*Rich, appley nose with good weight of oak. Very forward style. Confident and boisterous.*	£9.10	Widely available	(B)
KRONDORF SHOW RESERVE CHARDONNAY, KRONDORF 1994 South Australia	*Vanilla and lemon sherbet on nose. Wonderful mixture of citrus and melon in mouth.*	£9.20	WFB DBY ES TO	(B)
COLDSTREAM HILLS CHARDONNAY, COLDSTREAM HILLS 1994 Yarra Valley Victoria	*Delicious, smooth, oily emollience with a bright, crisp citrus bite. Full of Aussie character.*	£9.40	BWC DBY CPW OD AVH DL	(B)

AUSTRALIA • WHITE

INGLEWOOD SHOW RESERVE CHARDONNAY, INGLEWOOD VINEYARDS 1994 New South Wales	*Vanilla nose with light oak and good fruit on palate. Elegant and dry.*	**£9.50**	SVH W	Ⓑ
EILEEN HARDY CHARDONNAY, BRL HARDY WINE CO 1993 South Australia	*Lively, oaky Burgundian style. Tannins and Crème Anglais, vanilla pods. Overall ripe fruit.*	**£9.70**	HBR DBY OD	Ⓑ
CAPEL VALE CHARDONNAY, CAPEL VALE 1992 Western Australia	*Soft nose with floral aspects and touch of asparagus. Good acidity; sufficient tannins; luscious fruit.*	**£10.00**	M&S AHW	Ⓑ
KINGSTON ESTATE RESERVE CHARDONNAY, KINGSTON ESTATE 1993 Riverland	*Lemon and pencil shaving nose. Attractive vanilla style. Rich, golden structure with trim, French oak.*	**£10.00**	TO	Ⓑ
TIM KNAPPSTEIN LENSWOOD CHARDONNAY, TIM KNAPPSTEIN 1993 South Australia	*Sticky, butterscotch nose. Subtle vanilla fruit on palate, slightly warm moving towards hot. Still developing.*	**£10.00**	GRA OD WIN	Ⓑ
SCOTCHMANS HILL GEELONG CHARDONNAY, SCOTCHMANS HILL 1993 Victoria	*Attractive, lemon nose. Big, fruit extracts with spicy lemon acidity. Creative use of oak.*	**£10.00**	J&B	Ⓑ
PLANTAGENET MOUNT BARKER CHARDONNAY, PLANTAGENET WINES 1994 Western Australia	*Cheesy nose which hints at coconut milk and lanolin. On palate: easy ripe fruit, splash of citrus.*	**£10.00**	SG	Ⓢ
SPECIAL RESERVE CHARDONNAY, CAPEL VALE 1993 Western Australia	*Lovely nose with sweet vanilla and oak. Sweet, oily lanolin character with touch of mangoes.*	**£10.00**	AHW	Ⓑ

AUSTRALIA • WHITE

PETALUMA CHARDONNAY, PETALUMA 1991 South Australia	*Toasted Chardonnay nose with hints of nectarine, apricot, melon and strawberry. Vanilla and oak.*	**£11.50**	GRA DIR NI OD	(G)
PETALUMA CHARDONNAY, PETALUMA 1992 South Australia	*A delicate, yeasty nose with light, floral fruit and soothing, oily vanilla. Good New World style.*	**£11.70**	Widely available	(B)
MOUNTADAM CHARDONNAY, MOUNTADAM 1993 South Australia	*Aromas of deep, richly oaked vanilla and fresh tropical fruit. Glorious wine*	**£11.90**	Widely available	(S)
MOUNTADAM CHARDONNAY, ADAM WYNN 1991 South Australia	*Toasty, marshmallow sweetness. Fruity palate: glimpses of lychee and melon, fig and citrus.*	**£12.00**	BU BOO ADN WRC HF OD SHB	(S)
STONIERS RESERVE CHARDONNAY, STONIER 1993 Mornington Peninsula	*Subtle nose; tinges of lemon and lime. Spiciness, camomile and mint on mid palate. Good oak finish.*	**£12.20**	HOL DIR WAW OD	(B)
DRIFTWOOD CHARDONNAY, DRIFTWOOD WINERY 1994 Margaret River	*Toasty, complex nose featuring lychee, mango and lanolin. Overall, nicely integrated and smooth.*	**£13.00**	MPA	(B)
COLDSTREAM HILLS RESERVE CHARDONNAY, COLDSTREAM HILLS 1993 Victoria	*Buttery, vanilla pod nose. Plenty of lemony fruit and good, clean acidity. Touches of nuttiness.*	**£13.20**	BWC CPW OD HDL	(S)
DALWHINNIE CHARDONNAY, DALWHINNIE VINEYARDS 1993 Victoria	*Aromas of vanilla pod, papaya and grapefruit. Oaky flavours exuding creamy oiliness and exotic spices.*	**£13.70**	WTR UBC	(S)

AUSTRALIA • WHITE				
TYRRELLS VINEYARDS PRIVATE BIN VAT 47 CHARDONNAY, TYRRELLS VINEYARDS 1994 New South Wales	*Buttery, toasty, melony and lemony. Still a touch young but virile and exciting.*	£14.80	G&M JS AV	**B**
LEEUWIN ESTATE 'ART SERIES' CHARDONNAY, LEEUWIN ESTATE 1990 Margaret River	*Tropical nose with touch of zesty lemon and calming avocado. Creamy palate. Great length.*	£15.70	OD DD	**S**
ROSEMOUNT ESTATE ROXBURGH CHARDONNAY, ROSEMOUNT 1993 New South Wales	*Hot, toasty nose. Cool nectarine on palate with oily emollient. Fat and round.*	£15.80	ROS DBY WR BU TO CEB	**S**

RIESLING

PENFOLDS RIESLING 'BIN 202', PENFOLDS 1994 South Australia	*Fresh, greenish colour. Clean and crisp. Slightly vegetal, and full of juicy lime flavours.*	£4.00	Widely available	**B**
WYNNS COONAWARRA ESTATE RIESLING, WYNNS 1994 South Australia	*Rich, Riesling fruit character backed by some ennervating citrus acidity.*	£4.20	Widely available	**B**
TESCO CLARE VALLEY RIESLING, MITCHELL 1994 South Australia	*Clean, fresh fruit with citrus acidity. Hints of spice on the nose. Ideal summer drinking.*	£5.00	TO	**B**
WOLF BLASS SILVER LABEL RIESLING, WOLF BLASS 1993 South Australia	*Charming Riesling with hint of petroleum in the aroma. Full of lime with some toast.*	£5.10	WFB VW VDV	**S**

AUSTRALIA • WHITE

PFEIFFER CARLYLE ESTATE RIESLING, PFEIFFER WINES 1994 Victoria	*Youthful nose of spiced apples and grapefruit. Fruit salad flavours in mouth with fresh acidity.*	£5.80	REN	**B**
PEWSEY VALE EDEN VALLEY RIESLING, PEWSEY VALE 1994 Eden Valley	*Excellent example of Australian Riesling. Palate of fresh apples and cream backed by zesty acidity.*	£6.00	GRA TO VDV WIN	**S**
BROWN BROTHERS RIESLING, BROWN BROTHERS 1994 Milawa Victoria	*Ripe Riesling. Flowery with hints of honey. Lively lime and lemon citrus flavours. Steely finish.*	£6.00	DIR MD NY VIL	**B**
GLENARA ADELAIDE HILLS DRY RIESLING, GLENARA 1990 South Australia	*Rich Riesling nose of toffee apples and paraffin. Powerful punchy fruit. Soft and fleshy.*	£7.40	VDV	**B**
ORLANDO WINES, STEINGARTEN RHINE RIESLING, ORLANDO WINES 1992 South Australia	*Evocative of summer with smells of fresh grass and flavours of apricots and peaches.*	£8.00	CAX BI	**B**
BROWN BROTHERS FAMILY RESERVE RIESLING, BROWN BROTHERS 1991 Milawa Victoria	*Rich, Riesling nose of honeyed apples and petrol. Full, ripe fruit with acidity. Long finish.*	£8.70	MD ADN VDV CPW DIR NI NY	**B**

SEMILLON

LINDEMANS CAWARRA SEMILLON CHARDONNAY, LINDEMANS 1994 South Australia	*Developed, tropical fruit flavours with lovely integration of ripe peaches, and melons.*	£3.90	Widely available	**B**

AUSTRALIA • WHITE				
PENFOLDS RAWSON'S RETREAT 'BIN 21' SEMILLON CHARDONNAY, PENFOLDS 1994 South Australia	*Full of ripe, tropical Semillon flavours. Great depth and complexity and suggestion of vanilla oak.*	**£4.50**	Widely available	(S)
PENFOLDS SEMILLON CHARDONNAY, PENFOLDS 1994 South Australia	*Beautifully balanced oak and peaches. Rich, almost oily, cut with hint of lemon acidity. Luscious.*	**£5.00**	Widely available	(S)
ROSEMOUNT CHARDONNAY SEMILLON, ROSEMOUNT 1994 New South Wales	*Clean, fresh and full of fruit; ripe pineapples and lemons; easy drinking, with character.*	**£5.20**	ROS JS	(B)
SUTHERLAND HUNTER VALLEY SEMILLON, SUTHERLAND WINES 1991 New South Wales	*Pineapple and lychee flavours dominate.*	**£5.80**	PCE	(B)
BASEDOW SEMILLON, BASEDOW 1993 South Australia	*Rich, ripe fruit layered with warm, spicy oak. Clean, lemon acidity and long finish.*	**£5.80**	VWC BI VDV	(B)
IRONSTONE SEMILLON CHARDONNAY, IRONSTONE VINEYARDS 1994 Western Australia	*Grapey, gooseberry aromas - delicious, full flavoured wine with superb fruit character. Well-integrated acidity.*	**£6.00**	PRG MWW FUL	(B)
REDBANK SEMILLON, REDBANK 1994 Victoria	*Attractive and delicate on nose. Subtle oak is filled on palate by oily richness.*	**£6.50**	GRA WIN	(B)
GEOFF MERRILL SEMILLON CHARDONNAY, GOEFF MERRILL 1989 South Australia	*Powerful, ripe apple, honey and new oak with grassy tones. Supple fruit. Buttery, toasted oak.*	**£6.70**	PLE OD	(B)

AUSTRALIA • WHITE

BROWN BROS SEMILLON, BROWN BROTHERS 1991 Milawa, Victoria	*Deep golden colour; oaky nose. Citrus peel fruit and a hint of botrytis on palate.*	£6.90	Widely available	(S)
PENFOLDS BARREL FERMENTED SEMILLON, PENFOLDS 1994 South Australia	*Overtly oaky nose and grapey, floral, citrus peel fruit. Oak just dominating. Full and complex.*	£7.00	PEF BOO MWW VD VNI	(S)
SEMILLON, THE WILLOWS VINEYARD, THE WILLOWS VINEYARD 1993 South Australia	*Rich gold. Open complex aroma with botrytis. Juicy Semillon offset by buttery oak. Great depth.*	£7.00	AUC	(G)
MCWILLIAMS ELIZABETH SEMILLON, MCWILLIAMS 1989 New South Wales	*Bright yellow colour and intense aroma of ripe lemons, grassy herbs and fresh stone fruits.*	£7.20	WAV DBY ADN	(B)
SEMILLON, HERITAGE WINES, HERITAGE WINES 1993 South Australia	*Semillon nose with rich butter and toasty vanilla oak. Broad and oily in mouth.*	£7.60	AUC WR BU	(B)
CASSEGRAIN BLACK LABEL SEMILLON, CASSEGRAIN 1989 New South Wales	*Complex aromas of toffee, honey, butter and bread. Full and complex with perfect acidity.*	£8.60	GRB L&W NI	(B)
CHÂTEAU XANADU SEMILLON, CONOR LAGAN CHÂTEAU XANADU 1994 Western Australia	*Excellent nose in green, herbaceous style, with elements of spice and mineral edge.*	£9.50	MYS OXB GSH DIR	(B)

Pinpoint who sells the wine you wish to buy by turning to the stockist codes. If you know the name of the wine you want to buy, use the alphabetical index. If the price is your motivation, refer to the invaluable price guide index; red and white wines under £5, sparkling wines under £10 and champagne under £15. Happy hunting!

AUSTRALIA • WHITE

OTHER WHITE

BUCKLOW HILL DRY WHITE, SOUTHCORP South Australia	*Subtle on nose; clean, tropical, flowery bouquet with vanilla, sherbet, and spice. Crunchy fruit flavours.*	£3.80	PEF	(S)
SUNNYCLIFFE, DEAKIN ESTATE COLOMBARD/ CHARDONNAY, SUNNYCLIFFE 1994 South East Australia	*Fresh, grapey nose with floral, spicy aromas. Rich fruit on palate. Pleasing fullness of flavour.*	£4.00	VWC VW	(B)
KATNOOK ESTATE, RED CLIFFS ESTATE COLOMBARD CHARDONNAY, KATNOOK ESTATE 1992 Victoria	*Clean, grapefruity nose. Fresh, clean and attractive. Lively in mouth. Commercial style with sweetness.*	£4.20	KAT BI VDV	(B)
ROTHBURY TRIDENT, ROTHBURY 1993 New South Wales	*Sherbet lemon nose with hints of lime and melon. Slightly petillant; easy and soft.*	£5.10	RBW DBY DIR TRO COK	(B)
HOUGHTON WILDFLOWER RIDGE CHENIN BLANC, HOUGHTON 1994 Western Australia	*Crisp, green apples and hints of wax on nose. Very refreshing with zesty grapefruit flavours.*	£5.20	Widely available	(B)
ROSEMOUNT CHARDONNAY SEMILLON, ROSEMOUNT 1994 New South Wales	*Clean, fresh and full of fruit; ripe pineapples and lemons; easy drinking, with character.*	£5.20	ROS JS	(B)
MOONDAH BROOK VERDELHO, BRL HARDY WINE CO 1994 Western Australia	*Abundant bouquet of lemon, grapefruit and lychees. Full-flavoured, delicious and well-balanced.*	£5.30	Widely available	(B)

AUSTRALIA • WHITE

BROWN BROTHERS DRY MUSCAT BLANC, BROWN BROTHERS 1994 Milawa Victoria	*Fresh, grapey aromas. Excellent Muscat fruit character, full in body with a sweet follow-through.*	£5.40	Widely available	(S)
CRANSWICK ESTATE MARSANNE, CRANSWICK ESTATE 1994 New South Wales	*Citrus and green pepper. Creamy oak and tangerine fruit. Ripe, well-balanced with excellent length.*	£5.50	AUS	(B)
ROTHBURY VERDELHO, ROTHBURY 1994 New South Wales	*Clear, bright, pale yellow colour. Great, fresh, citrus aromas and rare delicacy.*	£5.60	RBW TO DIR	(B)
PENFOLDS ORGANIC CHARDONNAY SAUVIGNON BLANC, PENFOLDS 1994 South Australia	*Creamy, fat and citrussy, grapefruit flavours. Balanced, with intense greengage, lime nose. Oaky yet refreshing.*	£6.10	Widely available	(S)
KATNOOK ESTATE RIDDOCH SAUVIGNON BLANC, KATNOOK ESTATE 1994 South Australia	*Pale, gold wine with sweet honey and oak character on nose.*	£6.20	KAT WR BU BI VDV COK	(B)
CHENIN BLANC, PEEL ESTATE, PEEL ESTATE 1994 Western Australia	*Nose combines peaches, pineapples and cream. Layering of new oak and coconut. Grassy tones.*	£6.50	HA BOO ADN CHF DIR	(S)
BROWN BROTHERS SAUVIGNON BLANC, BROWN BROTHERS 1994 Milawa Victoria	*Elegant nose; delicious fruit salad. Touch of asparagus and smoke. Excellent fruit development.*	£6.70	Widely available	(B)
HILL SMITH ESTATE SAUVIGNON BLANC, S SMITH & SONS 1994 Eden Valley	*Nettle and grassy flavours; rounded, subtle style; plenty of gooseberry and crisp acid. Lingering finish.*	£7.00	GRA WIN	(S)

AUSTRALIA • WHITE

RESERVE CHARDONNAY, MITCHELTON WINES 1992 Victoria	*Waxy, ripe and honeyed. Big, golden colour. Broad in flavour and generously oaked.*	**£7.30**	JEF MTL RAV OD VIL	(B)
PETER DENNIS MCLAREN VALE SAUVIGNON BLANC, BABICH 1995 McLaren Vale	*Gooseberry jam nose. Clean wine with soft, ripe fruit and good, full palate. Creamy, mature.*	**£8.00**	THP	(S)
FLAXMANS TRAMINER, ORLANDO WINES 1990 Eden Valley	*Rich, spicy, apple aromas with sticky botrytis. Honeyed pineapples on palate. Clean with grape-fruit finish.*	**£8.00**	CAX	(B)

🍇

SWEET WHITE

TRENTHAM TAMINGA, TRENTHAM 1994 Murray River	*Attractive colour in glass. Pleasant lemon/golden syrup nose and flavour. Good balance and length.*	**£5.70**	BOO OXB VDV R NY	(S)
LINDEMANS BOTRYTIS SEMILLON, LINDEMANS 1987 South Australia	*Orange-coloured; rich toffee and oak bouquet. Obvious, rich, ripe, full flavours with great concentration.*	**£5.90**	Widely available	(S)
BETHANY ESTATE LATE HARVEST RIESLING, BETHANY ESTATE 1994 South Australia	*Good colour; some orange blossom aromas. Attractive palate with gentle, orange tastes and good acidity.*	**£6.30**	WSC DBY ADN	(B)
STANTON & KILLEEN RUTHERGLEN MUSCADELLE, STANTON & KILLEEN Victoria	*Elegant, nutty aromas. Soft caramel and sweet raisins. Full-bodied and sweet. Complex, long finish.*	**£6.50**	WSG BOO DBY VDV HOU NI NY	(B)

AUSTRALIA • SPARKLING

TESCO AUSTRALIAN NOBLE SEMILLON, WITTON ESTATE 1992 New South Wales	*Good colour and nose. A pleasant wine.*	**£7.00**	TO	(S)
HEGGIES BOTRYTIS RIESLING, S SMITH & SONS 1994 Eden Valley	*Lovely, fresh, honey, lemon nose. Delightful lemon flavour followed by some hints of butterscotch.*	**£7.30**	GRA DBY VDV OD WIN	(S)
CRANSWICK ESTATE BOTRYTIS SEMILLON, CRANSWICK ESTATE 1993 New South Wales	*Lemon, honey and nutmeg nose; creamy palate with lemon flavour following. Sweet, cloying after-taste.*	**£9.50**	AUS	(B)

SPARKLING

SEPPELT GREAT WESTERN ROSÉ, SEPPELT & SONS South Australia	*Sweet strawberries with hints of cherries. Quite ripe; balanced by lively, zesty acidity.*	**£5.30**	Widely available	(B)
SEPPELT PINOT ROSÉ, SEPPELT South Australia	*Soft, ripe fruit. Sweet with some toffee flavours. Excellent fruit and acidity. Good value.*	**£7.10**	Widely available	(B)
CUVÉE ONE PINOT NOIR CHARDONNAY, YALUMBA South Australia	*Fresh, zingy nose with good fruit. Crisp, attractive palate. Clean finish; grapefruit character.*	**£8.10**	GRA WR TH BU VW FUL OD	(B)
TALTARNI BRUT TACHE, TALTARNI Victoria	*Pretty pink colour; lean, delicate nose that develops well in glass. Lovely flavours and length.*	**£8.20**	Widely available	(S)

AUSTRALIA • SPARKLING/FORTIFIED

SEPPELT SPARKLING SHIRAZ, SEPPELT 1990 South Australia	*Complex, sparkling Shiraz with attractive blackberry. Warm spice and creamy texture. Good length.*	£8.60	Widely available	**S**
SEPPELT SALINGER, SEPPELT 1991 South Australia	*Simple, quite yeasty nose and high acid palate. Decent glass of bubble-softened out with sugar.*	£10.10	Widely available	**B**
CROSER, PETALUMA 1991 South Australia	*Light lemon colour; lemon peel and yeasty nose. Restrained style; good length.*	£10.50	GRA VW OD	**B**
E & E SPARKLING SHIRAZ, BRL HARDY WINE CO/VALLEY GROWERS CO-OP South Australia	*Wonderful, nose of nutmeg, cloves, oak, blackberries and cherries. Perfumed. Excellent fruit balanced by acidity.*	£11.80	HBR MTL DBY VDV OD R	**G**
SEPPELT SHOW SPARKLING SHIRAZ, SEPPELT 1985 South Australia	*Fruity nose of cassis, damsons and blackberries. Fabulous, soft fruit, ripe and rounded. Soft finish.*	£11.90	PEF ADN VDV HOU OD AMY	**B**

FORTIFIED

STANTON & KILLEEN, RUTHERGLEN OLD MUSCAT, STANTON & KILLEEN Victoria	*Burnt muscovado sugar, toffee aromas. Soft raisin and caramel fruit. Powerful. Good bite.*	£6.80	Widely available	**B**
YALUMBA MUSEUM SHOW RESERVE RUTHERGLEN MUSCAT, YALUMBA Rutherglen, Victoria	*Smooth and mature. Melange of dried fruits, toffee, caramel, figs, ginger. Smoky. Heady and warming.*	£7.00	GRA TO VW VDV NI WIN	**G**

AUSTRALIA • FORTIFIED

SEPPELT OLD TRAFFORD, **SEPPELT & SONS** South Australia	*A warm, reddy amber with spicy aromas. Smooth taste and a hint of caramel. Elegantly complex.*	**£8.60**	Widely available	**S**
BROWN BROTHERS, **RESERVE MUSCAT,** **BROWN BROTHERS** Milawa Victoria	*Elegant style of liqueur Muscat. Soft and grapey with orange peel and walnut flavours.*	**£8.50**	Widely available	**B**
MORRIS OF RUTHERGLEN **LIQUEUR MUSCAT,** **MORRIS WINES** Victoria	*Smooth caramel, toffee, spicy raisin. Balanced by tangy orange peel and bitter almonds. Full volume.*	**£9.20**	Widely available	**S**
OLD RUTHERGLEN **MUSCAT, CAMPBELLS** Victoria	*Sweet raisins and toasted nuts. Ripe, fresh figs and caramel. Luscious with delightfully tangy acidity.*	**£9.40**	Widely available	**B**
SHOW MUSCAT D.P. 63 **SEPPELT & SONS** Victoria	*Rich, syrupy, treacle with nuts on the nose. Palate offers fig, vanilla and truffle. Delicious wine.*	**£9.50**	WSG BOO NI NY	**B**
MCWILLIAMS, LIQUEUR **MUSCAT, MCWILLIAMS** South Australia	*Rich, black treacle and powerful fragrant nuttiness on nose. Rich and sweet on palate.*	**£21.20**	WAV DBY	**G**

AUSTRIA

A FTERMANY YEARS IN THE MAKING, Austria's winemakers are now teaching their neighbours across the German border a lesson in flavoursome winemaking. The most dazzling styles are the late-harvest wines, but the warmish climate is enabling the Austrians to make red and dry white wines which ought to be the envy of some of the big-name estates in the Rheingau.

RED

MALTESER RITTERORDEN CABERNET SAUVIGNON/MERLOT, 1992 Weinviertel	*Distinctive cherry and raspberry on the nose with a touch of vanilla pod and spicy leather.*	**£9.90**	FTH	**(B)**
PAUL ACHS PANNOBILE RED 1992 Burgenland	*Garnet red. Rich, distinctive smoky berry nose. Cherries, vanilla, and clean earthiness add to complexity.*	**£10.30**	NUM	**(S)**
WEINGUT JURIS-STIEGEL-MAR CABERNET SAUVIGNON, 1992 Burgenland	*Good solid tight Cabernet with resonant earthy spiciness and treacley richness.*	**£13.40**	BWC	**(B)**
UMATHUM FRAUENKIRCHNER ST LAURENT VOM STEIN, UMATHUM 1992 Neusiedler See	*Enticing nose of crisp summer fruits. Smoky, new oak and soft, spicy plum in abundance.*	**£16.60**	T&W	**(G)**

Pinpoint who sells the wine you wish to buy by turning to the stockist codes. If you know the name of the wine you want to buy, use the alphabetical index. If the price is your motivation, refer to the invaluable price guide index; red and white wines under £5, sparkling wines under £10 and champagne under £15. Happy hunting!

AUSTRIA • WHITE

WHITE

ALOIS KRACHER TRAMINER SPATLESE 1993 Neusiedler See	*Rounded nose of elder-flowers and gentle spice. Ripe, spiced peach and attractive nuttiness.*	**£9.80**	NY	**B**
ALOIS KRACHER TRAMINER SPATLESE 1990 Neusiedler See	*Delightful honey and mineral character. Soft, mature palate and steely acidic backbone give balance.*	**£9.80**	NY	**B**
WILLI BRÜNDLMAYER ZOBINGER HEILIGENSTEIN RIESLING ALTE REBEN 1993 Kamptal Donauland	*Rich fruit salad aroma. Peach and lychee flavours in the mouth with flowery character throughout.*	**£13.00**	NY	**B**

SWEET WHITE

SEEWINKLER IMPRESSIONEN, EISWEIN 1992 Neusiedler See	*Dried fruit, honey and sultana bouquet. Clean, balanced acidity; good intensity of fruit.*	**£7.00**	SAF	**B**
EISWEIN NEUSIEDLERSEE, WEINKELLEREI BURGENLAND 1992 Neusiedler See	*Dry, clean tropical fruit with a hint of caramel. Spicy bouquet with botrytis. Sweet and acid.*	**£7.50**	CAX	**G**
ALEX UNGER BOUVIER TROCKENBEERENAUSLESE 1991 Burgenland	*Likeable toffee apple character.*	**£8.30**	CAX	**B**

AUSTRIA • SWEET WHITE

PANNONISCHER TROCKENBEERENAUSLESE, 1989 Neusiedler See	*Good fruit and botrytis character. Biscuity. Fair acidity with hint of maderisation (oxidation) on palate.*	£12.00	NY	(G)
HEINRICH & KRACHER BEERENAUSLESE 1991 Neusiedler See	*Wonderfully sticky with lots of apricot, mango and thick honey. Beautiful balance.*	£13.00	L&W	(B)
ALOIS KRACHER TROCKENBEERENAUSLESE, ZWISCHEN DEN SEEN 1992 Neusiedler See	*Golden; marmalade nose. Lots of honey, lemon and acid. Very good balance.*	£19.00	NY	(B)
ALOIS KRACHER GRAND CUVÉE, BEERENAUSLESE 1991 Neusiedler See	*Deep, rich, golden, caramel colour; creamy, with fruit and good acidity. Well balanced.*	£19.00	NY	(B)
ERNST TRIEBAUMER, RUSTER AUSBRUCH 1991 Burgenland	*Golden; ripe pineapple nose. Concentrated pineapple flavours with good acidity on finish.*	£19.70	BWC CPW	(S)
ALOIS KRACHER SCHEUREBE BEERENAUSLESE 1987 Neusiedler See	*Oily nose; rich, soft, sweetness on palate. Sweet oranges with full concentration. Cleanish, hot finish.*	£20.00	NY	(G)
ALOIS KRACHER TRAMINER BEERENAUSLESE NOUVELLE VAGUE 1991 Neusiedler See	*Rich and honeyed, intense botrytis with orange nose. Fine, full flavour; sweet with high acid.*	£20.00	NY	(B)
ALOIS KRACHER CHARDONNAY & WELSCHRIESLING BEERENAUSLESE NOUVELLE VAGUE 1993 Neusiedler See	*Delicious, unctuous nose following through onto palate. Good acidity, concentration and length on finish.*	£25.00	NY	(G)

AUSTRIA • SWEET WHITE				
ALOIS KRACHER CHARDONNAY & WELSCH-RIESLING BEERENAUSLESE NOUVELLE VAGUE 1992 Neusiedler See	*Orange and powerful botrytis character; warm, toasty smoky nose. Rich flavours; superb acidity and long finish.*	£25.00	NY	(S)
ALOIS KRACHER CHARDONNAY & WELSCH-RIESLING BEERENAUSLESE NOUVELLE VAGUE 1991 Neusiedler See	*Golden with a green tinge; good intensity with floral and green fruit flavours. Excellent finish.*	£25.00	NY	(B)
WEISSER SCHILFMANDL, WILLI OPITZ 1992 Neusiedler See	*Magnificent colour and interesting nose. Good weight, well balanced and full of unusual flavours.*	£28.50	T&W ADN	(B)
OPITZ ONE RED TROCKENBEERENAUSLESE WILLI OPITZ 1993 Neusiedler See	*Dull black/red-brick; rich fruit nose. Complex baked fruit flavours.*	£31.50	T&W	(G)
WEISSER SCHILFMANDL WILLI OPITZ 1993 Neusiedler See	*Deep golden; rich, pineapple nose; good, fruity acidity. Apricots and pineapples; concentrated sweetness.*	£31.50	T&W	(G)

EASTERN EUROPE

T HE ADVENT OF PRIVATISATION and the arrival of flying winemakers on behalf of British retailers is helping to transform the face of Eastern European wine. Inevitably, however, development varies enormously from one country and region to another and it is impossible to generalise about trends, other than to say that, over the next few years, the challenge will often be between indigenous grape varieties and the 'international' styles demanded in the west.

BULGARIA • RED

SAFEWAY YOUNG VATTED MERLOT, VINPROM RUSSE 1994 Russe	*Sweet oak and ripe fruit. Great weight and soft, chewy tannins. Delightful, oaky finish.*	**£2.90**	SAF	**B**
SAFEWAY CABERNET SAUVIGNON, VINPROM SVISCHTOU 1991 Svischtou	*Enticing, ripe bouquet promising warmth and depth. Soft tannic damsons and a touch of figs.*	**£3.00**	SAF	**B**
GORCHIVKA VINEYARDS CABERNET SAUVIGNON, 1993 Russe	*Soft, hot fruit flavours. Intense, creamy character. Easy-drinking. A good value wine.*	**£3.40**	SAF	**B**
BULGARIAN RESERVE CABERNET SAUVIGNON STARAZAGORA WINERY 1990 Oriachovitza	*Earthy, soft and mature with good volume and raisins on palate. Dry and complex.*	**£3.50**	CRS CHF DIR FUL TAN	**B**
SPECIAL RESERVE CABERNET SAUVIGNON, LOVICO SUHINDOL 1990 Suhindol	*Delicate, elegant wine with discreet oak, lively fruit. Overall fresh, youthful style. Soft and appealing.*	**£3.50**	DBO SV JS	**B**

CZECH • WHITE

CZECH PINOT BLANC, NICK BUTLER & MARK NAIRN, 1994 Moravia	*Fat, baked apple character, gutsy and spicy with earthy pepper tones. Smooth, rounded palate.*	**£3.50**	VER	**B**

HUNGARY • RED

EGRI CSILLAGOK CABERNET SAUVIGNON, 1994 Eger	*Light, cherry nose with gunpowder. Hints of vanilla and pepper. Good, firm finish.*	**£3.00**	HAG	**B**
RIVER ROUTE MERLOT, CARL REH 1994 Szekszard	*Soft lolly on nose. Spicy, earthy character. Hot berry on palate, balanced against soft tannins.*	**£3.00**	RHC	**B**

HUNGARY • WHITE

VINUM BONUM CHARDONNAY, 1993 Etyek	*Fruity aromas and complexity on palate. Very dry.*	**£3.50**	MBL	**B**
DUNAVAR CHARDONNAY, DANUBIANA ST URSULA 1994 Matraalja	*Clean, pale yellow; fairly intense bouquet. Balanced acidity; creamy, ripe. Delicious.*	**£3.90**	TO SPR	**S**

CHAPEL HILL BARRIQUE AGED CHARDONNAY, BALATON BOGLAR 1993 South Balaton	*Attractive, woody nose. Delightful combination of lemon and toast. Good structure.*	**£4.00**	DBY CWS AV	**B**
CHAPEL HILL BARRIQUE CHARDONNAY, BALATON BOGLAR 1994 Balaton	*Ripe fruit and smoky bacon nose. Lovely weight; fresh, green apples dominate.*	**£5.00**	SAF	**B**

MOLDOVA • WHITE

CHARDONNAY HINCESTI, HDR WINES/PENFOLDS 1992 Hincesti	*Ripe, toasty nose with much fruit and acidity on palate.*	**£3.30**	WR	**B**
HUGH RYMAN/PENFOLDS KIRKWOOD CHARDONNAY, HUGH RYMAN/PENFOLDS Komrat	*Good oak nose with fruit; balance and length.*	**£3.30**	HAG	**B**

ROMANIA • RED

ROVIT WINERY CABERNET SAUVIGNON, 1986 Dealul Mare	*Aromas of cedar. Good concentration of hot raisin and juicy fruits.*	**£3.00**	HAE	**B**
VINEXPORT MERLOT, 1994 Dealul Mare	*Smoky, meaty, berry nose. Soft, jammy fruit, lightish and youthful with discreet tannins. Silky finish.*	**£3.00**	HAE	**B**

DEALUL CLASSIC PINOT NOIR, ROUIT WINERY 1990 Dealul Mare	*Soft, sweet nose of ripe strawberries and sugar beet. Ripe, developed palate. Finely-crafted, delicate finish*	**£3.00**	HAE CWS HOU VIL UBC TRO	**B**
VALEA MEILOR PINOT NOIR, VALEA MEILOR WINERY 1990 Dealul Mare	*Lovely, accessible mulberry interwoven with soft, vanilla oak. Good fruit extract and length.*	**£3.50**	HAE	**B**

ROMANIA • WHITE

SAINSBURY'S ROMANIAN CHARDONNAY, CARL REH 1994 Cernavoda	*Quite aromatic with a fat finish and nice length.*	**£3.20**	JS	**B**

ENGLAND

IMPROVING WITH EVERY HARVEST, today's English wines often have more in common with the dry wines of the Loire and the aromatic whites of Northern Italy than with anywhere else in the world. Thankfully, England's winemakers have mostly given up their efforts to make mock-German wines and are beginning to develop a strong identity for themselves.

WHITE

CHAPEL DOWN 'SL', 1993 West Sussex	*Freshly cut flowers and gooseberries with lively, grapefruit acidity. Refreshing citrus character.*	**£4.00**	CDL	(B)
BARKHAM MANOR KERNER, BARKHAM MANOR VINEYARD 1992 East Sussex	*Light, herbaceous nose. Sweet, green grapes and honey cut by lemony acidity. Rich and rounded.*	**£4.00**	TH BU WR BAK	(B)
SHAWSGATE MÜLLER THURGAU/SEYVAL BLANC, R A HEMPHILL/I S HUTCHESON 1993 East Anglia	*Pronounced, grapey nose. Subtle, medium-dry with interesting depths to apple and floral flavours.*	**£4.75**	SHA	(B)
THORNCROFT DRY, THORNCROFT VINEYARD LTD 1992 Southern Counties	*Peachy, tropical fruit aromas. Sweet, ripe honeydew melon and pear intermingled with crisp acidity.*	**£4.95**	THO	(B)
PILTON DRY RESERVE, HARVEST WINE GROUP 1993 Somerset	*Nettle and gooseberry aromas with a touch of green apple and passion-fruit. Crisp acidity.*	**£5.70**	PMV BU WR TH AV	(B)

ENGLAND • WHITE

DENBIES WINE ESTATE CHARDONNAY, DENBIES 1993 Surrey	*Perfumed, honey nose; traces of vanilla and melon. Zesty citrus mouth; well balanced acid. Weighty fruit.*	£6.10	DBS VIL	**B**
CARR TAYLOR 'ALEXIS', CARR TAYLOR VINEYARDS 1994 South East	*Soft, spicy, rounded and refreshing hint of gooseberry, grassy aromas and harmonious acidity.*	£6.50	CTV	**B**
SHARPHAM ESTATE SELECTION, HARVEST WINE GROUP 1994 Devon	*Young, fresh, floral nose. Ripe melons and pineapple balanced by green, gooseberry acidity.*	£7.00	WR BU TH SHR	**B**
THORNCROFT NOBLE HARVEST, THORNCROFT VINEYARD LTD 1994 Southern Counties	*Pineapple flavours and very good acidity with plenty of fruit; peaches and apricots. A dessert wine.*	£ 7.00	THO	**B**
CHANCTONBURY CLASSIC, CHANCTONBURY VINEYARDS 1993 West Sussex	*Refreshing on the palate, particularly floral on the nose. Classic combination of balanced acidity and good fruit.*	£7.50	CVY	**B**
CHANCTONBURY CLASSIC, CHANCTONBURY VINEYARDS 1992 West Sussex	*Mature nose of spice and rich, stewed gooseberries. Wet stone, mineral character. Fine balance and length.*	£8.30	NI CVY	**S**
VALLEY VINEYARDS FUME, HARVEST WINE GROUP 1992 Berkshire	*Rich, golden yellow. Well-rounded, ripe fruit on nose. Creamy, serious, well-judged oak.*	£8.50	TV VWR BU TH	**S**
SHARPHAM VINEYARD BARREL FERMENTED, HARVEST WINE GROUP 1993 Devon	*Open, floral aroma. Rich, full-flavoured lemon and oily richness offset by tinges of oak.*	£9.00	WR TH BU SHR	**B**

FRANCE

S TILL THE HEARTLAND of the wine world, despite the increasingly eager efforts of contenders from almost every continent, France is fighting back hard. The following pages reveal, however, that after the last few tricky vintages, France's strengths are far more apparent in some regions than others. The Rhône and southern France, for example, score more highly than wines from the Loire and lower-priced Bordeaux.

BORDEAUX • RED

SOMERFIELD CLARET, LOUIS ESCHENAUER Bordeaux	Good cabernet nose with a certain spiciness. Nice balance between oak and fruit, with soft acidity. Accessible.	**£3.20**	SMF	B
CALVET CLARET YVES BARRY, CALVET 1994 Bordeaux	Youthful colour, medium depth. Herbaceous claret nose, dark cherries on palate. Well-structured. Discreet tannins.	**£3.40**	GA MWW	B
VICTORIA WINE CLARET, CALVET Bordeaux	Characteristic Bordeaux nose. claret/French style continues on palate. Big tannins showing youth. Great potential.	**£3.80**	GA VW	B
CHATEAU ST MARTIN BARACAN, 1990 Bordeaux	Classic Clarety, vegetal nose. Mature styled claret for drinking now. Good, juicy fruit, tight tannins.	**£4.80**	EP	B
YVECOURT YVON MAU, 1993 Bordeaux	Pleasant, youthful mix of cherry, spice and oak. Vibrant and silky; good acidity. Full finish.	**£4.90**	YVM	B

COLLECTION ANNIVERSAIRE RESERVE CLARET, YVON MAU 1992 Bordeaux	*Mixed nose of light cherry and clean, spicy oak. Medium weight, decent grip. Well-defined.*	£5.00	U	**B**
'M' DE MONTESQUIEU ROUGE, VINS ET DOMAINES DE MONTESQUIEU 1992 Bordeaux	*Light, blackcurrant nose. Good, quaffable red fruits on palate. Simple, soft, rounded wine.*	£5.00	GRA	**B**
CHATEAU LAPLAGNOTTE BELLEVUE 1990 Bordeaux	*Sweet, chewy currants; mint nose. Light oak influence over curranty fruit. Full of complexity. Long.*	£5.00	TH PRW	**S**
NUMERO 1 DE DOURTHE, DOURTHE FRERES 1990 Bordeaux	*Pleasant on nose and palate. Characteristic, Bordeaux- style spicy aromas, ripe fruit and blended tannins.*	£5.10	GTA GSJ	**B**
LE VOYAGER, BENOIT ET VALERIE CALVET, 1990 Bordeaux	*Clean, herbaceous nose. Stalky, but evident Cabernet influence. Cassis on palate. Good, dry tannins.*	£5.50	CVP DBY	**B**
CHATEAU HAUT-MAZIERES, UNION DE PRODUCTEURS DE RAUZAN 1993 Bordeaux	*Light, floral bouquet. Powerful fruit and rather austere tannins. Very young, but good structure.*	£5.50	RA UM WW	**B**
CHATEAU CARSIN ROUGE, 1992 Bordeaux	*Pungent, hot nose full of character; round, con- centrated and chocolatey. Intense fruit flavours; moderate weight.*	£5.80	JS	**B**
CHATEAU PEYROU, CATHERINE PAPON, 1990 Bordeaux	*Blackcurrant and berry fruit cascade over the senses. Rich spice and chocolate add some com- plexity.*	£6.00	WCR	**B**

SAFEWAY CHATEAU CANTELOUP, M M FABRE 1992 Bordeaux	*Fruity nose with oak; somewhat metallic. Youthful, austere fruit; crisp, meaty style. Good tannic structure.*	£6.00	SAF	(B)
CHATEAU DE FRANCE, PATRICE CALVET 1990 Bordeaux	*Sophisticated nose of elegant fruit and oak. Delicious, firm tannin. Weighty, sound structure.*	£6.00	GRI DBY HLV	(S)
CHATEAU D'ARCINS, CASTEL FRÈRES 1992 Bordeaux	*Black cherry robe. Good Cabernet nose, herbaceous and spearmint notes, some oak. Jammy, spicy fruit.*	£6.20	MPA VW	(B)
CHATEAU LALANDE D'AUVION, 1990 Bordeaux	*Soft, cedar nose, ripe, jammy blackcurrant. Soft oak and good acidity, though slightly lean.*	£6.20	JS	(B)
SIRIUS RED, PETER A SICHEL 1993 Bordeaux	*Clear, bright aspect. Typical Cabernet herbaceous nose. Light, vivacious palate, with dryness and acidity.*	£6.50	SIP WR BU TH CNL	(B)
CHATEAU CAP DE FAUGERES 1990 Bordeaux	*Nose of chocolate, coffee and vanilla. Creamy, warm, ripe, with notable crisp acidity.*	£6.50	CP WBI	(S)
VIEUX CHATEAU NEGRIT, YVON MAU 1992 Bordeaux	*Interesting, earthy notes; a suggestion of pea pods. Austere and herbaceous on palate. Dry, typically Bordeaux.*	£6.50	U	(B)
GRAVES ROUGE BARON PHILIPPE DE ROTH-SCHILD, 1993 Bordeaux	*Slightly green, stalky fruit but showing good promise. Well made wine in an average year.*	£6.70	PR GM TL	(B)

CHATEAU LAMARCHE 'LUTE', VIGNOBLES BERNARD GERMAIN 1993 Bordeaux	*Cedar notes on the nose with a fine fresh berry palate. Notes of ripe cassis and cherry.*	£6.80	ALL	(B)
CHATEAU FOURNAS BERNADOTTE, 1990 Bordeaux	*Potent berry on the nose with fine, balanced tannins and fresh, full fruit.*	£7.50	JS	(B)
CHATEAU DE REIGNAC CUVÉE PRESTIGE, CHARLES LAGAUZERE 1990 Bordeaux	*Blackcurrants, eucalyptus and spicy leather on the nose. Matured fruit from an excellent year.*	£8.00	RW	(B)
CHATEAU LA VIEILLE CUVÉE, 1989 Bordeaux	*Typical Cabernet Sauvignon nose. Sweet, wild fruits. Tight, dry tannins in mature, classic, European style.*	£8.00	JS	(B)
CHATEAU MERCIER CUVÉE PRESTIGE, PHILIP CHETY 1991 Bordeaux	*Very good Bourg wine with a fine balance of juicy Merlot and more structured Cabernet.*	£8.00	WR TH BU	(B)
CHATEAU MERCIER CUVÉE PRESTIGE, PHILIP CHETY 1990 Bordeaux	*Much the same as above but a much better year, which means a much more balanced, satisfying claret.*	£8.00	WR BU TH	(B)
CHATEAU HAUT LAGRANGE, BOUTEMY, 1992 Bordeaux	*An unusually light claret but nevertheless containing good purple fruit and a fine tannin balance.*	£8.00	WR OD	(B)
SAINT JULIEN, RAOUL JOHNSTON 1993 Bordeaux	*Spicy nose with good clean fruit and berries on palate; leathery cassis*	£8.00	MWW	(B)

CHATEAU LAMARCHE VIGNOBLES BERNARD GERMAIN 1993 Bordeaux	*Bright, sharp, complex cassis nose. Raspberry, wild berries and strong oak flavours.*	**£8.30**	ALL	**B**
CHATEAU HAUT-LOGAT, CHEVAL QUANCARD 1989 Bordeaux	*Mature, cedary nose. Good length and direction; balanced acidity. Soft, curranty fruit.*	**£8.50**	ET	**B**
CHATEAU LA VIEILLE 1992 Bordeaux	*Strong, sappy, cedary nose revealing dusty, cherry oak and notes of eucalyptus. Good length.*	**£8.80**	DBY JS	**B**
LA ROSERAIE DE GRUAUD LAROSE, CORDIER 1992 St. Julien	*Luscious, chewy berry fruits in soft, plummy style. Moderate tannins. Gentle, cedar oak and a touch of glycerine.*	**£9.00**	W	**B**
CHATEAU LA CARDONNE, DOMAINES BARONS DE ROTHSCHILD, 1993 Bordeaux	*Good, rich tannins mean this wine is easy to enjoy young. No evidence of oak.*	**£9.10**	CP W MZ OD HDL	**B**
CHÂTEAU TOUR DE MARBUZET, HENRI DUBOSCQ 1992 Bordeaux	*Interesting aromas of spice and rubber. Old Bordeaux style, soft tannins, light fruit on palate.*	**£9.20**	BP MWW	**B**
CHÂTEAU LES HAUTS DE PONTET, YVES PAGES ET ASSOCIES 1991 Bordeaux	*Serious Bordeaux nose. Well-defined, full fruit character married with powerful tannins and backbone.*	**£9.50**	BP DBY CW SV	**B**
CHATEAU LE MEYNIEU, 1990 Bordeaux	*Heady aromas of mature fruits. Powerful tannins married to ripe cassis fruit, impression of high alcohol.*	**£9.80**	VW CW	**B**

CHÂTEAU LA CLARIERE LAITHWAITE, 1993 Bordeaux	*Fine Bordeaux Superieur. Well balanced tannins and berry fruit. Cedar and cigar on the nose.*	**£10.00**	BD	(G)
CHATEAU TRIMOULET, YVON MAU 1990 Bordeaux	*Subtle oak berry on nose and palate. Integrates well. Charming, light, well-made wine.*	**£10.00**	YVM	(B)
CHÂTEAU RAMAGE LA BATISSE 1990 Bordeaux	*Good cabernet nose with liquorice and hints of marzipan and vanilla. Tight tannins and fresh fruit.*	**£10.00**	Widely available	(B)
LES TOURELLES DE LONGUEVILLE, CHÂTEAU PICHON LONGUEVILLE 1992 Bordeaux	*Quite tight on the nose but opening up with earthy, fruity flavours on the palate. Getting better.*	**£10.99**	VWC MTL WR TH BU VW	(B)
CHATEAU MOULIN DE BRIDAINNE, YVES PAGES ET ASSOCIES 1991 Bordeaux	*Vanilla pod and ripe blackcurrant on nose with eucalyptus and a slight, green stalkiness on palate.*	**£11.00**	BP	(S)
CHATEAU PONTET CHAPPAZ 1990 Bordeaux	*Brambles and berries on nose, with earthy, musky mushrooms on palate. Rich, refined claret.*	**£12.00**	JN	(B)
CHATEAU LEOVILLE BARTON 1992 Bordeaux	*Bright red robe. Elegant, vanilla oak nose. Powerful, dry oak on palate. Mature, ripe tannins.*	**£12.20**	MTL BU WR BI TAN OD SAF	(S)
CUVÉE ARISTIDE, YVON MAU 1992 Bordeaux	*Notes of cassis and vanilla on nose, with a fresh, herbaceous palate. Give it a couple of years.*	**£13.00**	YVM	(B)

St Michael Chateau l'Hospitalet 1988 Bordeaux	*Beautiful, rich, Cabernet nose showing depth and maturity, with herbaceous aromas. Soft, smoky fruit. Elegant.*	£13.00	M&S	(S)
Chateau Carbonnieux 1992 Bordeaux	*Open nose with soft, pleasing bouquet of brambles. Rich, chewy fruit; medium weight, firm tannins.*	£13.00	WR BU VWC	(S)
Chateau Pichon Longueville Baron 1992 Bordeaux	*Seasoned oak and tobacco aromas. Tutti-frutti flavours and elegant, tannic structure. Dry tobacco finish.*	£13.50	BU WR BI OD	(S)
Chateau La Clusiere, Patrick Valette 1990 Bordeaux	*Meatiness balances hot, ripe fruits and powerful alcohol against good tannic structure. Classic Bordeaux.*	£14.80	L&W	(B)
Chateau Durfort-vivens 1986 Bordeaux	*Restrained berry with animal, meaty aromas. Traditional Merlot character. Intense fruit balanced by dry tannins.*	£14.99	MWW RW	(B)
Chateau La Tour Carnet 1990 Bordeaux	*Excellent year producing a wine combining delicious summer fruit with great balance. Good now but will improve.*	£15.00	VWC VW	(B)
St Michael Chateau Gazin 1989 Bordeaux	*Complex aromas of sandalwood, tobacco, moss and earth. Smooth. Excellent, compact flavours; dry finish.*	£15.00	M&S	(B)
Chateau Yon Figeac 1992 Bordeaux	*Smoky, spicy oak aromas. Deep, mature on palate; complex flavours of cedar and burnt fruits.*	£15.00	ALL NI	(B)

FRANCE • BORDEAUX RED

CHATEAU HAUT MARBUZET, HENRI DUBOSCQ 1992 Bordeaux	*Wonderful Cabernet nose of mint with cedary oak. Luscious, ripe berry and creamy, vanilla oak.*	**£15.00**	W CRD BY MWW HVW ABY	(S)
CHATEAU MERVILLE 1990 Bordeaux	*Wonderful concentration of chocolatey aromas and cooked, plummy fruit. Grippy tannins and dry tobacco oak.*	**£15.50**	EWC JS	(B)
CHATEAU HAUT BAGES AVEROUS 1989 Bordeaux	*Elegant, plummy fruit on nose. Smooth, ripe, sweet fruit with peppery overtones. Dry tobacco finish.*	**£15.50**	BWI TH WR BU MWW	(B)
FORTNUM AND MASON MARGAUX, CHATEAU RAUSAN-SEGLA 1988 Bordeaux	*Lovely notes of leather and spice on nose. Vegetal palate with hints of mushroom and marzipan.*	**£16.00**	F&M	(S)
CHATEAU CLERC MILON, BARON PHILIPPE DE ROTHSCHILD, 1991 Bordeaux	*Good, cedary, classic Medoc nose; delicious notes of chocolate and coconut. Broad, ripe fruit flavours.*	**£17.00**	Widely Avaialble	(B)
CHATEAU DESTIEUX 1988 Bordeaux	*Stylish, complex Claret nose. Deep, tarry, extracted flavours in nicely balanced proportions. Firm tannins.*	**£17.00**	GRA	(S)
CHATEAU D'ARMAILHAC, BARON PHILIPPE DE ROTHSCHILD, 1990 Bordeaux	*Very seasoned oak on nose. Elegant Margaux-like fruit with fine oak understructure. Dry.*	**£17.20**	PRG MTL	(B)
CHATEAU VILLEMAURINE, ROBERT GIRAUD, 1990 Bordeaux	*Plenty of vanilla oak on nose. Supple, soft, sweet juicy cherry on palate. Powerful oak.*	**£18.50**	MD HDL	(B)

CHATEAU LASCOMBES 1990 Bordeaux	*Rich, developed, rather earthy aromas. Soft, juicy fruit - sweet, hot and raisiny. Integrated, balanced, elegant.*	£19.60	MTL CHL	(B)
CHATEAU LASCOMBES 1991 Bordeaux	*Delicate coffee and chocolate aromas. Light Merlot on palate with cedar oak and berry.*	£19.70	Widely available	(B)
CHÂTEAU LEOVILLE BARTON 1989 Bordeaux	*Lovely, leafy, cedar aromas. Soft, ripe, warm, fruit with distinctive, claret character. Dry tannin backbone.*	£19.80	Widely available	(S)
CHATEAU LASCOMBES 1989 Bordeaux	*Gamey aromas. Good, full body and character. An elegant yet firm wine.*	£19.90	Widely available	(S)
CHATEAU LASCOMBES 1988 Bordeaux	*Sweet cabernet nose in good quality, lightish style. Good intrinsic cassis. Elegant and developed.*	£22.50	MTL CHL MWW	(B)
VIEUX CHATEAU CERTAN 1986 Bordeaux	*Elegant, fine, complete nose. Intense, rich, concentrated flavours of creamy vanilla and chewy berry fruits.*	£29.40	Widely available	(G)
CHATEAU PICHON COMTESSE LALANDE 1985 Bordeaux	*Rich fruitcake, tobacco on nose. Jammy fruit on palate, balanced with cigar-box overtones.*	£35.00	DBY BWI L&W BI CPW	(S)
CHATEAU MONTROSE 1992 Bordeaux	*Clean aromas of cedary liquorice with stalk. Fine, tangy fruit on palate.*	£35.10	CPW	(B)

CHATEAU LEOVILLE LASCASES 1985 Bordeaux	*Delicious, well-structured, hot fruit, harmoniously balanced by soft, blended tannins. Well-integrated.*	£35.60	Widely available	(S)
CHATEAU TROTANOY 1988 Bordeaux	*Subdued, concentrated Merlot nose. Classic Bordeaux structures of powerful fruit married to soft, mature tannins.*	£39.90	DBY	(G)
CHATEAU HAUT BRION 1992 Bordeaux	*Creamy, toasty oak and buttery fruit on nose. Soft, easy, brambly flavours on palate.*	£40.00	Widely Available	(S)
CHATEAU HAUT BRION 1986 Bordeaux	*Distinctive, complex nose with toasty coffee aromas. Strong fruit with firm, bitter, tannic structure.*	£47.70	Widely available	(S)
CHATEAU LATOUR 1983 Bordeaux	*Ripe, elegant nose with finesse. Massive, intense fruit with developed, cedary oak. Firm tannic structure.*	£52.60	Widely available	(S)
CHATEAU HAUT BRION 1990 Bordeaux	*Elegant, mature, gamey aromas. A fine, graceful, fully ripe wine with powerful tannins.*	£56.20	BWI WR BU BI	(S)
CHATEAU MOUTON ROTHSCHILD 1990 Bordeaux	*Jammy, cassis and coffee, cedary aromas. Fine, dry texture with elegant, undeveloped fruit. Excellent.*	£65.10	Widely Available	(G)
CHATEAU MARGAUX 1983 Bordeaux	*Superb, deep fruit. Ripe, integrated tannins, excellent length and full flavour. Wonderful balance and structure.*	£69.40	BI OD HDL	(G)

BORDEAUX • WHITE

SAFEWAY BORDEAUX OAK AGED, CAVE DE LANDERROUAT 1994 Bordeaux	*Clean, modern wine. Fresh and zesty. Aromas of pear and citrus peel. Crisp and lemony.*	**£4.00**	SAF	**S**
CHATEAU LA JALGUE CUVEE PRESTIGE, GINESTET 1993 Bordeaux	*Herbaceous, green fruit aromas on nose with whiff of botrytis; zesty lemon acidity. Melon finish.*	**£4.50**	W VW	**B**
CHATEAU HAUT MAZIERES BLANC 1992 Bordeaux	*Easy, attractive New World style: lemon zest and creamy oak*	**£5.00**	MWW	**B**
CHATEAU HAUT MAZIERES BLANC 1993 Bordeaux	*Rich, tropical melons, pineapples and passionfruit. New World ripeness balanced by gentle, creamy oak.*	**£5.00**	MWW	**B**
NUMERO 1 DE DOURTHE, DOURTHE FRERES 1993 Bordeaux	*Rounded, grassy nose. well-balanced wine with style and fine length.*	**£5.10**	GTA GSJ	**B**
MOUTON CADET BORDEAUX BLANC, BARON PHILIPPE DE ROTHSCHILD 1994 Bordeaux	*Good, all-round wine with well-weighted, solid appley fruit and an attractive character.*	**£5.10**	Widely available	**B**
CHATEAU HAUT RIAN BORDEAUX BLANC, MICHEL DIETRICH 1994 Bordeaux	*Spicy, peppery fruit with clean aromas of Sauvignon Blanc. Excellent balance.*	**£5.20**	TNH CPW	**S**

FRANCE • BORDEAUX WHITE

CHATEAU NICOT, BERNARD DUBOURG 1993 Bordeaux	*Classy grass and asparagus bouquet typical of Sauvignon. Aromatic and slightly spritzy. Good concentration.*	£5.50	L&W	(B)
CHATEAU DE SOURS BLANC 1993 Bordeaux	*Broad, ripe pineapple fruit with whiff of refreshing greenness; kiwi fruit palate with oak.*	£5.70	HAG HHR MWW	(B)
CHATEAU THIEULEY CUVÉE FRANCIS COURSELLE 1993 Bordeaux	*Classic Bordeaux aromas of grass, asparagus and gooseberry. Waxy flavours of Semillon on palate.*	£7.90	WCR ES MWW OD	(B)
CHATEAU FIEUZAL BLANC 1988 Bordeaux	*Creamy, buttery nose; hints of asparagus, coconut, lemon and vanilla. Lush and fruit-driven.*	£23.10	CPW OD	(G)

BORDEAUX • SWEET WHITE

CHATEAU RIEUSSEC, DOMAINES BARONS DE ROTHSCHILD, RESERVE SPECIALE SAUTERNES 1993 Bordeaux	*Very pretty-coloured wine with intense, orange marmalade flavours; thick style. Sweet and condensed.*	£7.50	MZ OD	(B)
SAUTERNES BARON PHILIPPE DE ROTHSCHILD 1991 Bordeaux	*Rich, full and honeyed nose. Weighty and full flavours with pleasant fruit and fresh acidity.*	£10.00	PRG MTL VW	(B)
SAUTERNES BARONNE MATHILDE, BARON PHILIPPE DE ROTHSCHILD 1990 Bordeaux	*Quite full, ripe wine with an appley nose. Young and concentrated with good balance.*	£12.50	PRG	(B)

CHATEAU BASTOR-LAMONTAGE SAUTERNES, CREDIT FONCIER 1989 Bordeaux	*Lovely, botrytis, honey and peaches nose. Intense, creamy marmalade flavours and long finish.*	£13.50	BWI SMF	(B)
CHATEAU SUDUIRAUT 1989 Bordeaux	*Lush, with intensely rich nose; raisiny and rich palate. Full, creamy texture, slightly medicinal flavour.*	£26.90	BI CPW HOU NI TAN OD AV	(B)
CHATEAU RIEUSSEC 1988 Bordeaux	*Classy, ripe botrytis nose; complex and spicy. Full, long, balanced palate. Good acidity.*	£27.70	Widely available	(G)

BURGUNDY • RED

SAINSBURY'S RED BURGUNDY PINOT NOIR, RODET Burgundy	*Lightly oaked. Old-fashioned style of Burgundy with dark, brooding cherry. Faint hint of dustiness.*	£5.00	JS	(B)
PINOT NOIR, BICHOT 1993 Burgundy	*Attractive raspberry and mint aromas. Hints of liquorice and spice. Full, juicy fruit. Easy drinking.*	£5.50	U	(B)
BURGUNDY CHARLES DE FRANCE RED, JEAN CLAUDE BOISSET 1993 Burgundy	*Fresh, soft strawberry comes to the fore on palate. Perfect balance. Good length. Classic style.*	£6.00	W VW	(B)
CÔTES DE NUITS LE PRIEURE, CAVE DES HAUTES CÔTES, 1992 Burgundy	*Ripe, fragrant strawberries. Oak on nose. Some complexity rich, chocolate, cherry stone and warm spice.*	£6.50	SAF	(B)

BOURGOGNE HAUTES COTES DE BEAUNE, CHATEAU DE DAVENAY, MICHEL PICARD 1992 Burgundy	*Powerful, sweet, juicy fruit in abundance. Soft, inviting Burgundy.*	£6.70	FWF JS	**B**
MALT HOUSE VINTNERS CÔTE DE BEAUNE VILLAGES, HONORE LAVIGNE 1993 Burgundy	*Lovely, clean red fruits and sprinkling of spice and pepper. Warm peppery finish.*	£7.50	MHV	**B**
BEAUNE, LUC JAVELOT, 1992 Burgundy	*Nose of black cherries, crunchy hedgerow berry, toasty oak. Concentrated and harmonious. Expansive, supple feel.*	£8.00	SAF	**B**
DOMAINE CHEVROT, FERNAND CHEVROT 1992 Burgundy	*Sweet, developing fruit aromas integrated with soft, creamy vanilla. Crisp raspberry on palate.*	£9.00	3D	**B**
GIVRY CLOS JUS, CHOFFLET VALDENAIRE 1992 Burgundy	*Fresh, ripe raspberry and redcurrant. Has a good damson fruit finish.*	£9.30	MK NY	**B**
MARSANNAY, LOUIS JADOT 1989 Burgundy	*Lovely maturity; soft summer fruit aromas with hints of newly cut meadow in rain.*	£9.40	DBY VWC	**B**
MONTHELIE, DAMY-DUVOIS 1989 Burgundy	*Lovely nose of sweet, ripe strawberries and linseed. Soft and alluring palate.*	£9.50	TRW	**B**
CÔTES DE BEAUNE, J DROUHIN 1992 Burgundy	*Soft, sweet strawberry and warm vanilla. Lovely, ripe fruit. Long, complex finish.*	£9.60	MZ OD R	**B**

CÔTE DE NUITS VILLAGES, PHILIPPE BATACCHI 1992 Burgundy	*Soft, ripe and jammy. Crisp, fresh, red fruits and firm tannins. Youthful vigour throughout.*	£10.00	HDL	B
SAVIGNY LES BEAUNE, J DROUHIN 1992 Burgundy	*Good value Burgundy from a satellite village. Pleasing, ripe raspberry and gentle oak.*	£10.00	MZ	B
SAVIGNY-LES-BEAUNE, DOMAINE MAILLARD PERE ET FILS 1991 Burgundy	*Lovely, generous basket-full of currants and truffles. Great richness and warm texture.*	£10.50	BU	S
BEAUNE 1ER CRU CLOS DU ROI, CHATEAU PHILIPPE-LE-HARDI 1993 Burgundy	*Ripe, soft fruit nose. Soft, fleshy style with plummy texture and gentle spiciness. Super intensity.*	£11.70	ABY	B
GIVRY 1ER CRU CLOS DE LA SERVOISINE, JOBLOT 1993 Burgundy	*Very forthcoming, with violets and creamy vanilla. Burst of ripe fruits on palate. Forward style.*	£11.80	HOH	S
LADOIX CLOS DES CHAGNOTS, PIERRE ANDRE 1992 Burgundy	*Old-fashioned style of Burgundy with crisp Pinot Noir fruit and slight mustiness.*	£12.00	SOB MTL	B
SANTENAY CLOS DE LA CONFRERIE, VINCENT GIRADIN 1993 Burgundy	*Complex cherry, blackcurrant flavours with marzipan. Velvety texture and creamy, toasted oak. Soft spices.*	£12.90	TNH CWI TAN HVW	B
ST MICHAEL VOLNAY, LOUIS JADOT 1989 Burgundy	*Attractive, evolved Burgundy with mellow and soft summer fruit. Excellent, ripe fruit with good finish.*	£13.00	M&S	S

NUITS-SAINT-GEORGES, DOMAINE DE L'ARLOT 1992 Burgundy	*Gorgeous coffee intensity. Full of ripe, fresh summer fruits backed by smoky meatiness.*	**£13.20**	ABY TH WR BU HR OD	**B**
BEAUNE 1ER CRU, LOUIS JADOT 1990 Burgundy	*Elegant, fragrant style. Meaty backbone. Layers of quality fruit. Fine example from a good year.*	**£14.60**	HM DBY TO	**B**
MALT HOUSE VINTNERS GEVREY CHAMBERTIN, HONORE LAVIGNE 1992 Burgundy	*Fresh summer fruit aromas - layers of raspberry and strawberry abound. Sensuous palate. Warming spice.*	**£15.60**	MHV	**B**
DOMAINE SIMON BIZE 1991 Burgundy	*Attractive plum and cherry stone intermingled with sweet oak. Developing well. Firm tannic finish.*	**£16.10**	ABY HHC	**B**
BEAUNE DU CHATEAU PREMIER CRU, BOUCHARD PÈRE & FILS 1989 Burgundy	*Aged style. Mellow, fleshy strawberry fruit and slight savoury aspect. Sweet ripe finish.*	**£16.40**	MMD	**B**
NUITS ST GEORGES PREMIER CRU, DOMAINE DE L'ARLOT 1992 Burgundy	*Lovely, delicate fruit and soft, violet character. Ripe, clean Pinot Noir. Good length. Well made.*	**£16.80**	THP BWI ABY HR	**B**
VOLNAY FREMIETS CLOS DE LA ROUGEOTTE PREMIER CRU, BOUCHARD PÈRE & FILS 1990 Burgundy	*Appealing, aged character. Rich, silky cherry and plum. Layered, velvet texture. Seductive, classy, good quality.*	**£17.90**	MMD	**S**
NUITS-SAINT-GEORGES, DOMAINE DE L'ARLOT 1991 Burgundy	*Fresh fruit character at its best now. Soft, easy drinking. Plums and creamy vanilla.*	**£18.80**	BWI ABY DIR	**B**

GEVREY CHAMBERTIN, VALLET FRERES 1989 Burgundy	*Rich cherry and mature gamey/meaty aromas. Shows elegance of age.*	£19.30	BP BOO DBY AV	(B)
NUITS-SAINT-GEORGES CLOS DE L'ARLOT, DOMAINE DE L'ARLOT 1991 Burgundyr	*Ripe, velvety Pinot Noir with firm, earthy back-bone. Delicate and for-ward.*	£19.90	ABY HR	(S)
VOLNAY EN CAILLERETS, DOMAINE DE LA POUSSE D'OR 1992 Burgundy	*Delicious, plummy, Pinot Noir. Confident and bursting with fruit. Touches of vanilla. A true, Burgundy.*	£20.20	ABY OD	(B)
VOLNAY 1ER CRU LES PITURES, BITOUZET PRIEUR, 1990 Burgundy	*Full, plummy nose with lovely chocolate and fresh coffee aromas. Layers of gorgeous bramble flavour.*	£21.20	MK HCK	(S)
NUITS ST GEORGES LES PERRIERES, ROBERT CHEVILLON, 1992 Burgundy	*Rich, meaty nose. Fleshy and voluptuous. Soft vanilla and crunchy cranberry add complexity. Classic.*	£21.60	WTR	(S)
NUITS ST GEORGES LES CHAIGNOTS, ROBERT CHEVILLON, 1992 Burgundy	*Powerful summer fruit and hints of liquorice, coffee and tobacco. Shows early signs of maturity.*	£21.60	WTR	(S)
CORTON, LOUIS JADOT, 1989 Burgundy	*Gentle oak, warming spice and elegant, ruby fruit. Soft, ripe, well-extracted berry. Fleshy texture.*	£25.00	HM TH WR BU	(S)
NUITS ST GEORGES CLOS DES FORETS, DOMAINE DE L'ARLOT 1991 Burgundy	*Delightful fragrance of a true Burgundy. Rich bouquet. Palate bursting with silky, red fruits. Persistent.*	£27.50	ABY L&W DIR	(S)

| **CHAMBERTIN GRAND CRU, DOMAINE ROSSIGNOL TRAPET 1992** Burgundy | *Deep, unctuous ripe fruit. Complex with vibrant berry, chocolate, coffee and violet. Seductive and smooth.* | **£32.10** | ABY OD | **G** |

BURGUNDY • WHITE

BOURGOGNE ALIGOTÉ, DOMAINE DES MANANTS, JEAN-MARC BROCARD 1993 Burgundy	*Fresh nose of nectarine kernels. Clean, concentrated, well flavoured peach. Good length.*	**£5.50**	JBF	**B**
MACON CHARDONNAY, DOMAINE LES ECUYERS, 1993 Burgundy	*Smoky nose with touches of simple, ripe peach and citrus. Ripe, sweet, full fruit palate.*	**£6.70**	JS	**B**
MONTAGNY PREMIER CRU MONTCUCHOT, CAVE DE BUXY, 1993 Burgundy	*Green, peach, floral nose. Lean palate with great fruit and sweet, light oak. Good length.*	**£6.80**	WHC HOU R	**S**
MACON CHARDONNAY, J. TALMARD 1993 Burgundy	*Some grip to this wine with good fruit, structure and length.*	**£7.00**	MVN ADN HHC G&M TAN	**S**
SAINT-VERAN, DOMAINE DES DEUX ROCHES, 1994 Burgundy	*Clean nose; well-balanced with good amount of oak. Clean palate and style.*	**£7.40**	FWM HHC OD	**B**
CHABLIS MOREAU, J MOREAU ET FILS 1994 Chablis	*Light, pure, varietal nose; uncomplicated. Easy drinking, classically made.*	**£7.70**	HV MTL HOU GSJ	**B**

FRANCE • BURGUNDY WHITE

CHABLIS, ETIENNE BOILEAU 1994 Chablis	*Bright, lemon/gold; strong nose. Quite chunky, soft style; pleasing middle palate.*	£8.00	WTR	**B**
CHABLIS VIEILLES VIGNES, LA CHABLISIENNE 1992 Chablis	*Moderate, bright, lemon-coloured wine; ripe, cool-climate bouquet. Tight, complex palate, good acid, structure, length.*	£8.50	ET WR	**S**
CHABLIS DOMAINE DES MARRENNIERS, BERNARD LEGLAND 1993 Chablis	*Clean, pure Chardonnay character; plenty to taste. Pleasing.*	£8.60	BI CHF VIL	**S**
CHATEAU DE DAVENAY RULLY PREMIER CRU, MICHEL PICARD, 1993 Burgundy	*Decent, well-built wine; rounded and becoming richer. Clean and fresh with developing fruit flavours.*	£8.90	FWF	**B**
MONTAGNY BLANC, J DROUHIN, 1993 Burgundy	*Delicious, buttery, nutty, apple-like Chardonnay fruitiness, crisp acidity, not unlike a Chassagne-Montrachet.*	£9.00	MZ	**B**
MARSANNAY BLANC, LOUIS JADOT, 1993 Burgundy	*Toast and a touch of vegemite. Smooth, full and oaky.*	£9.20	HM WR BU	**B**
CHABLIS 1ER CRU BEAUROY, LA CHABLISIENNE 1991 Chablis	*Complex, spicy nose; good flavours. Has depth, weight and excellent length.*	£9.40	WCR W	**B**
DOMAINE DES MANANTS CHABLIS 1ER CRU MONTMAINS, JEAN-MARC BROCARD 1993 Chablis	*Soft, creamy, sandy, buttery nose. Very restrained, attractive wine.*	£9.60	JBF ADN	**B**

CLOS DU PARADIS, DOMAINE EMILE VOARICK 1993 Burgundy	*Full of flavour with depth, complexity and length.*	£9.80	FWF	(B)
CHABLIS 1ER CRU FOURCHAUME, DOMAINE DU COLOMBIER 1993 Chablis	*Creamy; ripe, runny cheese. Fat, full, ripe and soft flavours. Attractive finish.*	£10.00	FWM	(B)
CHATEAU DE MARSANNAY CUVÉE CHARLES LE TEMERAIRE BLANC, NOEMIE VERNAUX 1993 Burgundy	*Concentrated, weighty nose with soft fruit palate of good character. Good depth and length.*	£10.80	SG	(S)
CHABLIS FOURCHAUME, BOUDIN 1993 Chablis	*Rich, full nose; spicy and leafy. Nice, full fat fruit grip, minerally centre.*	£11.00	MWW	(B)
CHABLIS VIEILLES VIGNES, GILBERT PICQ ET SES FILS 1993 Chablis	*Fresh, leafy, flinty nose; firm, creamy palate, a touch lean and with grip. Fresh.*	£11.50	GRA	(B)
ST AUBIN BLANC, LOUIS JADOT 1992 Burgundy	*Up-front, big nose; lots of big, fruit flavours. Classy acid on end; steely and green.*	£11.50	VWC BWI VW	(B)
MEURSAULT , J DROUHIN 1992 Burgundy	*Asparagus nose with green fruit on palate. Very little oak. Good, solid Burgundy.*	£12.00	MZ	(B)
PULIGNY MONTRACHET, J DROUHIN 1993 Burgundy	*Fine, zippy, citrus acidity merging with fine Burgundian oak. Still a bit tight but will age well.*	£12.00	MZ	(S)

FRANCE • BURGUNDY SPARKLING				
PULIGNY MONTRACHET, DOMAINE GERARD CHAVY, 1992 Burgundy	*Slightly musty with touches of vanilla pod, butter and hazelnut. Full, rich, classic taste.*	£12.90	CPW JS HR OD	B
MERSAULT LES GRANDS CHARRONS 1ER CRU, LEFLAIVE, 1993 Burgundy	*Good, solid white. Fruity character and fresh oak infusion.*	£13.00	SAF	B
CHABLIS GRAND CRU CHATEAU GRENOUILLE, LA CHABLISIENNE 1992 Chablis	*Creamy, oaky style. Good, classy wine; simple flavours.*	£16.50	ET HR	B
CHASSAGNE MONTRACHET 1ER CRU, JEAN NOEL GAGNARD 1992 Burgundy	*Crisp, bright, lemon nose with tinges of fresh vanilla. Sweet, fat, ripe fruit on palate.*	£22.60	J&B BWI	S
MEURSAULT GENEVRIERES, BOISSONVADOT 1992 Burgundy	*Rich, asparagus nose, hint of green peach. Tropical fruits. Green peach on palate. Complex acidity.*	£23.90	L&W ABY	G
MEURSAULT BLAGNY, LOUIS JADOT, 1990 Burgundy	*Chunky lemon fruit on nose, traces of new oak and vanilla. Sweet nuts and vanilla on palate.*	£26.50	HM WR BU	S

BURGUNDY • SPARKLING

CRÉMANT DE BOURGOGNE BRUT, DENIS FOUQUERAND 1992 Burgundy	*Creamy, light, appealing bouquet; some sharpness to palate. Slight sherbet and frothy character. Balanced*	£7.30	TRW	S

CRÉMANT DE BOURGOGNE BLANC DE BLANCS, DENIS FOUQUERAND 1992 Burgundy	*Clean fruit palate with some almond character.*	£7.50	TRW	B

BEAUJOLAIS • RED

MOULIN A VENT, FUT DE CHENE, GEORGES DUBOEUF 1993 Beaujolais	*Classic. Red fruits and gaminess on nose. Sweet cherry and redcurrant married to new oak.*	£5.40	MTL BWC GDS	G
BEAUJOLAIS VILLAGES CHATEAU DES VERGERS, ETS LORON ET FILS 1994 Beaujolais	*Lovely nose of violets and soft, gamey fruits. Good concentration of summer fruits on palate.*	£5.40	EG UBC	B
BROUILLY CHATEAU THIBAULT, CAVE CHAMPIER 1994 Beaujolais	*Ripe, raspberry character. Fragrant fruit nose. Excellent balance on palate. Ripe, sweet fruit. Soft tannins.*	£6.00	EG	B
BROUILLY, LES CELLIERS DE SAMSONS 1994 Beaujolais	*Fragrant nose of raspberries and redcurrants with hints of spice. Cherry stone and raspberry flavours.*	£6.10	NUR ABY	B
MALT HOUSE VINTNERS BROUILLY, THORIN 1994 Beaujolais	*Soft, sweet raspberry with herbal overtones. Crisp and refreshing. Attractive light style. Good, clean finish.*	£6.50	MHV	B
REGNIE, GILLES ET NEL DUCROUX, 1993 Beaujolais	*Plum and cherry with hints of violets. Fragrant palate of sweet strawberries and subtle spice.*	£6.60	WSC	B

FLEURIE DOMAINE DES CARRIERES, ETS LORON ET FILS 1994 Beaujolais	*Restrained, youthful nose. More open on palate. Lively cherries. Lively acidity. Could develop further.*	£7.00	EG U	**B**
MORGON LES CHARMES, GERARD BRISSON 1993 Beaujolais	*Juicy redcurrants on nose. Rich and full-bodied. Ripe raspberry with gamey overtones. Soft tannins.*	£7.20	CWS HW DN	**S**
FLEURIE F VERPOIX, 1994 Beaujolais	*Quite youthful. Fresh summer fruit and spice aromas. Good balance. Very refreshing now, will develop.*	£7.50	A CPW	**B**
BROUILLY DOMAINE DES SAMSONS, SYLVAIN FESSY, 1994 Beaujolais	*Creamy, raspberry and cherry aromas. Hint of spice. Lovely summer fruit character. Lively, crisp acidity.*	£8.00	GRA	**B**
JULIENAS DOMAINE DU CLOS DU FIEF, MICHEL TETE 1994 Beaujolais	*Ripe raspberry and red-currant aromas. Good concentration of flavour. Soft, opulent summer fruits. Silky texture.*	£8.00	L&W NY	**G**
FLEURIE, GEORGES DUBOEUF 1994 Beaujolais	*Ripe raspberry and redcurrant nose. Hints of spice and chocolate.*	£8.20	Widely available	**S**
BROUILLY CHATEAU DES TOURS, 1994 Beaujolais	*Light, elegant, cherry nose. Herbaceous overtones confirmed on palate. Soft fruit. Good complexity.*	£9.20	CPW CWI NI	**B**

Pinpoint who sells the wine you wish to buy by turning to the stockist codes. If you know the name of the wine you want to buy, use the alphabetical index. If price is your motivation, refer to the invaluable price guide index; red and white wines under £5, sparkling wines under £10 and champagne under £15. Happy hunting!

FRANCE • CHAMPAGNE

CHAMPAGNE

CHAMPAGNE DE NAUROY BLACK LABEL Champagne	*Crisp, fresh nose with some yeast; very clean yet complex palate. Full, rich and balanced.*	£7.50	TW MK	(S)
CHAMPAGNE ELLNER, MARQUIS D'ESTRAND, Champagne	*Good measure of fruit; clean nose; some acidity.*	£8.50	MVN MK G&M TAN	(B)
CHAMPAGNE MEDOT BRUT, MEDOT ET CIE Champagne	*Lemony, complex nose; nutty, creamy, leesy. Ripe and complex; lovely texture. Good grip to finish.*	£11.00	AUL	(B)
ANDRE SIMON CHAMPAGNE BRUT, MARNE ET CHAMPAGNE Champagne	*Complex, yeasty nose; fairly straightforward but attractive palate. Excellent acidity. Easy drinking; well made.*	£11.20	WRT MTL HOU GDS	(S)
PRINCE WILLIAM CHAMPAGNE, MARNE ET CHAMPAGNE Champagne	*Refreshing, lively, concentrated palate; good finish.*	£11.80	SMF	(S)
CHAMPAGNE MEDOT BRUT RESERVE, MEDOT ET CIE Champagne	*Caramel, butter and yeast aromas on nose; fruit on palate.*	£12.00	AUL	(B)
CHAMPAGNE FLEURY, 1988 Champagne	*Golden; yeasty nose; excellent palate. Pleasant, rich finish.*	£12.30	VR RW RAE	(B)

FRANCE • CHAMPAGNE				
CHAMPAGNE DE CLAIRVEAUX BRUT, MARNE ET CHAMPAGNE Champagne	*Farmyardy, earthy, yeasty nose; green fruit palate. Great, drinkable wine.*	£12.50	CWS	**B**
CHAMPAGNE DE TELMONT GRANDE RESERVE Champagne	*Clean, fruit nose; light and lemony. Crisp and fresh; young palate. Good balance and flavour.*	£13.00	MWW	**B**
CHAMPAGNE BONNET PRESTIGE, A. BONNET Champagne	*Complex, fruity bouquet; young and yeasty character. Creamy, medium palate.*	£13.00	RS W	**B**
CHAMPAGNE BILLIOT CUVÉE DE RESERVE BRUT, H. BILLIOT Champagne	*Rounded fruit nose; fruity. Well balanced; creamy finish.*	£13.10	ADN RW RAE	**S**
CHAMPAGNE BONNET, CARTE BLANCHE, CHAMPAGNE F. BONNET Champagne	*Big, broad nose; big, yeasty flavour. Dry, clean and gulpable.*	£13.50	ROI OD	**G**
AVERYS SPECIAL CUVÉE CHAMPAGNE, AVERYS OF BRISTOL Champagne	*Leesy, forthcoming wine; lifted, stylish flavours. Good richness on palate. Balanced and concentrated. Rich finish.*	£13.70	GDS AV	**S**
CHAMPAGNE H. BLIN & CIE Champagne	*Big, biscuity nose with a fine mousse on the palate. Dry, warm and pleasant.*	£13.90	JBF RAV OD	**B**
CHAMPAGNE OEIL DE PERDRIX, LÉONCE D'ALBE Champagne	*Spicy, soft Pinot Noir nose. Delicate strawberries and raspberries. Zesty acidity. Lovely, elegant finish.*	£14.00	MWW	**B**

CHAMPAGNE LE BRUN DE NEUVILLE BRUT ROSÉ, Champagne	*Yeasty nose. Full-flavoured, maturing style. Complex with ripe strawberry married to nutty, bready character.*	£14.10	WAW	**B**
CHAMPAGNE BONNET ROSÉ, CHAMPAGNE F. BONNET Champagne	*Raspberry comes through in mature Pinot Noir nose. Complex on palate. Strawberry with nutmeg aspects.*	£14.20	ROI OD	**G**
MERCHANT VINTNERS' BARON DE BEAUPRÉ CHAMPAGNE ELLNER Champagne	*Soft, creamy nose; easy, pleasant, soft flavours. Gulpable!*	£14.40	MVN G&M	**B**
CHAMPAGNE CUVÉE RESERVE BRUT, BOUCHÉ PÈRE ET FILS Champagne	*Lighter nose filling out on palate. Rich, mouthfilling fruit; clean with a dry finish.*	£14.60	GRA	**B**
CHAMPAGNE NICOLAS FEUILLATTE RESERVE PARTICULIERE BRUT 1ER CRU Champagne	*Lean, leesy; clean, young fruit flavours. Elegant style. Aggressive, yet rich. Complex and biscuity.*	£14.60	NF HCK U VW	**S**
WAITROSE VINTAGE CHAMPAGNE, F. BONNET, 1989 Champagne	*Toasty, seductive, apples and pears aroma. Full, rich Chardonnay character.*	£14.80	W	**B**
CHAMPAGNE DRAPPIER, CUVÉE SPECIALE, Champagne	*Bready, fruity nose; good balance on palate; fresh lemony character.*	£15.00	DBY ABY	**B**
CHAMPAGNE, LE BRUN DE NEUVILLE CUVÉE SELECTION Champagne	*Good, biscuity, yeasty nose. Soft, foamy and pleasant with a touch of sweetness.*	£15.00	HOU WAW TRO	**S**

FRANCE • CHAMPAGNE

CHAMPAGNE HERBERT BEAUFORT Champagne	*Yeasty tang on nose; signs of bottle age. Balanced palate with some complexity; fresh citrus.*	**£15.00**	LAW TO	**B**
CHAMPAGNE DUCHATEL BLANC DE BLANCS BRUT, ALAIN THIENOT Champagne	*Bready, yeasty, complex nose; light lemon on palate. Some complexity.*	**£15.00**	U	**B**
CHAMPAGNE JACQUART BRUT SELECTION, Champagne	*Subtle, Chardonnay nose; lighter style. Good acidity and length; apricot and fruit character.*	**£15.00**	PAT	**S**
CHAMPAGNE MERCIER BRUT Champagne	*Clean, yeasty nose; good fruit and depth. Ripe, peachy flavours; long finish. Classy.*	**£15.50**	Widely available	**B**
CHAMPAGNE DEVAUX CUVÉE ROSÉ, Champagne	*Lovely, delicate, fresh fruit - light raspberries and strawberries. Attractive, zesty acidity. Fine and elegant.*	**£15.50**	DVX W ENO CHF	**B**
CHAMPAGNE MERCIER DEMI-SEC Champagne	*Soft Champagne/ yeasty character on nose; firm biscuity backbone. Creamy sweetness to palate. Mellow.*	**£15.60**	Widely available	**S**
CHAMPAGNE JEEPER GRANDE RESERVE, Champagne	*Full, rich style; toasty character to nose; ripe, full, flavoursome palate. Fresh finish.*	**£15.75**	FOZ	**S**
CHAMPAGNE DRAPPIER CUVÉE SPECIALE, DRAPPIER 1990 Champagne	*Good mousse, lasts well. Light, refreshing aroma; firm acidity and good grip.*	**£16.00**	BOO DBY ABY	**S**

CHAMPAGNE BESSERAT DE BELLEFON, LA CUVÉE DES MOINES BLANC, BESSERAT DE BELLEFON Champagne	*Mid-gold colour; clean, ripe and yeasty nose. Crisp, lemon, gooseberry palate. Off-dry.*	£16.00	CBD	(B)
CHAMPAGNE MEDOT BRUT, MEDOT ET CIE Champagne	*Intense, apple nose; very fresh. Apples on palate; hint of herbs. Long finish.*	£16.00	AUL	(B)
CHAMPAGNE CHARTOGNE-TAILLET ROSÉ, CHARTOGNE-TAILLET Champagne	*Crisp fruit with grapefruit and vanilla. Yeastiness on palate. Fresh fruit backed by lemony acidity.*	£16.00	CAX	(B)
CHAMPAGNE LE BRUN DE NEUVILLE MILLESIME 1988 Champagne	*Pure Chardonnay nose; delightful. Delicate, dry and elegant with good fruit. Lovely, fresh, refined character.*	£16.20	WAW	(B)
CHAMPAGNE JEEPER, 1990 Champagne	*Elegant, rich, toasty style. Balanced and very quaffable. Stylish.*	£16.95	FOZ	(G)
CHAMPAGNE PHILIPPONNAT ROYALE RESERVE, PHILIPPONNAT Champagne	*Pale, straw-coloured; toasty, yeasty character. Good balance and very long finish.*	£17.00	WAV	(B)
CHAMPAGNE, LE BRUN DE NEUVILLE CUVÉE ROI CLOVIS Champagne	*Pale yellow; rich, toasty character. High acidity with long finish. Needs some time. Classy.*	£17.10	WAW	(B)
CHAMPAGNE POMMERY BRUT ROYAL, POMMERY Champagne	*Bready nose; nutty, spicy, ginger character. Clean flavours; good length.*	£17.20	Widely available	(B)

CHAMPAGNE PIPER-HEIDSIECK CUVÉE SAUVAGE, PIPER-HEIDSIECK 1985 Champagne	*Light, biscuity, toasty nose. Well balanced. Pleasant.*	£17.70	REM MTL	B
CHAMPAGNE LANSON BLACK LABEL, Champagne	*Clean, fresh, fruity nose with a honeyed edge. Well balanced and quite long.*	£17.80	Widely available	B
CHAMPAGNE MERCIER BRUT VINTAGE, 1988 Champagne	*Big, toasty oak nose and concentrated flavour. Simple style.*	£18.60	M&C MTL DBY AV AMY	B
CHAMPAGNE GEORGES VESSELLE BRUT, 1988 Champagne	*Light, biscuity, toasty nose; good balance and length. Elegant.*	£19.00	SOB	B
CHAMPAGNE MOËT & CHANDON BRUT IMPERIAL Champagne	*Intense bouquet; good fruit. Flavoursome and creamy palate.*	£19.00	Widely available	B
VICTORIA WINE VINTAGE CHAMPAGNE, MARNE ET CHAMPAGNE, 1989 Champagne	*Super, soft nose; clean, juicy, simple style but elegantly balanced. Dryish and clean.*	£19.00	VWC VW	G
CHAMPAGNE LE MESNIL, L'UNION DES PROPRIETAIRES RECOLTANTS 1988 Champagne	*Bready, yeasty nose; hint of digestive biscuit. Good follow-through on to palate.*	£19.20	TH WR BU RW	B
'R' DE RUINART BRUT CHAMPAGNE, RUINART Champagne	*Good fruit intensity; bready nose. Rich, ripe fruit in mouth; pleasant finish.*	£19.40	RUI BI	S

CHAMPAGNE CHARLES HEIDSIECK BRUT RESERVE Champagne	*Big, rich, toasty nose; full-flavoured, ripe, fruit palate. Pleasant, balanced and long.*	£19.60	Widely available	**G**
CHAMPAGNE BILLECART-SALMON Champagne	*Honeycomb nose; Rich wine; good acidity and length.*	£19.70	BIL DBY ADN CEB V&C OD	**S**
CHAMPAGNE HENRIOT BRUT VINTAGE, 1988 Champagne	*Slightly yeasty nose; good fruit base to palate; rich style. Green touch to finish.*	£19.70	MTL ABY	**B**
TESCO VINTAGE CHAMPAGNE, CHOUILLY 1985 Champagne	*Pronounced, fat, biscuity nose; some fruit on palate. Well made.*	£20.00	TO	**B**
CHAMPAGNE TAITTINGER BRUT RESERVE Champagne	*Green fruit on nose; dry, lighter elegant style. Slightly sweet palate. Long, concentrated finish.*	£20.20	Widely available	**B**
CHAMPAGNE AYALA CHATEAU D'AY BRUT VINTAGE, 1989 Champagne	*Nutty, toasty nose following through to good, meaty palate of crisp, savoury flavours.*	£20.50	GRA WIN	**B**
CHAMPAGNE POL ROGER WHITE FOIL EXTRA DRY, Champagne	*Delicate, honeyed fruit nose; yeasty and toasty character. Full-bodied; good balance.*	£20.70	Widely available	**S**
CHAMPAGNE VEUVE CLICQUOT WHITE LABEL DEMI-SEC Champagne	*Soft, ripe, biscuity nose, well balanced with slightly sweet, grapey fruit. Elegant and restrained.*	£20.90	Widely available	**B**

CHAMPAGNE DEVAUX CUVÉE DISTINCTION, DEVAUX 1988 Champagne	*Toasty, lemony fruit nose; crisp, lemony palate. Austere but with a rich toffee behind.*	£21.00	DVX	(S)
CHAMPAGNE JOSEPH PERRIER, CUVÉE ROYALE ROSÉ Champagne	*Quite mature with attractive, cheesecake-base aromas. Lovely, developed palate of strawberries and cream.*	£21.00	CHN ES TAN EVI	(B)
CHAMPAGNE CHARLES HEIDSIECK BRUT, 1985 Champagne	*Yellow to pink coloured wine with attractive nose; biscuity. Quite ripe fruit with some creaminess and acidity.*	£22.00	REM MTL CPW	(B)
CHAMPAGNE DRAPPIER, GRANDE SENDRÉE, 1988 Champagne	*Yeasty, rich nose; fruit flavours; good weight. Excellent length.*	£22.40	DBY ABY	(B)
CHAMPAGNE PHILIPPONNAT, LE REFLET Champagne	*Soft, creamy and lemony; gentle fruit palate. Nutty, savoury finish.*	£23.00	WAV	(G)
CHAMPAGNE MOËT & CHANDON BRUT IMPERIAL VINTAGE, 1988 Champagne	*Appealing, big, toasty nose. Clean cut; rich, bready. Complex.*	£23.50	Widely available	(S)
CHAMPAGNE LANSON VINTAGE, 1988 Champagne	*Broad, classy and full; showing ripe, yeasty, citric fruit. Clean, long finish.*	£23.50	Widely available	(B)
CHAMPAGNE TAITTINGER ROSÉ Champagne	*Classy rosé. Lovely, yeasty, biscuity aromas and elegant, crunchy, summer fruits.*	£24.50	DBY ES PF AV	(B)

FRANCE • CHAMPAGNE				
CHAMPAGNE TAITTINGER, 1989 Champagne	*Clean, balanced, complex nose; good mousse. Dry palate; good fruit; clean finish.*	£24.70	MTL DBY PF WIN	(B)
CHAMPAGNE BOUCHÉ SELECTION BLANC DE BLANCS, BOUCHE PÈRE ET FILS Champagne	*Gentle, lemony nose. Creamy, lemony palate. Slightly savoury; simple, lean style.*	£25.00	GRA	(B)
CHAMPAGNE DE VENOGE BRUT, 1989 Champagne	*Big, yeasty/toasty wine; Concentrated raspberry flavours. Creamy and complex.*	£26.00	GRB	(G)
CHAMPAGNE DE VENOGE BLANC DE BLANCS, 1990 Champagne	*Simple, clean palate with some savoury character. Crisp and light style.*	£26.00	GRB	(B)
CHAMPAGNE PHILIPPONNAT GRAND BLANC, 1988 Champagne	*Firm, yeasty nose; good flavour on middle palate. Elegant. Good length; dry finish.*	£27.00	WAV	(B)
CHAMPAGNE POL ROGER EXTRA DRY, 1988 Champagne	*Clean, balanced nose. Soft, restrained palate; length and crispness. Some yeast character.*	£27.60	Widely available	(B)
CHAMPAGNE HENRIOT CUVÉE DES ENCHANTELEURS, 1985 Champagne	*Balanced nose; good, mellow fruit. Crispy palate and good balance.*	£29.10	ABY	(B)
CHAMPAGNE BOLLINGER GRANDE ANNÉE, 1988 Champagne	*Firm, yeasty nose following through on to palate. Rich and full-bodied. Good length.*	£32.70	Widely available	(G)

CHAMPAGNE BOLLINGER GRANDE ANNÉE ROSÉ, 1985 Champagne	*Rich, yeasty, bready nose. Complex palate of mature summer fruits and freshly baked biscuits.*	£33.50	DBY ABY BI SEB DIR MZ TAN	(B)
CHAMPAGNE CHARLES HEIDSIECK BLANC DES MILLENAIRES 1983 Champagne	*Fine mousse lasts well; yeasty, biscuity nose. Sweet, ripe fruit palate. Well balanced; excellent length.*	£34.40	REM MTL CPW	(G)
CHAMPAGNE AYALA CHÂTEAU D'AY GRANDE CUVÉE 1988 Champagne	*Light, fresh, biscuity nose; full, rich flavours; lots of fruit. Good length; sweet finish.*	£38.50	GRA WIN	(S)
CHAMPAGNE DOM RUINART, BLANC DE BLANCS 1986 Champagne	*Fine mousse; bready nose. Huge flavours; honeyed edge on palate. Complex; perfect balance.*	£38.50	RUI BI	(G)
CHAMPAGNE POMMERY CUVÉE LOUISE POMMERY BRUT 1988 Champagne	*Big, bready palate. Honeyed depth to flavours.*	£40.40	TEL BI OD HDL	(B)
CHAMPAGNE NICOLAS FEUILLATTE PALMES D'OR BRUT 1ER CRU 1985 Champagne	*Herbal, fruity nose; yeasty, biscuity character. Appealing flavour; depth of fruit.*	£45.00	NF	(B)
CHAMPAGNE DE VENOGE, CHAMPAGNE DE PRINCES, 1989 Champagne	*Lemon colour; fine mousse; lovely bead. Gentle yeast and biscuit flavour. Elegant, lemony, creamy palate.*	£46.00	GRB	(S)
CHAMPAGNE VEUVE CLICQUOT LA GRANDE DAME 1988 Champagne	*Fine nose; lovely mousse. Soft, persistent and very creamy. Fine length.*	£51.40	Widely available	(G)

FRANCE • ALSACE WHITE

CHAMPAGNE MOËT ET CHANDON, CUVÉE DOM PERIGNON 1985 Champagne	*Lemon-coloured wine; gentle nose. Elegant, fruit palate; appealing length. Superbly made.*	**£57.50**	Widely available	**G**

ALSACE • WHITE

PINOT BLANC, DOMAINE J RIEFLE 1993 Alsace	*Fresh, clean apples with stalky, leafy tones. Good, ripe fruit palate and clean, intense finish.*	**£4.90**	WTR HLV	**B**
TOKAY PINOT GRIS CLOS DE HOEN, CAVE VINICOLE DE BEBLENHEIM 1994 Alsace	*Elegant, floral nose; richer honey aspects. Light and fruity. Appealing, with dry, citrussy finish.*	**£5.00**	W	**B**
WAITROSE GEWÜRZTRAMINER, CAVE DE BEBLENHEIM 1993 Alsace	*Floral style of Gewürztraminer. Fresh grapefruit with clean spiciness. Refreshing lemon zest finish.*	**£5.60**	W	**B**
MUSCAT, CAVE D'OBERNAI 1992 Alsace	*Fresh, floral and clean with plenty of ripe, characterful Muscat fruit. Firm, spicy finish.*	**£5.80**	FOZ	**B**
GEWÜRZTRAMINER, CAVE VINICOLE DE BEBLENHEIM 1994 Alsace	*Apple blossom nose. Elegant Gewürztraminer spiciness. Good concentration in mouth. Fresh acidity at finish.*	**£5.80**	NUR W	**B**
GEWÜRZTRAMINER, CAVES DE TURKHEIM 1994 Alsace	*Floral, zesty lime nose. Firm spiciness. Dry and clean with a steely backbone. Well made.*	**£5.90**	Widely available	**B**

FRANCE • ALSACE WHITE				
TOKAY PINOT GRIS CÔTES DE ROUFFACH, DOMAINE J RIEFLE, 1993 Alsace	*Soft, smoky aromas. Spicy toffee, honey and baked apple flavours and clean, underlying acidity.*	£6.80	WTR HLV	B
GEWÜRZTRAMINER RESERVE, CAVE DE TURCKHEIM, 1993 Alsace	*Gentle, scented nose. Spritzy lime and spicy backbone. Good concentration. Fat and rich. Spicy finish.*	£6.90	BP BOO DBY HOU FUL	B
TOKAY PINOT GRIS RESERVE PARTICULIÈRE, VINS D'ALSACE KUEHN, 1993 Alsace	*Soft with attractive bite of acidity. Emminently drinkable, with real spice. Pleasant, weighty finish.*	£7.30	CHN EVI	B
GEWÜRZTRAMINER CÔTES DE ROUFFACH, RÉNÉ MURÉ, 1993 Alsace	*Warm, spicy, apple aromas; like apple crumble. Powerful palate. Heady and alcobolic, but retains balance.*	£7.40	BWC DIR HDL	B
RIESLING GUEBERSCHWIHR, DOMAINE ZIND HUMBRECHT 1992 Alsace	*Elegant, clean nose. Floral with oily aspect; steely intensity characteristic of fine Alsatian Riesling.*	£7.60	TH DBY ABY TH WR BU	B
GEWÜRZTRAMINER RESERVE, LORENTZ 1993 Alsace	*Floral, berbaceous aromas. Off-dry, rich and easy-going. Clean, citrus fruit on finish.*	£7.80	FTH DBY TRO	B
PINOT D'ALSACE VIEILLES VIGNES, DOMAINE ZIND HUMBRECHT, 1992 Alsace	*Soft, dry and spicy with an attractive, characterful nose. Well-judged oak with a nutty flavour.*	£8.40	DBY ABY	B
GEWÜRZTRAMINER, DOMAINE ZIND HUMBRECHT, 1993 Alsace	*Distinctive, spicy nose. Rich, honeyed fruit with some botrytis. Delightful perfume on lengthy finish.*	£8.50	DBY ABY	B

FRANCE • ALSACE WHITE

PINOT D'ALSACE, DOMAINE ZIND HUMBRECHT, 1993 Alsace	*Lean, clean and delicate, with ripe mango and peach aromas. Hint of almonds.*	**£8.60**	DBY ABY WR	(S)
GEWÜRZTRAMINER WINTZENHEIM, DOMAINE ZIND HUMBRECHT 1992 Alsace	*Typical richness of Zind Humbrecht stable; warm, honeyed flavour.*	**£9.10**	DBY ABY	(B)
TOKAY PINOT GRIS HEIMBOURG, CAVE DE TURCKHEIM, 1993 Alsace	*Elegant style of Tokay Pinot Gris. Honeyed spice and delicate, floral character. Soft, ripe, rounded.*	**£9.40**	BP BOO DBY	(B)
GEWÜRZTRAMINER HERRENWÉG/TURCKHEIM, DOMAINE ZIND HUMBRECHT 1992 Alsace	*Subdued nose but bursts on palate with strong, cinnamon, peach and fat, creamy, honeyed texture.*	**£9.60**	DBY ABY WR	(B)
MUSCAT D'ALSACE, DOMAINE ZIND HUMBRECHT, 1993 Alsace	*Spicy, aromatic Muscat character. Clean, crisp, refreshing fruit on the palate. Quintessential Muscat.*	**£9.90**	DBY ABY	(B)
RIESLING GRAND CRU BRAND, CAVE DE TURCKHEIM 1985 Alsace	*Excellent, developed Riesling. Aromatic apples with hints of petrol and spice.*	**£11.30**	BP DBY	(B)
RIESLING BRAND, DOMAINE ZIND HUMBRECHT, 1992 Alsace	*Classic Riesling nose. Delicate balance of ripe fruits, herbal and floral flavours. The finish is long and lemony.*	**£11.30**	DBY ABY	(S)
GEWÜRZTRAMINER GRAND CRU BRAND, CAVE DE TURCKHEIM, 1990 Alsace	*Classic nose of ripe, honeyed lychee. Rich texture with sweetness and racy spice. Apricot finish.*	**£12.60**	Widely available	(S)

FRANCE • ALSACE WHITE				
TOKAY PINOT GRIS VIEILLES VIGNES, ZIND HUMBRECHT, 1992 Alsace	*Delicate floral nose. Apples and greengages. Initial soft banana gives way to mineral character.*	£12.90	WR DBY ABY CEB	**B**
TOKAY PINOT GRIS VIEILLES VIGNES, DOMAINE ZIND HUMBRECHT 1993 Alsace	*Rich, oaky nose with spicy raisins and some smokiness. Creamy oak finish.*	£14.00	DBY ABY WR	**B**
GEWÜRZTRAMINER CUVÉE DES SEIGNEURS DE RIBEAUPIERRE, F E TRIMBACH, 1990 Alsace	*Spiced peach nose. Full of sweet lychee. Fat and full-bodied. Still youthful.*	£14.90	PRG DBY AV HDL	**S**
TOKAY PINOT GRIS CLOS WINDSBUHL, DOMAINE ZIND HUMBRECHT 1993 Alsace	*Nose of cloves and apples. Well-integrated toasty oak and caramel flavours. Honeyed fruit.*	£15.30	DBY ABY	**S**
RIESLING CUVÉE FREDERIC EMILE, TRIMBACH, 1989 Alsace	*Honeyed apple and lime – rich, spicy and creamy. Lovely weight of fruit but good acidity.*	£15.80	Widely available	**B**
GEWÜRZTRAMINER CLOS WINDSBUHL, DOMAINE ZIND HUMBRECHT 1990 Alsace	*Elegant, classic nose. Ripe fruit with delicious spiciness. Sweet peaches balanced by acidity. Creamy depth.*	£15.80	DBY ABY BU WR	**G**
TOKAY PINOT GRIS CLOS JEBSAL, DOMAINE ZIND HUMBRECHT, 1993 Alsace	*Mature nose of spice and petrol. Palate of Seville oranges, candied peel and kiwi fruit.*	£17.80	ABY	**B**
GEWÜRZTRAMINER GOLDERT VENDANGE TARDIVE, DOMAINE ZIND HUMBRECHT 1989 Alsace	*Ripe, honeyed, botrytis nose. Palate of sweet bananas, toasted nuts and raisins. Complex.*	£21.30	DBY ABY	**G**

FRANCE • ALSACE SPARKLING					
RIESLING RANGEN DE THANN, DOMAINE ZIND HUMBRECHT 1993 Alsace	*Rich guava and apple fruit aromas. Hints of spice and botrytis. Enticing floral quality.*	**£23.60**	ABY		(B)

ALSACE • SWEET WHITE

TOKAY PINOT GRIS VENDANGES TARDIVE, CAVE DE TURCKHEIM, 1992 Alsace	*Lovely, lemony nose and palate.*	**£15.90**	BP DBY		(B)
TOKAY CLOS JEBSAL VENDANGES TARDIVE, DOMAINE ZIND HUMBRECHT 1992 Alsace	*Soft, classy wine with good acidity and fruit balance. Some bitterness on finish.*	**£19.40**	ABY		(B)
TOKAY ROTENBERG SELECTION DES GRAINS NOBLES, DOMAINE ZIND HUMBRECHT 1991 Alsace	*Liquid loveliness! Beautiful balance and length with great sweetness and acidity. Deep rich flavours; elegant.*	**£91.80**	DBY ABY		(G)

ALSACE • SPARKLING

MAYERLING BRUT CRÉMANT D'ALSACE, CAVE DE TURCKHEIM Alsace	*Good mousse and richness; aristocratic nose. Complex, lean, elegant and biscuity. Lovely richness on palate.*	**£8.30**	BOO DBY U HVW AMY		(B)

Pinpoint who sells the wine you wish to buy by turning to the stockist codes. If you know the name of the wine you want to buy, use the alphabetical index. If price is your motivation, refer to the invaluable price guide index; red and white wines under £5, sparkling wines under £10 and champagne under £15. Happy hunting!

LOIRE • RED

SAUMUR CHAMPIGNY, BOUVET LADUBAY, 1990 Loire	*Some complexity: cherry and raspberry combined with farmyard, spicy characteristics.*	**£7.70**	DBY PF	(B)
LANGLOIS CHATEAU, SAUMUR ROUGE VIEILLES VIGNES, 1993 Loire	*Elegant, interesting. Lovely, intense raspberry and cherry on palate, integrated with subtle oak. Long finish.*	**£8.70**	DBY DIR MZ	(B)
SANCERRE ROUGE LES CAILLIERS, DOMAINE VACHERON, 1993 Loire	*Sweet, rose petal nose. Light, fragrant with gentle, herbaceous aspect. Delicate fruit. Super summer drinking.*	**£9.60**	ET DBY	(B)

LOIRE • WHITE

VOUVRAY DEMI-SEC, CHÂTEAU VAUDENUITS, 1990 Loire	*Nose of honey and greengages. Soft apples on palate. Heather honey overtones and gentle acidity.*	**£3.80**	BWC ABY	(B)
DOMAINE DE LA HALLOSIERE CHARDONNAY, LES VIGNERONS DE LA NOELLE 1994 Loire	*Intense nose of creamed rice pudding and coconut. Good acidity on palate; builds well. Complex.*	**£4.00**	T&T	(B)
SANCERRE GUE D'ARGENT, DOMAINE SERGE LALOUE, 1993 Loire	*Delicate, lemon varietal nose. Fresh balance of acidity and fruit. Subtle bite, stylish and pleasant.*	**£4.00**	ABY CPW	(B)

VOUVRAY DEMI SEC, BOURILLON DORLEANS 1993 Loire	*Wonderful example of demi-sec Vouvray. Toffee apples and honey with lovely, fresh, floral acidity.*	£6.10	TO NY	(S)
VOUVRAY SEC, DOMAINES BOURILLON D'ORLEANS, 1994 Loire	*Nose of apples, gooseberries, almonds, minerals and honey. Zippy apple acidity gives it verve.*	£6.60	T&T R	(B)
MALT HOUSE VINTNERS POUILLY FUMÉ DOMAINE DES VALLÉES, DOMAINE LUMEREUX, 1994 Loire	*Grassy nose with ripe passion-fruit and grapefruit. Well balanced acidity. Good length and finesse.*	£6.70	MHV	(B)
SANCERRE DOMAINE BONNARD, 1993 Loire	*Pale, straw-coloured with tropical fruit nose and supple, full palate. Good length.*	£6.90	MCA	(B)
VOUVRAY, JEAN CLAUDE AUBERY, 1992 Loire	*Classic Chenin Blanc. Greengage and apple with hints of spice and honey. Rounded and creamy.*	£7.30	3D	(S)
SAUMUR BLANC VIEILLES VIGNES, LANGLOIS CHATEAU, 1992 Loire	*Herbaceous nose. Ripe apple and gooseberry well integrated with the oak. Coconut and warm vanilla.*	£9.90	DIR MZ	(S)
VOUVRAY MOELLEUX, CAVE DES VITICULTEURS DU VOUVRAY, 1989 Loire	*Classic Chenin Blanc nose of honey and apples. Ripe pear and melon flavours. Minerally backbone.*	£10.00	ABY U	(S)
FORTNUM AND MASON SANCERRE, VACHERON, 1993 Loire	*Clean, soft fruit; fragrant and attractive. Good balance throughout; fresh, light quality.*	£10.00	F&M	(S)

LOIRE • SPARKLING

VOUVRAY BRUT, DIDIER CHAMPALOU Loire	*Clean, fairly intense nose; off-dry palate; slightly coarse fruit.*	£6.00	SOM	B
SPARKLING VOUVRAY BRUT, CHATEAU MONCONTOUR, 1992 Loire	*Crisp, lemony middle palate; medium-high acidity.*	£7.50	ET	B
SAUMUR BRUT, BOUVET LADUBAY Loire	*Fresh, green bouquet; good acidity and weighty palate. Good length. Rich fruit flavours.*	£8.20	DBY ES PF EVI	B
CRÉMANT DE LOIRE LANGLOIS CHATEAU Loire	*Good colour; strong yeasty character to nose; weighty, soft and emollient. Good richness.*	£8.50	DBY MWW GDS DIR MZ UBC	S

RHONE • RED

LA VIEILLE FERME RESERVE ROUGE, PIERRE PERRIN, 1992 Rhone	*Deep, bright purple. Good, strong, farmyard character. Rich, ripe and with good depth.*	£3.30	MIS TO HOL	B
UVICA MERLOT, UVICA 1994 Ardeche	*Claret nose with black-currant, peppery over-tones. Intense berry flavours enhance the richness.*	£3.50	SAF WOI	B

GAMAY / SYRAH VIN DE PAYS DES COTEAUX DE L'ARDECHE, LES VIGNERONS ARDECHOIS 1994 Rhone	*Fresh, gurgling Gamay meets a spicy roasted Syrah. Lovely combination.*	£3.60	DAM W DIR	**B**
LE CORDON, GABRIEL MEFFRE, 1994 Rhone	*Rich, fruity nose with undertones of brambles and spices. Fruit prevalent on palate.*	£4.00	GA	**B**
CÔTES DU RHONE DOMAINE ST ETIENNE, M COULCOMB,1993 Rhone	*Crimson/purple; smoky, blackcurrant bouquet. Decent body; ripe fruit; balanced acidity. Oak, dry finish.*	£4.80	H&H NY	**B**
CÔTES DU RHONE DOMAINE DES MOULINS, GEORGES DUBOEUF 1994 Rhone	*Good colour; fresh, spicy bouquet. Firm fruit and tannins with good balance.*	£4.80	BWC HDL	**S** WINE OF THE YEAR
CÔTES DU RHONE CUVÉE DES CAPUCINES, DOMAINE DU VIEUX CHÊNE 1992 Rhone	*Pale red; light, stewed fruit bouquet. Soft and sweet palate.*	£4.90	J&B	**B**
CÔTES DU RHONE DOMAINE DIONYSUS, GABRIEL ALIGNE, 1994 Rhone	*Juicy, ripe fruit; pleasing, sweet fruit palate. Firm tannins.*	£5.00	DN	**B**
CROZES HERMITAGE, LOUIS MOUSSET,1992 Rhone	*Purple; big, fruit bouquet; light and pleasant wine that is very quaffable.*	£5.20	CWS U	**B**
CÔTES DU RHONE DOMAINE DES JONQUIERS OGIER & FILS 1994 Rhone	*Clean, vibrant purple, ruby; mild raspberry aromas. Juicy character and flavours; good length.*	£5.20	GRA WIN	**B**

CHATEAU VAL JOANIS 1992 Rhone	*Light nose, some perfume; soft, fruit palate; medium acidity.*	£5.30	BOO ABY CEB	(B)
CÔTES DU RHONE ELEVÉ EN FOUDRES DE CHENE, A OGIER & FILS, 1992 Rhone	*Clean, medium-ruby colour with pinkish rim. Classic Southern wine with raspberry palate. Very tasty.*	£5.50	GRA	(B)
CÔTES DU RHONE VILLAGES LA PRESIDENTE CAIRANNE, DOMAINE MAX AUBERT 1994 Rhone	*Young, tart berries with a hint of ripeness.*	£5.60	SG SV	(B)
DOMAINE LE CLOS DE CAVEAU VACQUEYRAS, GERARD BUNGENER 1993 Rhone	*Deep, thick, red wine with big nose; sweet berries on palate. Massive tannins.*	£5.80	VER BG	(B)
MALT HOUSE VINTNERS CROZES HERMITAGE, CAVE DE TAIN L'HERMITAGE Rhone	*Good, chunky nose following on to palate. Lovely full fruit; easy to drink.*	£6.00	MHV	(B)
DOMAINE DE LA MACHOTTE, CAVES BESSAC 1991 Rhone	*Nice fruit and structure with dry, lean finish. Big, softish mouthful of fruit.*	£6.00	MIS	(S)
CROZES-HERMITAGE CUVÉE JEAN-ETIENNE GUIBERT, CAVE DE TAIN L'HERMITAGE 1992 NORTHERN Rhône	*Attractive peppery nose. Good plum/peppery palate. Well made with good balance. Gentle fruit finish.*	£6.10	BP BOO DBY OD ABY	(S)
CÔTES DU RHONE E GUIGAL, 1992 Rhone	*Young wine. Great for drinking now with lovely feel in mouth. Elegant finish.*	£6.30	Widely available	(B)

FRANCE • RHONE RED

CÔTES DU RHONE CUVÉE PRIVÉE, CELLIER DAUPHINS 1989 Rhone	*Spicy, complex nose; good concentration on palate.*	**£6.50**	HOT	(B)
DOMAINE DE LUNARD, FRANCOIS MICHEL 1989 Rhône	*Spicy fruit flavours; dry finish.*	**£6.50**	MK	(B)
VACQUEYRAS BOISERAIE, A OGIER & FILS 1993 Rhone	*Subdued nose; spicy, fruit palate and ripe tannins. Medium weight; spicy character.*	**£6.60**	GRA WIN	(B)
VACQUEYRAS, CAVE DE VACQUEYRAS 1992 Rhone	*Lovely, sweet, heady aromas; gutsy, satisfying warm berry palate. Ripe, elegant; great style.*	**£6.80**	DBY CWS	(B)
CHATEAUNEUF DU PAPE LES GRANDES SERRES 1992 Rhone	*Mature, complex wine. Good bottle age and warm style.*	**£7.00**	EH JS	(B)
VALREAS DOMAINE DE LA GRANDE BELLANE , JEAN COUSTON 1993 Rhône	*Black cherry aromas. Good spicy character and tannic finish.*	**£7.20**	VER BG	(B)
CHÂTEAU VAL JOANIS LES GRIOTTES 1989 Rhone	*A delightful wine, but perhaps need a little more time to be ideal. Still fresh and light.*	**£7.20**	MTL ABY	(B)
CROZES HERMITAGE LES LAUNES, DELAS 1991 Rhone	*Black/red cherry; sweet wildflower and fruits on nose. Some medicinal character to palate.*	**£7.30**	FTH DBY HOU	(B)

CHÂTEAUNEUF DU PAPE DOMAINE ST BENOIT 1992 Rhone	*Slightly confected but exciting bouquet; clean fruit and spice. Soft strawberries.*	£8.20	WTR HLV	**B**
CHÂTEAUNEUF DU PAPE DOMAINE ANDRE BRUNEL 1992 Rhone	*Ripe, sweet, jammy nose following on to palate with fair acid balance. Astringent finish.*	£9.90	JS HVW	**B**
CROZES HERMITAGE 'LA GUIRAUDE', GRAILLOT 1991 Rhone	*Classic, mature, French Syrah bouquet; tasty, pungent middle palate. Good length; serious wine.*	£10.10	DBY ABY OD YAP	**B**
CHATEAU DE ST. GEORGES CUVÉE SYRAH, DOMAINE ST. GEORGES 1993 Rhone	*Wonderful, ripe nose; vegetal, pungent. Magnificent, spicy palate. Soft fruit; firm finish. Great potential.*	£10.20	CPW	**S**
CORNAS, CAVE DE TAIN L'HERMITAGE 1991 Northern Rhone	*Warm, soft fruit; complex bouquet. Sweet, ripe palate.*	£10.70	BP BOO DBY CNL	**S**
DOMAINE FONT DE MICHELLE, LES FILS D'ETIENNE GONNE, 1992 Rhone	*Pungent vanilla nose; clean fruit flavours on palate.*	£10.80	WSG TH WR BU WSO AMY	**B**
CHÂTEAUNEUF DU PAPE SOLEIL ET FESTINS, DOMAINE ST BENOIT 1993 Rhone	*Sweet fruit, vegetal and earthy nose. Strong tannins.*	£10.90	WTR	**B**
CHÂTEAUNEUF DU PAPE MONT REDON 1990 Rhone	*Elegant wine, warm style; less obviously fruity but with ripe and rounded flavours.*	£10.90	DBY PF	**B**

CHATEAUNEUF DU PAPE CUVÉE DE CARDE, DOMAINE ST BENOIT 1993 Rhone	*Forward, vegetal and slightly confected aromas; softly spicy and sweet. Pleasant finish.*	£11.00	WTR	(S)
CHATEAUNEUF DU PAPE DOMAINE CHANTE CIGALE, SABON-FAVIER 1990 Rhone	*Highly-perfumed wine with good wood and grip.*	£11.40	BP DBY CHF EVI AMY	(S)
CHATEAU LA NERTHE 1991 Rhone	*Superb, peppery, creamy nose; well-balanced palate and ripe tannins. Complex and long.*	£11.70	HAL OD	(B)
HERMITAGE, BROTTE 1988 Rhone	*Full-bodied wine with raspberries and tannin. Very 'big' flavour with style.*	£13.50	WMK	(S)
DOMAINE FONT DE MICHELLE CUVÉE ETIENNE, LES FILS D'ETIENNE GONNET 1992 Rhone	*Light style, tobacco and shoe leather aromas; metallic finish.*	£15.80	WSG HVW AMY	(S)
CÔTE ROTIE, JAMET 1992 Rhone	*Soft, mulberry nose; long, cool fruit leading to blueberries and blackberries on finish.*	£17.10	DBY MWW BI CHF HVW	(B)
CÔTE ROTIE, M CHAPOUTIER 1991 Rhone	*Lean, closed, white pepper nose. Soft, fragrant palate; white pepper and soft, bramble flavours.*	£18.70	CEB DIR MZ AV	(B)
CÔTE ROTIE BRUNE ET BLONDE, E GUIGAL 1991 Rhone	*Closed nose; soft, creamy fruit on palate; new oak and vanilla. Fruit flavours last well.*	£19.90	JEF ABY HVW	(S)

FRANCE • RHONE WHITE

HERMITAGE, GUIGAL 1990 Rhone	*Good, young Syrah; peppery and ripe. Good texture and length. Grips and lasts.*	£20.10	VWC VW NI HVW JEF	(B)
CÔTE ROTIE, GUIGAL, GUIGAL 1990 Rhone	*Youngish nose; flavoursome, youthful palate; balanced fruit and crisp acidity. Good definition.*	£20.40	Widely available	(G)
CÔTE ROTIE, M CHAPOUTIER 1990 Rhone	*Intense, gamey, pungent nose; damsons and truffle. Fullish body; ripe, peppery fruit. Brambles and plums.*	£21.00	ES W DIR MZ	(B)
HERMITAGE LA CHAPELLE, JABOULET AINÉ 1986 Rhone	*Ruby red; blackberry/ minty nose; burnt coffee, earthy, plummy character. Blackberry and black cherry palate.*	£22.80	ADN TAN OD AV TRO CNL	(S)

RHONE • WHITE

GABRIEL MEFFRE GALET VINEYARDS CHARDONNAY 1994 Rhone	*Clean wine with juicy flavours and some length to finish.*	£4.00	GA VW	(B)
CONDRIEU LA CÔTE CHERY, A OGIER & FILS 1993 Rhone	*Complex and concentrated with pungent grape aroma. Oily and waxy with excellent spicy wood.*	£25.50	GRA	(B)

Pinpoint who sells the wine you wish to buy by turning to the stockist codes. If you know the name of the wine you want to buy, use the alphabetical index. If price is your motivation, refer to the invaluable price guide index; red and white wines under £5, sparkling wines under £10 and champagne under £15. Happy hunting!

PROVENCE • RED

CHATEAU LA CANORGUE, J.P. MARGAN 1993 Provence	*Good colour; fruity nose. Quite long with fruit flavours carrying through.*	**£6.50**	VR	B
CHATEAU ROUTAS CUVÉE INFERNET, CHÂTEAU ROUTAS 1993 Provence	*Fresh, fruity nose with balance of fruit and oak. Full-bodied; good structure.*	**£7.00**	DBY M&V	B
DOMAINE RICHEAUME SYRAH, HENNING HOESCH 1992 Provence	*Herby and peppery, full of character; well made and good balance.*	**£8.00**	VER BG	B
TERRES BLANCHE CUVÉE DE TAVEN, LES TERRES BLANCHE 1990 Provence	*Deep, dark colour. Blackcurrant and bitter raisin bouquet. Light palate, undertones of toffee and spices.*	**£11.10**	ABY	S

PROVENCE • WHITE

CHATEAU MIRAVAL VIN BLANC, CHÂTEAU MIRAVAL 1993 Provence	*Rich, ripe and complex; cinnamon, apple, spices, botrytis, apricots and peaches.*	**£4.00**	BWC MK DBY	B

Pinpoint who sells the wine you wish to buy by turning to the stockist codes. If you know the name of the wine you want to buy, use the alphabetical index. If price is your motivation, refer to the invaluable price guide index; red and white wines under £5, sparkling wines under £10 and champagne under £15. Happy hunting!

FRANCE • SOUTH WEST WHITE

SOUTH WEST • RED

CLOS L'ENVEGE CÔTES DE BERGERAC, YVES PAGES ET ASSOCIES 1993 Bergerac	*Ripe nose, slightly herbaceous with notes of tobacco. Abundant fruit extract and Cabernet flavours.*	**£4.60**	BP	(S)
CHATEAU DE SABAZAN PRODUCTEURS PLAIMONT 1990 South West	*Rich ruby colour. Youthful taste with balanced sweet fruits on palate. Flavoursome, with excellent aftertaste.*	**£6.00**	WSO	(B)
CHATEAU BOUSCASSE, ALAIN BRUMONT 1992 South West	*Dark rich colour. Oaky, plummy nose with spices and tar intermingling. Classy tannic gulp.*	**£7.70**	H&H HOL RD	(B)
CHATEAU BOUSCASSE VIEILLES VIGNES, ALAIN BRUMONT 1989 South West	*Inky black with spices and berries on nose. Mineral blackcurrant on palate, hints of eucalyptus.*	**£10.00**	H&H	(B)
CHATEAU MONTUS, ALAIN BRUMONT 1992 South West	*Spicy, smoky, woody nose. Powerful flavours on palate. Strong, firm tannins. Overtones of ripe cassis.*	**£11.20**	H&H HOL	(B)

SOUTH WEST • WHITE

VIN DE PAYS DES CÔTES DE GASCOGNE DOMAINE PLANTERIEU, GRASSA, GRASSA 1994 South West	*Intensely aromatic, floral, delicate and just off-dry. Full of elegant zingy fruit and length.*	**£3.60**	W	(B)

LANGUEDOC ROUSSILLON • RED

LA CROIX ROUGE 1994 Languedoc Roussillon	*Remarkably fruity aroma with spicy undertones and full colour. Good structure.*	**£3.70**	BI CWI	**B**
CHATEAU DE MURVIEL, R M D I 1994 Languedoc Roussillon	*Deep, rich colour with good balance and pleasant froth on mid-palate. Strong finish.*	**£3.70**	FWF	**S**
DOMAINE ROCHEVUE, JEANJEAN 1993 Languedoc Roussillon	*Powerful raspberry/dark cherry aroma. Good weight of fruit and balance between acidity and tannin.*	**£3.90**	SAF	**B**
SYRAH CHAIS CUXAC, VAL D'ORBIEU 1993 Languedoc Roussillon	*Sherbety, peppery, baked fruit aroma; undertones of oak. Medium-bodied with fresh acidity and tannins.*	**£3.90**	VDO SPR CPW	**S**
CHATEAU DU CAPITOUL 1993 Languedoc Roussillon	*Deep, cherry colour and rich, chocolate flavour. Intense fruit on the palate.*	**£4.00**	VWC VW	**B**
DOMAINE DE COUDOUGNE, TERROIRS D'OCCITANIE 1992 Languedoc Roussillon	*Rich cherry and currants on nose with rustic, creamy, classy grip and fruit. Good structure.*	**£4.00**	CHN	**B**
DOMAINE BASSAC SYRAH, DELHON FRÈRES 1994 Languedoc Roussillon	*Deep purple colour. Great fruit and character are dominant traits. Concentrated sweet fruits.*	**£4.00**	VR	**B**

DOMAINE DE LA LOUVETERIE, R M D I 1993 Languedoc Roussillon	*Grand, deep ruby colouring. Full of gorgeous, soft, ripe fruits. Great structure and lovely finish.*	**£4.10**	FWF UBC	**B**
MERLOT CHAIS CUXAC, VAL D'ORBIEU 1993 Languedoc Roussillon	*Clean, plummy fruit and raspberry aroma. Soft, pleasant texture. Well made.*	**£4.20**	SPR VW VDO	**B**
LA SERRE CABERNET SAUVIGNON 1994 Languedoc Roussillon	*Richly fruity, delicious, complex flavours of mellow oak and berries. Good backbone and tannic structure.*	**£4.40**	BIC WI	**B**
LA SERRE CABERNET SAUVIGNON 1994 Languedoc Roussillon	*Richly fruity, delicious complex flavours of mellow oak and berries. Good backbone and tannic structure.*	**£4.40**	BI CWI	**B**
CHAIS BAUMIERE CABERNET SAUVIGNON, DOMAINE DE LA BAUME 1993 Languedoc Roussillon	*Essence of raspberries on nose, traces of bacon and pepper. Dark fruits on palate. Unusual.*	**£4.40**	HBR CWS JS	**B**
CHAIS BAUMIERE SYRAH, DOMAINE DE LA BAUME 1994 Languedoc Roussillon	*Leathery, tarry, cherry aroma. Sweet ripe fruits on palate. Good, firm finish.*	**£4.40**	HBR JS	**B**
CHAIS BAUMIERE SYRAH, DOMAINE DE LA BAUME 1993 Languedoc Roussillon	*Jammy fruit and fine French oak on nose, soft fruits on palate. Fresh acidic finish.*	**£4.40**	HBR JS	**B**
DOMAINE ST EULALIE MINERVOIS 1992 Languedoc Roussillon	*Great, sweet, fruity elegant aroma with traces of pepper. Big, generous, earthy finish.*	**£4.40**	MVN TH WR BU HHC TAN	**B**

SAINT CHINIAN SIALA, MAUREL VEDEAU 1993 Languedoc Roussillon	*Brilliant cherry and cassis aroma. Deep red fruits with soft, balanced tannins. Crisp acidity.*	£4.50	T&T	(B)
SYRAH DOMAINE DU BARRES, CAROLINE DE BEAULIEU 1993 Languedoc Roussillon	*Light colour and delightful light bouquet. Soft berry on palate. Well balanced combination.*	£4.60	CVR L&W	(S)
CHATEAU LES OLLIEUX, FRANCOISE SURBEZY-CARTIER 1991 Languedoc Roussillon	*Great depth of fruit on nose, cherries and berries with chocolate. Approachable, well-made wine.*	£5.30	AUL DBY TH WR BU RD	(B)
CHATEAU ST JAMES, CORBIERES GUALCO 1992 Languedoc Roussillon	*Impressive balance of flavours. Subtle redcurrant palate. Soft, fruity nose with trace beetroot.*	£5.50	BWC HVW	(B)
LA CUVÉE MYTHIQUE, VAL D'ORBIEU 1993 Languedoc Roussillon	*Deep, youthful garnet. An excellent balance of ripe fruits, oak and acidity.*	£6.20	VDO VW SAF	(B)
CHATEAU D'OUPIA CUVÉE BARON 1992 Languedoc Roussillon	*Deep, thick, herbaceous and complex. Exceedingly well made. Great length and good aftertaste.*	£6.50	CPW	(B)
LES CHEMINS DE BASSAC CUVÉE PIERRE ELIE, R & I DUCELLIER 1993 Languedoc Roussillon	*Sweet, ripe blackcurranty nose with clove undertones. Good ,ripe palate. Approachable.*	£6.50	WTR	(B)
SAINT CHINIAN LA FONSALADE, MAUREL VEDEAU 1992 Languedoc Roussillon	*Inky, plummy, vinous aroma. Very good balance. Super fruits on palate.*	£7.20	T&T TO WSO	(B)

| **Chateau Real Martin Rouge De La Provence, Jacques Clothilde 1990** Languedoc Roussillon | *Delicious, soft, spicy flavour with abundant fruit on nose including passion-fruit, melon.* | £8.00 | CRM | B |

LANGUEDOC/ROUSILLON • WHITE

Ryman Chardonnay 1993 Languedoc Roussillon	*Tropical, oaky nose. Ripe apples, touch of citrus; complex.*	£3.00	HHR BTH JS	B
Terret Chardonnay J & F Lurton 1994 Languedoc-Rousillon	*Fresh, lemony nose; crisp, fresh palate with good fruit intensity. Lemony, lively and light.*	£3.50	W SAF	B
Fortant De France Chardonnay, Skalli 1994 Languedoc Roussillon	*Full nose with some malolactic fermentation flavours; good acid and length.*	£4.00	SKA W VW	B
Le Piat De Chardonnay, Piat Père Et Fils 1994 Languedoc Roussillon	*Clean, full-flavoured nose; quite zingy. Fullish, creamy palate with good depth and rich fruit.*	£4.10	IDV MTL CWS SMF TO U VW	B
St Michael Domaine Virginie Mandeville Chardonnay 1994 Languedoc Roussillon	*Straightforward, slightly scented grapefruit aromas on nose; soft palate, lasting well throughout.*	£4.30	M&S	B
Chais Baumière Sauvignon Blanc, Domaine De La Baume 1994 Languedoc-Roussillon	*Clean, fresh nose; develops quite well in the glass. Pleasant texture and nice balance.*	£4.30	DBY HOU JS	B

FRANCE • LANGUEDOC ROUSSILLON WHITE

DOMAINE DE LA BAUME CHAIS BAUMIERE CHARDONNAY 1994 Languedoc Roussillon	*Subtle aromas of melon and nectarine. Young, fruity flavours. Balanced; rich, full-bodied finish.*	**£4.40**	HBR JS	**B**
LAPEROUSE, VIN DE PAYS D'OC PENFOLDS & VAL D'ORBIEU 1994 Languedoc Roussillon	*Floral nose with citrus and honey tones. Young, fresh and crisp. Good weight of ripe fruit.*	**£4.50**	Widely available	**B**
DOMAINE DE LA BAUME PHILIPPE DE BAUDIN CHARDONNAY 1993 Languedoc Roussillon	*Citrus with kiss of lime. Fino sherry finish.*	**£4.50**	HBR CWS HVW R	**B**
SAUVIGNON, PHILIPPE DE BAUDIN 1994 Languedoc Roussillon	*Pale green with subtle nose, but big, up-front fruit. Clean and crisp.*	**£4.50**	SAF MTL DBY HOU R	**B**
CHARDONNAY BOISE, MAUREL VEDEAU 1994 Languedoc Roussillon	*Toasted oak aromas. Strong oak does not overwhelm fruit but brings out complexity.*	**£4.60**	T&T W JS	**B**
CHARDONNAY, DOMAINE VIRGINIE 1994 Languedoc Roussillon	*Good fruit and oak balance; pleasing palate.*	**£4.70**	SAF CWS ADN HHC G&M TAN	**S**
ST MICHAEL MANDEVILLE VIOGNIER, DOMAINE VIRGINIE 1994 Languedoc Roussillon	*Creamy nose with gentle, elegant lime and white peach notes. Ripe fruit flavours. Fresh acidity.*	**£5.00**	M&S	**S** WINE OF THE YEAR
CHARDONNAY, DOMAINE DE REGISMONT 1994 Languedoc Roussillon	*Quite a floral, perfumed nose; less obvious fruit palate. Vanilla finish. Elegant.*	**£6.50**	BD	**B**

GERMANY

G ERMANY IS THE SOURCE of some of the world's greatest white
wines, made in styles unparalleled elsewhere. Sadly, many
producers are chasing the rainbow of dry wine while some of
the biggest names are letting themselves down with shoddy
winemaking. All of which helps to explain the presence of
new-wave winemakers as medal winners, who are often more
quality-conscious than many of their forebears.

RED

BADEN PINOT NOIR, BADISCHER WINZERKELLER 1991 Baden	*Light, clean fruit character with soft strawberry and raspberry. Very refreshing and well made.*	**£3.99**	LAY	B

WHITE

MALT HOUSE VINTNERS OBERMEISTER LIEBFRAUMILCH, URBANBERGER Rhein	*Sweet vanilla and pear-drop aromas. Sweet apples with floral overtones. Gentle, grapefruit acidity.*	**£ 2.60**	MHV	B
RIESLING ST URSULA/HUGH RYMAN, ST 1994 Pfalz	*Lovely, perfumed nose, clean and fragrant with hints of apple skin. Backed by fine steeliness.*	**£ 3.80**	SAF	B
ST MICHAEL RÜDESHEIMER ROSENGARTEN RIESLING SPÄTLESE, FRANZ REH 1993 Nahe	*Clean, lemon nose. Ripe, apple and peaches. Fat and rounded, but lively acidity for balance.*	**£ 4.00**	M&S	B

GERMANY • WHITE

WONNEGAU AUSLESE, LANGENBACH 1992 Rheinhessen	*Nose of pot-pourri. Concentrated, rich and sweet. Floral, honeyed flavours. Rich, chunky fruit.*	**£4.20**	RHC TH WR BU	(S)
FORSTER JESUITGARTEN RIESLING SPÄTLESE, BASSERMANN-JORDAN, 1988 Pfalz	*Mature aromas - honey, pears, peaches and petrol. Ripe fruit with citrus acidity to balance.*	**£5.60**	VWC VW RW	(S)
HALLGARTENER SCHÖNHELL QBA, SCHLOSS VOLLRADS MATUSCHKA – GREIFFENCLAU 1986 Rheingau	*Beautiful Riesling nose - crisp apples, honey, botrytis and petrol. Lovely pineapple on palate.*	**£5.70**	EP EVI	(S)
BURRWEILER ALTENFORST SCHEUREBE KABINETT, WEINGUT HERBERT MESSMER 1993 Pfalz	*Rich, grapey fruit. Quite soft and spicy. Lovely, gentle sweetness.Great with Japanese food.*	**£6.00**	RHC OD	(B)
AVELSBACHER ALTENBERG RIESLING KABINETT, HOHE DOMKIRCHE 1986 Mosel-Saar-Ruwer	*Classic Riesling. Yellow/green in colour with lemon and lime tanginess. Elegant and well made.*	**£6.00**	VWC VW	(S)
RIESLING QBA, DR. LOOSEN 1992 Mosel-Saar-Ruwer	*Aromatic, spicy apple nose. Honey and citrus flavours marry to produce wonderful fresh Riesling.*	**£6.10**	Widely available	(B)
KIEDRICHER SANDGRUB RIESLING KABINETT, SCHLOSS GROENESTEYN 1988 Rheingau	*Nicely structured with good fruit flavours and clean tartness to finish.*	**£6.50**	VW	(B)
SERRIGER HEILIGENBORN RIESLING SPÄTLESE, STAATLICHEN WEINBAUDOMANEN TRIER 1983 Mosel-Saar-Ruwer	*Classy nose. Fresh, green apples backed by firm mineral character. Lively acidity. Maturing but youthful.*	**£6.60**	VWC VW	(S)

GERMANY • SWEET WHITE				
NIERSTEINER PETTENTHAL RIESLING AUSLESE, WEINGUT METTERNICH, 1993 Rheinhessen	*Enticing nose of grapes, raisins and orange blossom. Citrus peel flavour. Wonderful elegance. Great balance.*	£7.00	RHC	(S)
ELLERSTADTER SONNENBERG, SPÄTLESE CASTELL VOLLMER 1992 Pfalz	*Clean, fresh, floral aromas. Hints of spice and exotic fruits. Lively palate of fragrant apples.*	£9.00	RS	(B)
NIEDERHAUSER HERMANN-SHOLE RIESLING, STAAT-LICHE WEINBANDOMÖNE NIEDERHAUSEN-SCHLOSS-BÖCKELHEIM 1988 Nahe	*Showing good age. Rich Riesling nose of green apples, honey and petrol. Intense, ripe fruit.*	£9.50	VWC VW G&M	(S)
PIESPORTER GOLD-TROPFCHEN RIESLING AUSLESE, REICHSGRAF VON KESSELSTATT 1990 Mosel-Saar-Ruwer	*Rich, petrol nose. Honeyed apples with steely quality behind. Light, delicate spiciness. Firm, mineral character.*	£11.90	DBY MWW HDL AHW	(G)
WEGELER-DEINHARD RHEINGAU RIESLING SPÄTLESE, DEINHARD 1990 Rheingau	*Warm and rich with unusual tropical fruits, balanced by a racy acidity.*	£13.00	DN	(B)
BRAUNEBERGER JUFFER SONNENUHR RIESLING AUSLESE, FRITZ HAAG, 1990 Mosel-Saar-Ruwer	*Delicately sweet with floral aromas and myriad fruits, including lime, grapefruit and pineapple.*	£17.90	J&B	(G)

SWEET WHITE

KIRCHHEIMER GEISSKOPF GEWÜRZTRAMINER BEERENAUSLESE HAMMEL 1992 Pfalz	*Attractive citrus nose; good balance and stylish palate. pleasing finish.*	£4.30	EHA	(B)

GERMANY • SWEET WHITE

UNGSTEINER WEILBERG RIESLING AUSLESE, WINZERGENOSSENSCHAFT HERRENBERG HONIGSÄCKEL 1992 Pfalz	*Attractive, boneyed botrytis nose; noticeable alcohol and bitterness on finish.*	£8.60	RWI	**B**
FORSTER SCHNEPFENFLUG HUXELREBE BEERENAUSLESE, WZG VIER JAHREZEITEN 1993 Pfalz	*Deep gold; marmalade and butterscotch bouquet. Balanced acidity and long, rich finish.*	£9.00	RHC	**S**
DURKHEIMER FRONHOF SCHEUREBE TROCKENBEERENAUSLESE, KURT DARTING 1993 Pfalz	*Floral perfume with grapey palate; appealing and sweet.*	£10.00	OD	**B**
OPPENHEIMER SACKTRAGER RIESLING WEINGUT KUHLING - GILLOT 1992 Rheinhessen	*Pale lime; delicate lime cordial bouquet, slightly sweet. Honeyed, gentle, elegant, lighter style. Dry finish.*	£13.50	WSC	**B**
ELLERSTADTER BUBENECK CASTELL VOLLMER 1992 Pfalz	*Intense, spicy ginger in syrup nose; luscious, gingery, sweet palate. Zippy finish.*	£14.00	RS	**S**
WEINGUT KUHLING - GILLOT BODENHEIMER BURGWEG PINOT NOIR WEISHERBST 1992 Rheinhessen	*Golden/amber colour; raisiny, butterscotch nose. Simple and straightforward.*	£39.50	WSC	**B**
EITELSBACHER MARIENHOLZ RIESLING, BISCHOFLICHES KONVIKT 1989 Mosel-Saar-Ruwer	*Gold wine with grapefruit and lime character. Medium length and balanced acidity. Tangy and refreshing.*	£85.00	J&B	**S**

Pinpoint who sells the wine you wish to buy by turning to the stockist codes. If you know the name of the wine you want to buy, use the alphabetical index. If price is your motivation, refer to the invaluable price guide index; red and white wines under £10 and champagne under £15. Happy hunting!

SPARKLING

CO-OP SPARKLING LIEBFRAUMILCH, RUDESHEIMER WEINKELLEREI 1992 Rhine	*Light-coloured wine with big bubbles and fresh, Muscat nose. Lemony, clean fruit flavours.*	**£4.20**	CWS	**B**

ITALY

Not so much a country as a loosely attached collection of regions, Italy defies vinous description. There is everything to be found here: from reds produced using methods almost as ancient as the grape varieties from which they are made, to ultra-modern Bordeaux and Burgundy look-alikes and inventive Vini da Tavola unlike wines produced anywhere else in the world.

PIEDMONT • RED

GIORDANO BARBERA DEL PIEMONTE, GIORDANO 1994 Piedmont	*Fresh, lively fruity nose. Attractive, jammy fruit on palate, well-structured and with great length.*	**£4.10**	U HVW	(B)
ARALDICA CEPPI STORICI BARBERA D'ASTI, ARALDICA 1991 Piedmont	*Savoury, woody nose with good fruit concentration on palate. Marvellous balance and great length.*	**£5.20**	Widely available	(B)
RUCHE DI CASTAGNOLE MONFERRATO, CANTINE BAVA 'CASA BRINA' 1992 Piedmont	*Intense, rose petal aromas on nose. Dry tobacco flavours. Floral, creamy palate. Marshmallow yet dry.*	**£7.80**	VIN WSO	(S)
VEGLIO BAROLO, VEGLIO 1990 Piedmont	*Light in colour, showing some age. Earthy nose, full palate with fruit and subtle tannins.*	**£8.50**	RT	(B)
BAROLO DOCG SCANAVINO, SCANAVINO 1991 Piedmont	*A soft nose opens in the mouth to reveal sweet fruit. Well-balanced and good length.*	**£8.50**	MCA	(B)

GIORDANO BAROLO, GIORDANO 1988 Piedmont	*Mature colour and warm, cherry nose. Rich, spicy palate balanced by solid tannic structure.*	**£8.50**	EH GDS JS HVW	(B)
VILLA DORIA BAROLO ALBEISA, VILLADORIA 1991 Piedmont	*Brick-red colour. Good fruit on nose and ripeness comes through on palate; softly tannic.*	**£8.60**	AFI MTL	(S)
GIORDANO BAROLO, GIORDANO 1991 Piedmont	*Mature colour and port-like nose. Soft fruit on palate with creamy texture. Great Barolo.*	**£9.50**	U GDS V&C HVW	(S)
AURELIO SETTIMO BAROLO, AURELIO SETTIMO 1990 Piedmont	*Almost opaque colour. Concentrated nose with peppery overtones. Cherry fruit, good concentration and complexity.*	**£9.60**	WAW	(B)
VIBERTI BARBERA D'ALBA, VIBERTI 1991 Piedmont	*Smoky, Barolo-style nose, concentrated and soft. Complex fruit flavours and smooth tannins on palate.*	**£10.00**	BI	(B)
BATASIOLO BAROLO, BATASIOLO 1990 Piedmont	*Brick colour, chocolate and liquorice nose. Juicy, lingering fruit.*	**£10.00**	MON	(B)
ASCHERI BRIC MILIEU, ASCHERI 1992 Piedmont	*Nice balance of good fruit and oak on nose. Sweet cherries on palate with soft tannins.*	**£10.30**	BOO ENO CWI DIR V&C	(S)
CASCINA CASTLET POLICALPO, CASCINA CASTLET 1990 Piedmont	*Rich, deep colour. Oaky nose balanced with luscious fruit on palate; clean finish. Will age well.*	**£11.50**	BI	(S)

ITALY • TUSCANY RED

CASCINA CASTLET PASSUM, CASCINA CASTLET 1990 Piedmont	*Soft summer fruits on nose and palate with undertones of cinnamon. Powerful structure; will develop.*	£13.00	BI V&C	(S)
FRANCO CESAR & FIGLI BAROLO VIGNA SCARRONE SINGLE VINEYARD 1990 Piedmont	*Ruby colour. Spicy nose, ripe, fresh cherries and plums on palate. Elegant, well constructed.*	£13.70	AFI	(B)
PRUNOTTO BAROLO CRU BUSSIA, PRUNOTTO 1990 Piedmont	*Rich, red-brick intensity. Concentrated nose with excellent structure. Massive, spicy fruit, ripe black cherries.*	£18.90	BLN SV DBY V&C	(B)
BATASILO BAROLO VIGNETO LA CORDA DELLA BRICCOLINA, BATASOLI 1989 Piedmont	*Plum colour. Complex medley of pepper, spice, soft tannin and low acidity. Clean, lingering finish.*	£28.00	MON	(B)

TUSCANY • RED

PICCINI ROSSO TOSCANO, PICCINI 1994 Tuscany	*Deep purple colour. Weighty nose and soft berry fruits on palate with lingering finish.*	£3.80	WST	(B)
CHIANTI VILLA SELVA, VILLA SELVA 1994 Tuscany	*Good colour. Spicy, smoky nose and fresh, sweet fruit on the palate, ending with a long, flavoursome finish.*	£4.00	U	(B)
CHIANTI CLASSICO MONTECCHIO, MONTECCHIO 1990 Tuscany	*Youthful, ruby colour. Soft, warm fruit flavours with ripe cherries on palate. Vigorous, attractive wine.*	£4.10	SMF	(B)

Wine	Tasting Notes	Price	Availability	Rating
LA PIEVE CHIANTI RUFINA RISERVA, LA PIEVE 1985 Tuscany	*Smoky, curranty nose. Berry fruits on palate backed up by good licquorice, chocolaty finish.*	£5.00	JS	(S)
VINO NOBILE, CECCHI 1991 Tuscany	*Delicate, ripe and sweet curranty fruit on nose backed up by firm tannins on palate.*	£5.20	IT JS	(B)
CAPEZZANA BARCO REALE, CAPEZZANA 1994 Tuscany	*Ripe cherry fruit flavours on nose. Well-balanced, attractive palate with spicy overtones.*	£6.30	Widely available	(B)
CHIANTI CLASSICO, CASTELLO DI FONTERUTOLI 1992 Tuscany	*Subtle, attractive berry fruits backed with soft tannins to create structured wine.*	£6.50	EUW	(B)
CAMPO AI SASSI, MARCHESI DE FRESCOBALDI 1993 Tuscany	*Oaky, leathery, complex bouquet. Attractive palate with massive fruit and multi-layered flavours.*	£6.80	GRA W U V&C	(B)
CECCHI VILLA CERNA RISERVA, CECCHI 1991 Tuscany	*Deep colour. Herby, leafy nose with cherry. Intense palate with nicely balanced tannins.*	£7.00	IT	(B)
FELSINA BERADENGA CHIANTI CLASSICO, FELSINA BERADENGA 1992 Tuscany	*Attractive depth. Good, herbaceous, berry nose. Complex structure. Soft berry flavours.*	£8.10	Widely available	(S)
ARGIANO ROSSO DI MONTALCINO, ARGIANO 1993 Tuscany	*Open, plummy nose with intense raspberry aromas. Palate is rich, jammy with complex, floral overtones.*	£8.40	Widely available	(G)

MARCHESI DE FRESCOBALDI POMINO ROSSO 1991 Tuscany	*Dark plum colour. Dusky, intense nose. Dark fruits and pepper on palate; creamy texture. Good length.*	£8.70	GRA V&C OD WIN	**B**
FONTODI CHIANTI CLASSICO, FONTODI 1992 Tuscany	*Loganberry red. Classic blackberry style with soft, elegant nose. Lots of structure and great finish.*	£8.70	DBY ENO DIR V&C WSO	**S**
MARCHESI DE FRESCOBALDI LAMAIONE 1992 Tuscany	*Leafy, blackcurrant nose - classic Claret. New oak produces surprisingly soft tannins. Young berry fruits.*	£10.50	GRA OD WIN	**S**
ANTINORI TENUTE MARCHESE CHIANTI CLASSICO, ANTINORI 1990 Tuscany	*A peppery nose opens out on palate to reveal rich, ripe fruits and herbs.*	£10.90	BLN SV DBY L&W DIR V&C AV	**B**
AVIGNONESI GRIFI, AVIGNONESI 1990 Tuscany	*Good, rich colour and young minty, herby nose. Dark, rich fruit and subtle oak.*	£12.50	EUW W V&C	**S**
BANFI BRUNELLO DI MONTALCINO, CASTELLO BANFI 1990 Tuscany	*Deep red in colour. Youthful on nose. Herby, creamy palate with good fruit.*	£15.10	VIN MWW ENO V&C	**B**
ARGIANO BRUNELLO DI MONTALCINO, ARGIANO 1990 Tuscany	*Deep red with rounded fruit on nose. A tarry palate with oak and sweet fruit.*	£15.20	Widely available	**G**
COL D'ORCIA BRUNELLO DI MONTALCINO, COL D'ORCIA 1990 Tuscany	*Lovely, deep fruits, richly peppered on palate. Long, rich, softly tannic.*	£15.90	ALI V&C	**B**

ALTESINO ALTE D'ALTESI ROSSO, ALTESINO 1990 Tuscany	*A ripe, fat nose. Soft fruit with underlying tannins on the palate, mellowing out beautifully.*	£16.00	PF	(B)
PODERI CASTELLARE DI CASTELLINA I SODI DI SAN NICCOLO, PODERI 1991 Tuscany	*Bright, clear colour. Ripe nose, and palate full of autumnal fruit and modern, oaky flavours.*	£16.60	GRA	(B)
PODERI CASTELLARE DI CASTELLINA CONIALE, 1991 Tuscany	*Ripe, intense fruit and dried grass aromas. Good cherry on palate with complex, minty overtones.*	£17.00	GRA	(S)
ISOLE E OLENA CEPPARELLO, ISOLE E OLENA 1991 Tuscany	*Heavy, deep colour and good, balanced nose with spice and damsons. New oak and ripe fruit.*	£17.10	Widely available	(B)
RUFFINO CABREO IL BORGO CAPITOLARE DI BITURICA, RUFFINO 1988 Tuscany	*Ruby coloured with ripe, fruity nose, hints of new oak. Sweet, spicy palate. Good weight.*	£18.10	ALI V&C	(B)
FONTODI FLACCIANELLO DELLA PIEVE, FONTODI 1991 Tuscany	*Ruby colour and choco-laty nose. Hefty fruits on palate; new oak, stewed plums, soft tannins.*	£18.60	ENO V&C	(S)
ISOLE E OLENA CABERNET SAUVIGNON, ISOLE E OLENA 1991 Tuscany	*Spearmint nose. Clean, soft, elegant modern wine in straightforward style. Dry, youthful and good length.*	£19.50	ENO V&C	(B)
BANFI SUMMUS, BANFI 1990 Tuscany	*Deep cherry/plum aromas on nose. Balanced, with some oak and ripe, sweet fruit.*	£20.00	VIN	(S)

ANTINORI TIGNANELLO, ANTINORI 1991 Tuscany	*Pungent cigar-box, bramble nose. Intense, ripe berry on palate balanced by elegant tannins.*	£21.40	Widely available	(S)
POGGIO ANTICO BRUNELLO DI MONTALCINO, POGGIO ANTICO 1990 Tuscany	*Dark, ruby colour and full, ripe brambly nose. Concentrated, sweet and spicy fruit on palate.*	£22.00	BLN V&C	(G)
BANFI POGGIO ALL ORO BRUNELLO DI MONTALCINO RISERVA, BANFI 1988 Tuscany	*Old oak mixed with blackcurrants on nose. Rich, opulent, sweet-ripe fruit.*	£25.00	VIN	(B)

OTHER REGIONS • RED

COLTIVA IL ROSSO, GRUPPO COLTIVA 1994 Emilia-Romagna	*Light, balanced nose with soft fruits. Cherry on palate with herby overtones and long finish.*	£2.40	A	(B)
ASDA SICILIAN ROSSO, SIV SPA Sicily	*Pale crimson colour and soft, cherry nose. A crisp, clean palate - light with soft fruits. Lingering finish. Well made.*	£2.70	A	(B)
CALATRASI SAFEWAY SICILIAN RED, CALATRASI 1994 Sicily	*Deep, ruby colour. Soft, fresh nose and nicely balanced fruits and tannin on the palate. Good structure and weight.*	£2.90	SAF	(B)
PASQUA VALPOLICELLA, PASQUA 1993 Veneto	*Vibrant nose with intense raspberry flavours and young fresh fruit on palate. Underlying tannic structure.*	£3.30	M&M SMF	(B)

Wine	Tasting Notes	Price	Stockists	
CA'VIT TRENTINO PRINCIPATO ROSSO VALDADIGE, CA'VIT TRENTINO 1994 Valdadige	*Strong, raspberry fruit on nose, fresh palate. Youthful berry balanced by smooth underlying tannins.*	**£3.40**	BP CWS DBY AMY	**B**
SOMERFIELD CABERNET SAUVIGNON DEL VENETO, PASQUA 1994 Veneto	*Deep purple colour, with a herbaceous nose. Intense, concentrated fruit on the palate; well-balanced, soft tannins.*	**£3.50**	M&M SMF	**B**
CORDEVINO CABERNET MERLOT TRE VENEZIE, PASQUA, 1993 Veneto	*Complex nose of baked, sweet fruit and cedary oak. Spiced palate balanced by berry.*	**£3.90**	M&M	**S**
BARONE DI TUROLIFI LIBECCHIO ROSSO, BARONE DI TUROLIFI 1992 Sicily	*Elegant nose, slightly tarry with blackcurrant and cherry. Well-rounded palate; herby over-tones, good tannins.*	**£4.30**	RAV ALI	**S**
CANTINA SOCIALE MIGLIONICO MONTEPULCIANO D'ABRUZZO Abruzzo	*Plum colour. Pleasant cherry and almond aromas. Smooth, good body with ripe, spicy tannins.*	**£4.50**	U ENO CWI HVW EVI	**B**
TRENTINO CABERNET SAUVIGNON, CA'VIT TRENTINO, 1992 Trentino	*Ruby coloured. Youthful, vigorous, raspberry fruit nose and ripe cherry fruit on the palate.*	**£4.60**	BP BOO DBY	**B**
TEDESCHI VALPOLICELLA CLASSICO SUPERIORE, TEDESCHI 1991 Veneto	*Dark red colour. Nice spicy, herby nose. good forward fruit on palate. Well-rounded flavours.*	**£4.60**	L&W MWW	**B**

Pinpoint who sells the wine you wish to buy by turning to the stockist codes. If you know the name of the wine you want to buy, use the alphabetical index. If price is your motivation, refer to the invaluable price guide index; red and white wines under £5, sparkling wines under £10 and champagne under £15. Happy hunting!

COPERTINO RISERVA, C S COPERTINO 1992 Puglia	*A fistful of blackcurrants and redcurrants help produce a truly fruity flavour on the palate*	**£4.90**	Widely available	B
GEOFF MERRILL CABERNET SAUVIGNON ATESINO, BARRIQUE AGED, GEOFF MERRILL Atesino	*Good fruit and new wood on nose. Herbaceous fruit on palate. Well-structured; good length.*	**£5.00**	JS	B
VILLA PIGNA ROZZANO, VILLA PIGNA 1992 Marche	*Ripe, sweet wildberries and blackcurrants on nose. Big, New World style: plenty of fruit and spices.*	**£5.00**	WST	B
TAURINO SALICE SALENTINO RISERVA, TAURINO 1990 Puglia	*A good nose, mouth-watering cherry fruits with oaky undertones. Elegantly structured.*	**£5.10**	Widely available	B
BROGAL VINI ROSSO DI TORGIANO VIGNABALDO, BROGAL VINI SRL BASTIA UMBRIA 1991 Umbria	*Dark colour, ripe, warm fruits on nose. A complex fruit, herbs and spices. Supple, good length.*	**£5.20**	AFI BI	B
CESARI SANGIOVESE DI ROMAGNA RISERVA, CESARI 1992 Emilia-Romagna	*Pleasant, light, fruity style, balanced by soft tannins. Finishes well.*	**£5.40**	ALI	B
CANDIDO SALICE SALENTINO, CANDIDO 1990 Puglia	*Unusual smoky oak and fruit nose. Good, firm structure on palate; complex fruit flavours.*	**£5.40**	Widely available	B
TAURINO NOTARPANARO, TAURINO 1986 Puglia	*Perfumed nose with plummy, redcurrant fruit on palate and good, clean finish. Shows ageing potential.*	**£5.70**	MWW DIR WIN	S

CABERNET RISERVA SCHLOSSHÖF, VITICOLTORI ALTO ADIGE 1991 Alto Adige	*Aromatic with notes of blackcurrants and elder-flower. Delicious mouth-fuls of drying, sweet fruit and mint.*	**£5.90**	GRA	(B)
VILLA PIGNA CABERNASCO, VILLA PIGNA 1991 Marche	*Very deep colour. Soft, oaky, plummy nose. Rich, dark fruits. Wonderful complexity.*	**£6.00**	TO	(B)
CANNONAU DI SARDEGNA RISERVA, SELLA E MOSCA, SELLA E MOSCA 1990 Sardinia	*Attractive, pale purple colour. Brambly fruit on the nose and juicy, ripe fruit on palate with a pleasant finish.*	**£6.00**	RAV ALI V&C	(B)
VALPOLICELLA, ITALY 1993 Veneto	*Intense, cherry nose. Rich, full-bodied palate with plenty of soft fruits and artichoke aromas.*	**£6.00**	FBG	(B)
CABERNET RONCACCIO, CASA VINICOLA E COLLAVINI 1993 Friuli	*Cedary, spicy nose. Smooth, ripe, warm spicy fruit on palate. Good crisp style.*	**£6.10**	GRA V&C	(B)
TEDESCHI CAPITEL SAN ROCCO ROSSO, TEDESCHI 1990 Veneto	*Mature colour and well-developed, complex nose. Palate is up-front with full fruit. Good structure.*	**£6.50**	GRA MWW WIN	(B)
VIGNETI DI MARANO, BOSCAINI 1990 North East Italy	*Peppery, spicy nose. Intensely fruity palate of plums and cherries balanced by firm, soft, tannins.*	**£6.80**	VWC CWS	(B)
BELLAVISTA FRANCIACORTA ROSSO, BELLAVISTA 1991 Lombardy	*Blackcurrants and cher-ries on nose. Attractive, jammy fruits and soft tannins on palate.*	**£7.80**	RAV ALI V&C	(B)

DINO ILLUMINATI ZANNA MONTEPULCIANO D'ABRUZZO, DINO ILLUMINATI 1990 Abruzzo	*Good, fruity nose and intensely fruity palate balanced by soft tannins and good length.*	£8.00	BLN CUM	(B)
SANTADI CARIGNANO DEL SULCIS ROCCA RUBIA, SANTADI 1991 Sardinia	*Savoury, fruity nose. Full, ripe raspberry palate with overtones of dark chocolate. Nicely balanced.*	£8.20	Widely available	(B)
ROCCA SVEVA AMARONE, ROCCA SVEVA 1988 Veneto	*Warm, rich, scented nose and lovely, smoky palate balanced by ripe fruits. Creamy, elegant finish.*	£8.50	Widely available	(S)
ALLEGRINI VALPOLICELLA LA OROLA, ALLEGRINI 1991 Veneto	*Gorgeous morello cherry on gamey nose. Complex, rich palate, loads of ripasso, plenty of depth.*	£8.80	BOO ENO V&C	(B)
LOREDAN GASPARINI VENEGAZZU DELLA CASA, LOREDAN GASPARINI 1991 Veneto	*Interesting vegetal, foresty nose. Hefty with fruit extract and tannin; earthy reminders of mushrooms. Jammy.*	£8.90	ENO CWS V&C CUM	(B)
LIBRANDI CIRÒ RISERVA DUCCA SAN FELICE, LIBRANDI 1990 Calabria	*An attractive Nebbiolo/Barolo style pungency on the nose. Firm fruit on the palate, lingering nicely.*	£9.00	ENO CWI V&C VIL	(B)
VALPOLICELLA PALAZZO DELLE TORRE, ALLEGRINI 1991 Veneto	*Ripe blackcurrant on nose. Full-flavoured palate with crisp cherry and integrated oak aromas.*	£9.30	Widely available	(B)
TEDESCHI RECIOTO DELLA VALPOLICELLA, TEDESCHI 1988 Veneto	*Rich, complex nose with luscious, intense Amarone fruits on palate.*	£9.80	ADN MWW V&C WIN	(B)

IL ROSSO DI ENRICO VALLANIA, VIGNETO DELLE TERRE ROSSE, VIGNETO 1990 Emilia-Romagna	*Lightish nose, smooth oak, slightly papery. Ripe fruit and firm, dry tannins. Youthful, well-balanced.*	£9.90	WTR	(B)
ZENATO RECIOTO DELLA VALPOLICELLA AMARONE CLASSICO, ZENATO 1988 Veneto	*Deep colour and powerful nose. Elegant fruits balanced by peppery flavours on palate.*	£10.00	EUW V&C	(S)
MASI AGRICOLA TOAR ROSSO, VINO DA TAVOLA, MASI AGRICOLA 1992 Veneto	*Cool, floral and refined, summer fruits on palate. Good length; intense, almost sweet finish.*	£10.50	BLN DIR V&C	(B)
ROI, LA VIARTE, 1988 Friuli	*English summer fruits such as blackcurrants and raspberries combine together, creating rich colour and flavour.*	£11.00	BI	(B)
AMARONE CLASSICO DELLA VALPOLICELLA SPERI, CASA GIRELLI 1988 Veneto	*Rich, ruby fruits on nose, balanced by soft palate of peppers and spices. Lingering finish.*	£11.00	CGI CHF GSJ	(B)
BOLLA CRESO ROSSO CABERNET SAUVIGNON VINO DA TAVOLA, BOLLA 1990 Veneto	*Vibrant, tobacco-peppery nose with rich, full fruits on palate and lovely, long finish.*	£11.20	ALI	(B)
ARGIOLAS TURRIGA, VITIVINICOLA ARGIOLAS 1990 Sardinia	*Light, mulberry nose. Big, open fruit flavours on palate balanced by oak and soft tannins.*	£12.30	EUW RD	(B)
PASQUA VIGNETI CASTERNA AMARONE, PASQUA 1988 Veneto	*Light, youthful colour. Intense, Italianate nose. Heaps of luscious fruit and soft tannins on palate.*	£12.50	MCA	(B)

Wine	Tasting Notes	Price	Stockist	
D'ANGELO CANNETO, D'ANGELO 1988 Basilicata	*Smoky nose with rich, peppery fruits on palate balanced by soft tannins.*	£13.10	ALI V	(B)
ALLEGRINI AMARONE, ALLEGRINI 1988 Veneto	*Dense, smoky nose, with sweet fruits, Excellent palate: bitter-sweet fruit and mellow wood; intense finish.*	£13.60	Widely available	(G)
SANTADI TERRE BRUNE, SANTADI 1990 Sardinia	*Meaty, rounded nose with concentrated black fruit aromas. Powerful palate: chocolate and rich, new oak.*	£13.90	Widely available	(B)
GERRARDO CESARI AMARONE VIGNETO BOSCO, CASA VINICOLA 1988 Veneto	*Mature russet colour. Old wood and berry fruit on nose. Stewed plums and soft wood tannins.*	£14.80	AFI MTL	(B)
CASAL DEI RONCHI RECIOTO AMABILE SEREGO ALIGHIERI 1990 Veneto	*Ruby red. Sweet, ripe berry fruit on nose. Good structure and balance on palate.*	£16.80	BLN DBY V&C	(B)
ROSSO RISERVA DEGLI ORZONI, RUSSIZ SUPERIORE 1990 Friuli-Venezia Giulia	*Peppery on the nose and soft tannins on palate create well-balanced and colourful wine.*	£17.00	BLN	(S)
MASI AGRICOLA MAZZANO AMARONE DELLA VALPOLICELLA, MASI AGRICOLA 1988 Veneto	*Rich colour. Ripe, powerful cherry fruits overlaid with spices. Almost Port-like flavour.*	£19.90	BLN DBY	(B)

Pinpoint who sells the wine you wish to buy by turning to the stockist codes. If you know the name of the wine you want to buy, use the alphabetical index. If price is your motivation, refer to the invaluable price guide index; red and white wines under £5, sparkling wines under £10 and champagne under £15. Happy hunting!

WHITE

FRASCATI SUPERIORE, CANTINA DEL BACCO 1994 Lazio	*Clean, buttery nose with grassy apple fruit, well-textured palate and great balanced flavours.*	£2.90	BUC	(B)
TESCO SICILIAN DRY WHITE, PELLEGRINO Sicily	*Spritzy, green apple fruit. Crisp, clean wine with refreshing acidity that opens nicely. Long finish.*	£2.90	GRA TO	(B)
CONCILIO ATESINO CHARDONNAY, CONCILIO 1994 Trentino	*Light and spritzy wine with nice fruit and pleasant lift. Good length.*	£3.50	IT	(B)
NURAGUS DI CAGLIARI, CANTINA SOCIALE DI DOLIANOVA 1994 Sardinia	*Clean, simple fresh fruit with slight petillance on palate and delicious, silky texture.*	£3.70	EUW L&W WTO V&C	(B)
SAINSBURY'S CHARDONNAY DELLE TRE VENEZIE, GEOFF MERRILL Veneto	*Nice, lemony nose; spritzy, uncomplicated flavours.*	£3.80	JS	(B)
I FRARI BIANCO DI CUSTOZA, SANTI 1994 Veneto	*Lively, open, fresh nose with nice depth of fruit on palate and crisp, lifted acidity.*	£3.80	SAF	(B)
SANTI LUGANA, G I V, 1994 Veneto	*Fresh, clean and easy with grape and pepper flavours. Some complexity.*	£4.00	SAF	(B)

ITALY • WHITE

LENOTTI BIANCO DI CUSTOZA, LENOTTI 1994 Verona	*Great, bright, vibrant colour and an aroma bursting with banana and pear. Light, lemony zingy.*	**£4.00**	WST	(S)
CHARDONNAY DEL PIEMONTE, ARALDICA 1993 Piedmont	*Good light nose; decent wine. Easy drinking and clean.*	**£4.40**	Widely available	(B)
VILLA FONTANA, FONTANA CANDIDA, PIEDMONT 1992 Piedmont	*Rounded with good flavours, character and some style. Touch of citrus spritz; fragrant fruit.*	**£4.60**	VWC W VIL	(B)
SOAVE CLASSICO, TEDESCHI 1993 Soave	*Pale green/yellow in colour. Youthful, aromatic fruit; pepper and spice on palate.*	**£4.80**	L&W ADN MWW WIN	(B)
CORTESE ALASIA, ARALDICA, ARALDICA 1994 Piedmont	*Greeny gold and full of peachy tropical fruit. Smooth, characterful and drinkable.*	**£4.90**	BOO TH WR BU ENO	(B)
LUGANA CRU VILLA FLORA, ZENATO, 1994 Lombardy	*Fresh lemons and yeast on nose. Rich palate with juicy fruit and good bite.*	**£5.00**	EUW W WAW	(B)
CA' BOLANI CHARDONNAY, TENUTA CA' BOLANI CERVIGNANO 1994 Aquileia	*Pleasant, fresh, characterful bouquet; floral and chewy palate. Fresh and light with bready finish.*	**£5.70**	CVZ ZON	(B)
FALANGHINA, TABURNO 1994 Campania	*Fine, ripe fruit with gentle, aromatic tones of lychee and pear drops. Abundant fruit.*	**£6.00**	IT	(B)

ITALY • SWEET WHITE				
CHARDONNAY DEI SASSI CAVI, CASA VINICOLA E COLLAVINI 1994 Grave del Friuli	*Closed fruit nose; good fruit flavours at the end and good finish.*	£6.10	GRA V&C	(B)
TALLINAIO, LOCOROTONDO, LOCOROTONDO 1993 Puglia	*Very pale in colour with lovely, fresh citrus nose. Peppery, spicy, lemony flavours.*	£6.50	ALI	(B)
TRENTINO CHARDONNAY MASO ROSABEL, CA'VIT TRENTINO 1993 Trentino	*Perfumed, floral nose following on to palate. Lemon character and crisp acidity. Clean, lemony finish.*	£9.00	BP	(B)
BORGO CONVENTI CHARDONNAY COLLIO, BORGO CONVENTI 1991 Friuli	*Rich, toasty, woody nose. A touch sappy on palate, but with fruit concentration and acidity.*	£12.20	ALI	(B)
JERMANN WHERE THE DREAMS HAVE NO END, JERMANN 1992 Friuli	*Flavour of lemon and crumpets. Subtle, home-made marmalade bitterness; hint of pineapple and lime.*	£29.70	ENO V&C VIL NY	(S)

SWEET WHITE

BANFI, MOSCADELLO DI MONTALCINO, BANFI 1992 Tuscany	*Pure, unadulterated Muscat. Lovely baked apple and honeyed raisins. Intense marmalade flavours. Good complexity.*	£15.00	VIN	(S)
COL D'ORCIA, PASCENA MOSCADELLO DI MONTALCINO, COL D'ORCIA 1990 Tuscany	*Aroma of orange peel and apples stewed with cinnamon. Sweet, viscous, honeyed palate. Soft apricot.*	£15.60	ALI	(B)

SPARKLING

Moscato d'Asti, Araldica, Araldica 1994 Piedmont	*Light and refreshing, marshmallow-style wine melts on the palate, leaving a well-balanced and tidy finish.*	£3.70	Widely available	B
Moscato Spumante 'Regional Classics' Santero, Santero Piedmont	*Light, grapey nose; well-balanced grapey palate with good finish. Clean, fresh acidity.*	£4.50	TH TH WR BU	B
Asda Asti, Capetta Piedmont	*Clean, medium-sweet. Good acidity; sherbety style on palate.*	£4.50	A	B
Borelli Asti, Fratelli Martini Asti	*Fresh, grapey, floral, pungent nose. Surprisingly dry palate with good acidity. Soft and light quality.*	4.70	WRT	B
Il Grigio Spumante, Collavini, Casa Vinicola e Collavini Friuli	*Fat, creamy, lifted aromatic nose; blossom. Balanced palate and good beading.*	£4.70	GRA ALI WIN	B
Co-op Asti Spumante, Fratelli Martini Piedmont	*Medium-sweet, with a pungent yeasty nose and hint of peaches. Attractive, full palate; powerful length.*	£4.80	CWS	B
Malt House Vintners Asti Spumante, Santero Piedmont	*Lovely, light, enticing bouquet; gentle, creamy, peach flavours. Delicious and balanced.*	£4.90	MHV	S

ITALY • FORTIFIED					
ASTI SPUMANTE, SPERONE Asti	*Soft, grapey, floral nose; rich, gentle palate. Sweet, but pleasantly balanced.*	**£5.00**	U		**B**
MARTINI BRUT SPECIAL CUVÉE, MARTINI & ROSSI Pessione	*Medium intense nose; simple, slightly yeasty character. Citrus and grapefruit. Clean, dry, crisp.*	**£6.50**	WET CWS SMF V&C WSO EVI TMW		**S**
MONDORO ASTI, BARBERO 1994 Piedmont	*Pungent Muscat aromas; soft, straight and very fresh. Grapey, full palate and clean, long finish.*	**£6.50**	IT		**B**
LESSINI DURELLO, FONGARO 1989 Veneto	*Good, yeasty nose; clean, high acid. Lean fruit on palate. Biscuity and elegant.*	**£9.30**	VR		**B**

FORTIFIED

VERMOUTH NO. 1 EXTRA DRY, WINE SERVICES EUROPE Northern Italy	*Lemony, herbal nose. Light, fresh grapefruit and rose petal flavours. Citrus, salty finish.*	**£2.70**	DWI		**B**
VERMOUTH NO. 1 BIANCO, WINE SERVICES EUROPE Northern Italy	*Light, delicate, herbal, nettle aromas. Soft and sweet raisin character. Good length.*	**£2.70**	DWI		**B**

Pinpoint who sells the wine you wish to buy by turning to the stockist codes. If you know the name of the wine you want to buy, use the alphabetical index. If price is your motivation, refer to the invaluable price guide index; red and white wines under £5, sparkling wines under £10 and champagne under £15. Happy hunting!

NEW ZEALAND

For too long in the shadow of its Antipodean neighbour, New Zealand produces wines which are unlike those made anywhere else in the world. Here is a combination of pure, often tropical, fruit flavours with the freshness only found in grapes grown in quite cool climate conditions. Sauvignon is already an international success, but Chardonnays, sparkling wines and reds are all developing.

CABERNET SAUVIGNON

DELEGATS HAWKES BAY CABERNET SAUVIGNON/ MERLOT, DELEGATS 1994 Hawkes Bay	*Cassis on nose with herbaceous notes of sweet pea. Straightforward, raspberry flavour. Grassy, fruity, direct.*	**£6.70**	DBY DIR WIN	(B)
MONTANA WINES CHURCH ROAD CABERNET SAUVIGNON, MONTANA 1992 Hawkes Bay	*Rich, ripe fruit, giving balance to a fully rounded wine, leaving clean finish on the palate.*	**£7.80**	Widely available	(B)
VIDAL CABERNET SAUVIGNON / MERLOT, VIDAL 1992 Hawkes Bay	*Hot, stewy, meaty stuff. Ripe fruit nose. Rich, raisin flavours and integrated wood. Well defined.*	**£8.50**	MTL VWC HVW DD	(B)
LINCOLN VINEYARDS AUCKLAND CABERNET SAUVIGNON/MERLOT THE HOME VINEYARD1992 Auckland	*Well developed nose; distinct fruity flavours, namely blackcurrant and raspberry. Good depth.*	**£8.60**	BP ENO	(B)
MATUA VALLEY SMITH DARTMOOR CABERNET SAUVIGNON, MATUA VALLEY WINERY 1992 Hawkes Bay	*Powerful, berry-like aromas invade the nose. A subtle oakiness on the palate. Overall, well-balanced.*	**£9.50**	MZ MRF HDL	(B)

C. J. PASK CABERNET SAUVIGNON, C.J. PASK 1991 Hawkes Bay	*Open, warm, spicy nose. Toasty, cedary notes enhance character of berry, oak and firm tannins.*	£9.60	MVN HHC TAN AV	**B**
WAIMARAMA ESTATE CABERNET SAUVIGNON, WAIMARAMA ESTATE 1993 Hawkes Bay	*Good fruit character, with a perfect marriage of fresh cassis and cherry. Plenty of depth, good balance.*	£11.00	BI FUL	**B**
BABICH IRONGATE CABERNET SAUVIGNON / MERLOT, BABICH 1992 Hawkes Bay	*Attractive nose, appealing to all sweet fruit enthusiasts. Full-flavoured, with soft tannins and oak.*	£11.70	HCK DBY DN EVI	**S**
LINCOLN VINEYARDS AUCKLAND CABERNET SAUVIGNON/MERLOT VINTAGE SELECTION 1991 Auckland	*Powerful, rich, spicy nose, slightly oaked with toast. Concentrated cassis married to ripe tannins.*	£12.10	BP ENO	**S**
VILLA MARIA RESERVE CABERNET SAUVIGNON, VILLA MARIA ESTATE 1989 Hawkes Bay	*Intense nose of stalky, sappy mulberry; some vegetal, cedary notes. Lacking middle but nice complexity.*	£14.80	HM CEB	**B**
GOLDWATER CABERNET MERLOT, GOLDWATER 1990 Waiheke Island	*Serious Cabernet nose. Chocolate box aromas with pencil shavings and discreet oak. Serious blackcurrant.*	£18.30	HOH MTL AV	**S**
MATUA VALLEY ARARIMU CABERNET SAUVIGNON / MERLOT, MATUA VALLEY WINERY 1993 Auckland	*Big aromas of American oak and powerful, capsicum and green bean. Youthful flavours of juicy fruits. Hard tannins.*	£19.00	MZ	**S**

Pinpoint who sells the wine you wish to buy by turning to the stockist codes. If you know the name of the wine you want to buy, use the alphabetical index. If price is your motivation, refer to the invaluable price guide index; red and white wines under £5, sparkling wines under £10 and champagne under £15. Happy hunting!

OTHER • RED

MORTON ESTATE HAWKES BAY PINOT NOIR, MORTON ESTATE 1994 Hawkes Bay	*Soft, strawberry jam nose with hints of herbs and spearmint. Layers of chewy cherry.*	£7.80	BWC	**(B)**
TE KAIRANGA PINOT NOIR, TE KAIRANGA 1993 Martinborough	*Softly-spiced redcurrant with lovely perfume. Silky, succulent and ripe.*	£9.50	BI	**(B)**
MORTON ESTATE CABERNET MERLOT BLACK LABEL, MORTON ESTATE 1992 Hawkes Bay	*Ripe nose, with rich fruit intensity. Slight acidity complemented by soft tannins. Will age well.*	£9.80	BWC DBY	**(S)**
MARK RATTRAY PINOT NOIR, MARK RATTRAY VINEYARD 1993 Waipara	*Nose of plummy New World fruit, warm vanilla and fresh herbs. Coffee, chocolate. Velvety.*	£12.00	HOL DIR WAW OD	**(G)**

CHARDONNAY

CORBANS COOKS CHARDONNAY, CORBANS 1994 Gisborne	*Pleasant, clean, apple blossom fragrance. Nuts, citron, vanilla pods on palate.*	£5.00	WR TH BU W TO G&M CAX AMY	**(B)**
MILLTON VINEYARD SEMILLON/CHARDONNAY, J MILLTON 1994 Gisborne	*Fine, spicy aroma. Lightly creamy oak with good weight of fruit on palate. Lots of juicy acidity.*	£5.20	CWS CWI SAF HVW BG	**(B)**

NEW ZEALAND • WHITE

STONELEIGH CHARDONNAY, CORBANS 1993 Marlborough	*Herbaceous, green leaf nose. Deep, long, fresh and satisfying.*	£7.20	Widely available	(B)
MONTANA ST MICHAEL KAITUNA HILLS CHARDONNAY, MONTANA 1994 Gisborne	*Bright, clear, yellow-coloured wine. Waxy nose; ripe, sweet exotic fruits. Crisp acid; subtle oak.*	£7.30	M&S DYB	(G)
CORBANS PRIVATE BIN CHARDONNAY, CORBANS 1991 Gisborne	*Burnt tropical oak with warm vanilla, offset by zippy lime acid. Resonant and sherried.*	£7.70	CAX UBC	(B)
MONTANA WINES CHURCH ROAD CHARDONNAY, MONTANA 1993 Hawkes Bay	*Medium intensity; warm fudge and toffee on palate. Lovely, fruity flavours.*	£7.90	Widely available	(B)
OYSTER BAY CHARDONNAY, OYSTER BAY MARLBOROUGH WINES LTD 1994 Marlborough	*Heady, warm, bread nose. Mango/melon flavours. Good integration of oak. Fine length.*	£7.90	ADN MWW DIR JS WIN HVW	(B)
JACKSON ESTATE CHARDONNAY, JACKSON ESTATE 1994 Marlborough	*Discreet, full fruit nose with melon, honey and oily coconut. Tidy oak infusion. Firm acidity.*	£8.20	Widely available	(S)
CORBANS PRIVATE BIN CHARDONNAY, CORBANS 1992 Marlborough	*Straw colour. Vanilla oak on nose. Complex. Mango, melon and papaya.*	£8.30	CAX	(S)
TE KAIRANGA MARTINBOROUGH CHARDONNAY, TE KAIRANGA 1994 Martinborough	*Brown, grey colour. Mango and lychee aromas. Nutty oak with simple vanilla.*	£8.90	BI WOI	(S)

NEW ZEALAND • WHITE

DELEGATS PROPRIETORS RESERVE CHARDONNAY, DELEGATS 1993 Hawkes Bay	*A certain freshness and medium intensity on nose. Hints of lemon sorbet on palate. Good drinking.*	£9.00	DBY DIR	(G)
HERMANN SEIFRIED REDWOOD VALLEY CHARDONNAY, HERMANN SEIFRIED 1994 Nelson	*Medium intensity; toasty, straw bale aromas. Dry and balanced. Soft, pleasing fruit.*	£9.50	FNZ RD	(B)
MORTON ESTATE BLACK LABEL CHARDONNAY, MORTON ESTATE 1993 Hawkes Bay	*Deep golden colour; sweet, ripe fruity nose supported by underlying creaminess. Round, supple oak.*	£9.80	BWC DBY	(B)
COOPERS CREEK CHARDONNAY SWAMP RESERVE, COOPERS CREEK 1992 Hawkes Bay	*Electric nose with lime and lemon peel. Sweet wood. Good weight.*	£10.00	EH	(B)
MONTANA RENWICK ESTATE CHARDONNAY, MONTANA 1991 Marlborough	*Dry, dignified French nose. Well-integrated wood. Long, toasty, creamy, biscuity finish.*	£10.20	MTW DBY OD TMW	(B)
PALLISER ESTATE CHARDONNAY, PALLISER ESTATE 1993 Martinborough	*Lychees and pronounced tropical nose. Orange peel, virile. Well made.*	£10.30	Widely available	(B)
MARTINBOROUGH CHARDONNAY, MARTINBOROUGH VINEYARD 1993 Martinborough	*Elegant nose of vanilla pod, green fruit, coconut and melon. Balanced mouth; lychee and ginger.*	£10.90	BOO L&W ADN WR OD AMY	(S)
VAVASOUR CHARDONNAY, VAVASOUR 1994 Marlborough	*Elegant and well-pronounced nose. Rounded flavours of peaches and pears reaching the palate. Clean finish.*	£11.00	DBY FUL AHW	(S)

NEW ZEALAND • WHITE				
JACKSON ESTATE RESERVE CHARDONNAY, JACKSON ESTATE 1994 Marlborough	*Grapefruit and continental fruits on palate. Almondy, vanilla and caramel. Fun, yummy and smooth.*	**£11.20**	SV HW VIL	(S)
BABICH IRONGATE CHARDONNAY, BABICH 1992 Hawkes Bay	*Ripe, aromatic style with a good nose; lemony. Great mouthful; soft, creamy and superb.*	**£11.50**	DBY DN TAN AV EVI	(G)
TE MATA ESTATE ELSTON CHARDONNAY, TE MATA 1993 Hawkes Bay	*Rich, oaky, leesy, toasty nose. Full, fat, rich and long.*	**£12.50**	Widely available	(B)
NEUDORF MOUTERE CHARDONNAY, NEUDORF 1993 Nelson	*Toasty lemon aromas; touch of vegetal boiled rice. Nutty creaminess on palate. Good acid/fruit balance.*	**£16.80**	HA ADN DIR	(S)
MATUA VALLEY ARARIMU CHARDONNAY, MATUA VALLEY WINERY 1993 Hawkes Bay	*Gentle, greenish tropical fruits on nose. Slightly spritzy on palate.*	**£19.00**	MZ	(B)

SAUVIGNON BLANC

MONTANA KAITUNA HILLS SAUVIGNON BLANC, MONTANA 1994 Marlborough	*Bold, gooseberry character. Grassy on palate with rich fruit.*	**£5.00**	M&S	(S)
MONTANA MARLBOROUGH SAUVIGNON BLANC, MONTANA 1994 Marlborough	*Pure gooseberries and fresh fruit attack. Full-flavoured, complex, balanced and clean. Good finish.*	**£5.10**	Widely available	(S)

NEW ZEALAND • WHITE

MILLS REEF MERE ROAD SAUVIGNON, MILLS REEF 1994 Hawkes Bay	*Varietal, shy nose; mineral, leafy character. Well-integrated flavours of spice, fruit and richness.*	£5.80	FTH HVW		(S)
MARTINBOROUGH VINEYARD SAUVIGNON BLANC, MARTINBOROUGH VINEYARD 1993 Martinborough	*Strong, fruity, herbaceous nose; lemon and asparagus. Fair fruit palate with good acidity. Rich style.*	£5.80	HA L&W ADN CHF		(B)
VILLA MARIA PRIVATE BIN SAUVIGNON BLANC, VILLA MARIA ESTATE 1994 Marlborough	*Tropical fruit bouquet leading on to palate. Grassy, clean, bracing acidity; citric but with creamy finish.*	£5.90	Widely available		(S)
NOBILO SAUVIGNON BLANC, NOBILO VINTNERS 1994 Marlborough	*Smoky nose. Excellent flavours, texture and length. Soft, with bite of fruit and acidity.*	£6.10	HCK DBY CEB GDS HOU AV EVI		(S)
MATUA VALLEY, SHINGLE PEAK SAUVIGNON, MATUA VALLEY 1993 Marlborough	*Elegant, pale, straw-coloured wine with full, grapefruit and gooseberry nose. Classic Sauvignon style.*	£6.30	VWC VW		(S)
MATUA VALLEY SAUVIGNON BLANC, MATUA VALLEY 1994 Hawkes Bay	*Light nose; pleasant, ageing gooseberry. Good fruit palate with length and up-front flavours. Soft finish.*	£6.30	RAVU MZ JS MRF		(S)
STONELEIGH SAUVIGNON BLANC, CORBANS 1994 Marlborough	*Bright, lime green colour. Grassy, ripe asparagus and herby bouquet. Grapefruit character. Good body.*	£6.30	Widely available		(S)
ROTHBURY ESTATE MARLBOROUGH SAUVIGNON BLANC, ROTHBURY 1994 Marlborough	*Intense, elegant wine with aromatic, varietal nose. Lovely, lychee/gooseberry flavours; creamy finish.*	£7.10	Widely available		(G)

NEW ZEALAND •WHITE				
GROVE MILL SAUVIGNON BLANC, GROVE MILL WINE COMPANY LTD 1994 Marlborough	*Pale, straw-coloured with ripe, blackcurrant leaf character on nose; some smokiness. Clean, balanced finish.*	£7.40	Widely available	(S)
NAUTILUS ESTATE MARLBOROUGH SAUVIGNON BLANC, NAUTILUS ESTATE 1994 Marlborough	*Full, spicy, herb and gooseberry bouquet. Ripe passion-fruit palate. Good depth and balance.*	£7.60	GRA DBY WIN	(G)
SELAKS MARLBOROUGH SAUVIGNON BLANC, SELAKS 1994 South Island	*Rich, spicy fruit aromas; tropical fruit character on palate. Clean, well-balanced with crisp edge.*	£7.70	SG DBY ADN	(S)
JACKSON ESTATE SAUVIGNON BLANC, JACKSON ESTATE 1994 Marlborough	*Gentle and attractive; clean fresh style. Very good nose; concentrated, herba-ceous character. Good acidity and long finish.*	£7.80	Widely available	(S)
VAVASOUR DASHWOOD SAUVIGNON BLANC, DASHWOOD 1994 Marlborough	*Fruit nose; green and gooseberry character. Rounded, fruit palate; well-structured with good finish.*	£8.50	DBY ABY BTH FUL OD HDL AHW	(S)
SELAKS MARLBOROUGH SAUVIGNON BLANC-SEMILLON, SELAKS 1994 South Island	*Powerful nose with classy, gooseberry char-acter. Delicious wine with lovely oak treatment and good fruit.*	£9.00	SG	(S)
VILLA MARIA RESERVE MARLBOROUGH SAUVIGNON BLANC, VILLA MARIA ESTATE 1994 South Island	*Lovely, delicate nose with good concentration of fruit. Ripe, gooseberry flavours. Herbaceous quality.*	£9.00	HM WR	(B)
PALLISER MARTINBOROUGH SAUVIGNON BLANC, PALLISER ESTATE 1994 Martinborough	*Restrained, classy bouquet. Balanced with good fruit and length. Complex but not over-stated; rounded fruit.*	£9.50	WR BWI HOU HVW	(S)

NEW ZEALAND • WHITE

HUNTERS WINES, SAUVIGNON BLANC, HUNTERS WINES 1994 Marlborough	*Flowery, delicate nose. Well-constructed with intense, fruity flavour. Fresh and clean.*	**£9.90**	Widely available	(S)
MONTANA BRANCOTT ESTATE MARLBOROUGH SAUVIGNON BLANC, MONTANA 1993 Marlborough	*Lovely, buttery nose; creamy character. Good concentration of fruit on palate.*	**£10.30**	MTW OD TMW	(B)
HERMANN SEIFRIED REDWOOD VALLEY SAUVIGNON, HERMANN SEIFRIED 1994 Nelson	*Lightish-coloured wine with subtle nose. Full, fruit character with good acidity. Crisp balance.*	**£23.00**	FNZ WAW	(S)

OTHER • WHITE

MATUA VALLEY CHENIN BLANC CHARDONNAY, MATUA VALLEY WINERY 1994 Hawkes Bay	*Full of ripe pineapple and papaya with asparagus/herbal overtones. Extremely well made.*	**£6.10**	MZ HDL	(B)
HERMANN SEIFRIED REDWOOD VALLEY DRY RIESLING, HERMANN SEIFRIED 1994 Nelson	*Ripe, full and creamy with defined petrol Riesling character. Tones of toffee and lime.*	**£6.90**	FNZ VDV	(B)
CORBANS PRIVATE BIN RHINE RIESLING, CORBANS 1991 Amberley	*Mature Riesling showing petrol and honeyed aromas. Rich ripe fruit and a creamy texture.*	**£7.50**	CAX	(B)
SAUVIGNON BLANC, VAVASOUR, VAVASOUR 1994 Marlborough	*Beautiful, yellow-green colour; lean blackcurrant bush aroma with hints of fresh citrus and apples.*	**£9.20**	AHW DBY HDL	(B)

NEUDORF MOUTERE SEMILLON, NEUDORF 1994 Nelson	*Rich green pepper/nettle aromas; grassy/ gooseberry. Pungent, but the limey acidity holds it together.*	**£10.10**	HA ADN DIR	**B**

SPARKLING

NAUTILUS CUVÉE MARLBOROUGH, NAUTILUS ESTATE Marlborough	*Moderate lemon/gold wine. Big, rich, full palate. Powerful, with great fruit.*	**£10.60**	GRA MWW WIN TMW	**G** WINE OF THE YEAR

NORTH AMERICA

NORTH AMERICA IS A FAR MORE DIVERSE source of wine than is generally recognised. Washington State and Oregon both make wines sufficiently distinctive to be considered in their own right, while, within California, there are a growing number of up-and-coming regions which challenge the notion of Napa Valley supremacy.

CALIFORNIA • CABERNET SAUVIGNON

AUGUST SEBASTIANI CABERNET FRANC, SEBASTIANI VINEYARD 1993 California	*Unusual concentrated cherry, bubblegum nose with spicy overtones. Attractive, supple, ripe, juicy fruit.*	**£4.50**	FBG	(B)
AUGUST SEBASTIANI CABERNET SAUVIGNON, SEBASTIANI VINEYARD 1993 California	*Closed, complex, leafy aromas. Soft, ripe fruit on palate and long, dry, cherry finish.*	**£4.80**	FBG MTL TO	(B)
FIRESTONE VINEYARDS PROSPERITY RED, FIRESTONE VINEYARDS California	*Fruity nose suggests modern winemaking techniques with interesting, smoky, red fruits. Vibrant flavours. Salty tang.*	**£5.70**	TH DBY WR BU WIN	(S)
MOUNTAIN VIEW CABERNET SAUVIGNON, MOUNTAIN VIEW VINTNERS 1989 California	*Closed bouquet of berry fruits. Soft but plentiful tannins. Good acidity and balance.*	**£6.00**	CKB.	(B)
FETZER STONY BROOK CABERNET SAUVIGNON, FETZER 1992 California	*Enticing aromas of deep plum, vanilla oak and toast. Silky, ripe fruit and some spiciness.*	**£6.00**	GRA SAF DIR	(B)

MARKHAM VINEYARDS GLASS MOUNTAIN CABERNET SAUVIGNON, MARKHAM VINEYARDS 1992 California	*Rich and intensified fruit nose, good tannic structure. Velvety finish on the palate.*	**£6.60**	TO	(B)
MONTEVINA CABERNET SAUVIGNON, MONTEVINA WINERY 1991 California	*Spicy, warm nose, hinting at Bordeaux-style fruits. Soft and mellow in the mouth. Great balance.*	**£7.00**	PRG HW	(S)
STERLING VINEYARD CABERNET SAUVIGNON, STERLING VINEYARD 1989 California	*Closed on nose. Discreet tannins delicately complement intense fruit. Good grip and structure.*	**£7.00**	SEA	(B)
IVAN TAMAS CABERNET SAUVIGNON, IVAN TAMAS 1991 California	*Attractive, elegant nose. A rich, ruby colour adds to the cabernet intensity of the fruit flavours.*	**£7.00**	GRB	(B)
QUIVIRA CABERNET SAUVIGNON CUVÉE, QUIVIRA VINEYARDS 1991 California	*Good Cabernet nose, the palate is immediately filled with blackcurrants and plums. Good length.*	**£7.00**	SKW	(B)
NEWTONIAN CABERNETS, NEWTON VINEYARD 1991 California	*Ripe, fruity nose. Aromas of berries and chocolate. A full-bodied, concentrated wine. Good ageing potential.*	**£7.60**	Widely available	(S)
LAUREL GLEN TERRA ROSA, LAUREL GLEN 1992 California	*Medium intensity, with soft aromas and tannins. Plenty of cassis, standing out above other vibrant flavours.*	**£7.80**	JN	(B)
BERINGER MERITAGE RED, BERINGER 1991 California	*A gutsy wine with rich, mature, ripe flavours. Plenty of oak on the finish. Ages well.*	**£8.00**	BWC	(B)

BERINGER CABERNET SAUVIGNON, BERINGER 1991 California	*Impressive nose of berry and bramble. Heavy, flavours of stewed fruits and spicy tannins. Tarry.*	£9.80	BWC SMF MWW VW HDL	(S)
ROBERT MONDAVI CABERNET SAUVIGNON, ROBERT MONDAVI WINERY 1991 California	*Magnificent black robe. Generous nose of choco-late and berry. Concen-trated blackcurrant. Hugely rich and bold.*	£10.30	DBY MWW MZ	(G)
FROG'S LEAP CABERNET SAUVIGNON, FROG'S LEAP 1991 California	*Spirited blackcurrant nose. Youthful, with poignant, ripe fruit flavours. Alcoholic heat fills palate. Heavy tannin.*	£11.90	L&W BOO DBY MZ	(B)
MERRYVALE CABERNET SAUVIGNON, MERRYVALE 1991 California	*Turkish Delight nose with minty overtones and warm alcohol. Ripe, juicy blackberry; fine varietal character.*	£12.20	ABY	(B)
VILLA MT. EDEN CABERNET SAUVIGNON, VILLA MT. EDEN 1990 California	*Broad nose of liquorice, chocolate and mint. Soft, integrated flavours on palate. Smooth, sweet fruit.*	£12.70	HOH SEB	(S)
SEQUOIA GROVE CABERNET SAUVIGNON, SEQUOIA GROVE VINEYARDS 1989 California	*Exciting nose filled with mature bramble fruits. deep, ruby colour. Fresh cassis flavours.*	£13.20	WTR TRO	(B)
STAGS LEAP CABERNET SAUVIGNON, STAGS LEAP WINE CELLARS 1992 California	*Powerful, big wine, full-bodied and characterful. Weighty sweet fruit. Supportive structure of tannin.*	£13.20	WTR DD	(S)
SHAFER VINEYARDS CABERNET SAUVIGNON, SHAFER VINEYARDS 1991 California	*Austere, woody nose with plums and cherry; typi-cal Cabernet character. Ripe tannins, lean char-acter.*	£13.50	WTR	(B)

CABERNET SAUVIGNON STAGS LEAP DISTRICT, CLOS DU VAL 1991 California	*Blackcurrant nose, some mineral hardness. Light tannins and strong acidity. Good fruit, though severe.*	**£13.60**	DBY CWI MDN AD	**B**
CARMENET CABERNET FRANC, CARMENET 1991 California	*Bright red fruit. Complex bouquet of raspberries and liquorice. Hot alcohol and new oak palate.*	**£13.70**	DBY BI	**S**
NEWTON CABERNET SAUVIGNON, NEWTON VINEYARD 1990 California	*Mellow black cherry and Merlot. Soft, integrated raisin on palate. Chunky, hot and well-balanced.*	**£15.10**	HA DIR	**B**
RIDGE SANTA CRUZ MOUNTAINS CABERNET SAUVIGNON, RIDGE 1992 California	*Rich, fruitcake nose. Sappy, tannic structure. Elegant cassis and rich cherry with caramel toffee.*	**£15.30**	Widely available	**S**
SWANSON VINEYARDS CABERNET SAUVIGNON, SWANSON VINEYARDS 1991 California	*Lively, blackberry nose with rich, intense, New World ripeness. Terrific concentration of flavour on palate.*	**£15.80**	AV	**S**
CLOS DU BOIS, MARLSTONE, CLOS DU BOIS/THE WINE ALLIANCE 1991 California	*Pungent nose of blackcurrant, oak and eucalyptus. Soft, light, full, sweet, vanilla middle; dry finish.*	**£15.80**	GRA WIN	**B**
TREFETHEN HILLSIDE VINEYARD CABERNET SAUVIGNON, TREFETHEN 1985 California	*Good, deep colour and rich, plummy nose. Excellent structural tannins, palate is fully rounded and soft.*	**£15.90**	ADN	**S**
BERINGER PRIVATE RESERVE CABERNET SAUVIGNON, BERINGER 1990 California	*Pruney, figgy, plummy nose with liquorice and light gaminess. Big, meaty, juicy mouthfuls of cassis.*	**£19.40**	MTL BWC CPW HDL	**S**

WENTE MURRIETA'S WELL VENDEMIA, WENTE BROTHERS 1991 California	*Strong, fruity nose, hot and well-knitted. Simple bramble fruits and spicy, rosehip, oak flavours.*	£22.50	HBJ	**B**
SHAFER CABERNET SAUVIGNON HILLSIDE SELECT, SHAFER VINEYARDS 1990 California	*Fine combination of fruit, terroir and wood aromas. Supple palate with intense flavours blended in modern style.*	£24.30	WTR	**G**
JOSEPH PHELPS INSIGNIA, JOSEPH PHELPS VINEYARDS 1991 California	*Young, intense nose with wood and some beetroot. Gutsy, ripe fruits with underlying dry tannins.*	£30.00	GRA WIN	**S**
ERNEST & JULIO GALLO NORTHERN SONOMA ESTATE CABERNET SAUVIGNON 1991 California	*Youthful on nose but great intensity. Powerful and inky with retro-nasal aromas. Smoky, creamy flavours.*	£30.00	E&J U	**G**
ROBERT MONDAVI CABERNET SAUVIGNON RESERVE, ROBERT MONDAVI WINERY 1990 California	*Some farmyard on nose. Hot, sweet fruit on palate with excellent quality of under-structure.*	£34.00	MWW MZ AV	**B**
MONDAVI/ROTHSCHILD OPUS ONE, MONDAVI/ROTHSCHILD 1991 California	*Sweet cassis nose. Ripe, firm oak, pronounced tannins and tangy acidity.*	£45.10	PRG DBY TAN HDL CNL	**S**
STAGS LEAP CASK 23 CABERNET SAUVIGNON, STAGS LEAP WINE CELLARS 1991 California	*Ripe aromas. Rich, fruity style with sweet vanilla oak, nutty flavours and ripe cassis.*	£52.60	WTR	**B**

Pinpoint who sells the wine you wish to buy by turning to the stockist codes. If you know the name of the wine you want to buy, use the alphabetical index. If price is your motivation, refer to the invaluable price guide index; red and white wines under £5, sparkling wines under £10 and champagne under £15. Happy hunting!

CALIFORNIA • PINOT NOIR

SOUTH BAY VINEYARDS CALIFORNIA PINOT NOIR, SOUTH BAY VINEYARDS California	*Warm bramble and spicy vanilla bouquet. Pleasingly rich. Smooth texture and great definition. Good finish.*	£5.00	JS	(B)
FETZER VINEYARDS SANTA BARBARA COUNTY PINOT NOIR, FETZER 1993 California	*Developed, warm, spicy bouquet. Ripe and supple, spiced plum married to some sweet oak.*	£7.00	GRA W DIR	(B)
AU BON CLIMAT PINOT NOIR, AU BON CLIMAT 1993 California	*Layers of ripe quality fruit and creamy texture. Exciting.*	£8.80	DBY M&V RD	(B)
SAINTSBURY GARNET PINOT NOIR, SAINTSBURY 1993 California	*Ripe forest fruits and cherry oak. Seductive. Good concentration and persistence of flavour.*	£8.90	HA ADN HHC FUL	(B)
LA CREMA RESERVE PINOT NOIR, LA CREMA WINERY 1993 California	*Delicate Pinot Noir nose. Velvety and open. Soft strawberry held in check by firm acidity.*	£9.00	PAC VW	(S)
PELLEGRINI OLIVET LANE PINOT NOIR, PELLEGRINI FAMILY VINEYARDS 1993 California	*Gentle, warm vanilla, Juicy red berries and lively acidity. Refreshing.*	£9.30	WTR	(B)
ROBERT MONDAVI LENSWOOD VINEYARD PINOT NOIR, ROBERT MONDAVI WINERY 1993 California	*Rich, full plummy nose and some toastiness. Full, ripe palate reminiscent of Christmas pudding.*	£10.00	MZ	(B)

ACACIA PINOT NOIR, ACACIA 1993 California	*Ripe, creamy fruit held together in firm tannic structure. Peppery spice, vanilla oak and prune.*	£11.40	DBY BI	**B**
SAINTSBURY CARNEROS PINOT NOIR, SAINTSBURY 1993 California	*Classic: beautiful, warm, alluring, fruit; good acidity and tannins; luscious palate.*	£11.80	HA DBY ADN HHC CHF DIR R	**G**
MORGAN PINOT NOIR, MORGAN 1993 California	*Enticing, fresh cherry/ raspberry aromas. Very clean and fresh. Complex. Soft, raspberry ripple finish.*	£12.50	BU BI	**B**
MARIMAR TORRES PINOT NOIR, MARIMAR TORRES 1992 California	*Rich aromas of beetroot, redcurrants, coffee, creamy oak and spice. Rich and substantial. Big structure.*	£14.00	JEF DIR	**S**
ETUDE PINOT NOIR, ETUDE 1992 California	*Young, crunchy cherry aromas with liquorice. Softer on palate; pure raspberry/strawberry flavours.*	£14.70	DD	**B**
ROBERT MONDAVI PINOT NOIR RESERVE, ROBERT MONDAVI WINERY 1993 California	*Warm spiciness. Layers of soft summer pudding. Subtle, creamy oak mixed with cinnamon and nutmeg.*	£18.60	MZ TAN AV	**S**
SANFORD BARREL SELECT PINOT NOIR, SANFORD WINERY 1992 California	*Aromas of rose petal and violets. Creamy oak gives silky texture. Intense clove and nutmeg.*	£18.70	GRA DIR NI	**B**
SAINTSBURY RESERVE CARNEROS PINOT NOIR, SAINTSBURY 1992 California	*Bold, spicy, peppery nose. Quite chunky. Full of minty plummy fruit. Big and bold.*	£20.00	HA ADN	**B**

SAINTSBURY RESERVE CARNEROS PINOT NOIR, SAINTSBURY 1993 California	*Complex, ripe, spicy fruit in abundance backed by strong, new oak. Violets and strawberries.*	£20.00	HA ADN	(S)
CHALONE VINEYARD PINOT NOIR, CHALONE 1990 California	*Soft, smooth and fat. Lovely, pure strawberry/raspberry. Creamy texture. Layered fruit; gentle vanilla.*	£21.99	BI	(B)

CALIFORNIA • OTHER REDS

BROOKHOLLOW RED, BROOKHOLLOW California	*Soft, earthy, smoky nose. Sweet fruit carries through to the palate. Great length.*	£3.50	SAF	(B)
STRATFORD ZINFANDEL, STRATFORD California	*Light in body and simple. Good herbaceous fruit combined with spice and savoury characters.*	£4.90	VWC VW	(B)
PARDUCCI PETITE SIRAH, PARDUCCI 1992 California	*Abundant blackcurrant with chocolate, tobacco, spice and cigar. Well integrated oak. Velvety, rich, full bodied.*	£5.50	PAC VW	(G)
FETZER ZINFANDEL, FETZER 1992 California	*Spice and pepper integrated with raspberries, cherries and blackberries. Pepper palate, joined by subtle oak.*	£5.80	DBY DIR NI OD WIN SAF HVW	(B)
BERINGER ZINFANDEL, BERINGER 1991 California	*Vibrant raspberry. Juicy cherries and fresh, succulent blackberries balanced by dry fruit finish.*	£6.60	Widely available	(S)

RUTHERFORD RANCH ZINFANDEL, RUTHERFORD RANCH 1992 California	*Vibrant Zinfandel characteristics of juicy cherries and brambles. Firm tannins and chewy, rustic finish.*	£7.70	L&W	(B)
GUNDLACH - BUNDSCHU ZINFANDEL, GUNDLACH - BUNDSCHU 1992 California	*Vanilla oak and sweet fruit. Powerful, spicy wine with chewy tannins – quite a mouthful.*	£8.10	EP	(S)
WILLIAM WHEELER WINERY ZINFANDEL, WILLIAM WHEELER 1991 California	*Elegant, aromatic wine. Pepper and spice are softened by vanilla and integrated oak. Quite hot on palate.*	£9.00	SV HW	(S)
QUPÉ SYRAH, BOB LINDQUIST, QUPÉ 1993 California	*Sweet, herbaceous nose; unctuous ripe fruit. Rich plum/berry palate; hints of chocolate and spice.*	£9.90	DBY M&V	(B)
CLOS DU BOIS ZINFANDEL, CLOS DU BOIS / THE WINE ALLIANCE 1993 California	*Warm, floral, spicy nose, sweaty hint, and toasty oak undertones. Long, refined palate. Intensely fruity.*	£10.00	GRA	(B)
CLOS DU VAL ZINFANDEL STAGS LEAP DISTRICT, CLOS DU VAL 1991 California	*Sophisticated, spicy nose: strawberry combined with chocolate, mint and spice. Medium weight with high acidity.*	£10.10	DBY MD NAD	(B)
NALLE ZINFANDEL, NALLE 1992 California	*Subtle, with ripe, raspberry, oaky tones. Creamy texture with soft tannins.*	£12.30	DD	(B)
ATLAS PEAK RESERVE SANGIOVESE, ATLAS PEAK VINEYARDS 1991 California	*Ruby colour. Creamy toffee-vanilla nose. Berry fruit and ripe cherries on palate. Good balance and structure. Nice, long finish*	£12.80	GRA DBY VW DIR WIN	(S)

SWANSON VINEYARDS, SYRAH, SWANSON VINEYARDS 1992 California	*Deep colour; big, rich character. Ripe cassis and spicy nose. Massive, but balanced. Needs time.*	**£14.00**	AV	(B)
RIDGE ZINFANDEL LYTTON SPRINGS, PAUL DRAPER RIDGE 1992 California	*Soft, rich oak integrated well with heady, warm blackcurrant. Sweet coconut, and concentrated fruit.*	**£14.40**	JN DBY ADN CPW OD WIN HVW	(B)

CALIFORNIA • CHARDONNAY

GLEN ELLEN PROPRIETOR'S RESERVE CHARDONNAY, GLEN ELLEN 1993 California	*Green/gold colour. Fat, fudge aromas. Creamy, nutty butter.*	**£4.70**	WAV CWS W TO EVI UBC	(S)
STONEY BROOK CHARDONNAY, STONEY BROOK VINEYARDS 1993 California	*Fresh, smoky nose. Lean acidity; warm, creamy, buttery fruit. Good balance.*	**£5.00**	SAF	(B)
FETZER VINEYARDS SUNDIAL CHARDONNAY, FETZER 1993 California	*Restrained, elegant; tasty oak. Full bodied and emollient.*	**£6.70**	GRA DIR OD WIN HVW MRF EVI	(B)
CUVAISON CHARDONNAY, CUVAISON WINERY 1993 California	*Zippy lime, pineapple and grass nose. Mellow fruit with eastern spiciness.*	**£6.80**	GRA DBY	(S)
VILLA MOUNT EDEN CHARDONNAY, VILLA MOUNT EDEN 1992 California	*Attractive, dainty, floral nose. Soothing oak on middle palate.*	**£8.00**	HOH W	(B)

FETZER VINEYARDS BONTERRA CHARDONNAY, FETZER 1993 California	*Bananas and pineapple mellowed by malo cream on nose. Broad presence in mouth; smoky.*	£8.10	GRA DBY WIN	(S)
NEWTONIAN CHARDONNAY, NEWTON VINEYARD 1993 California	*Sweet, rich nose with ripe kiwi fruit. Subtle oak with tinges of vanilla pod and caramel.*	£8.10	Widely available	(B)
JEKEL GRAVELSTONE VINEYARD CHARDONNAY, JEKEL VINEYARDS 1993 California	*Great, new oak nose; fresh vanilla and caramel. Hot, fruity flavours in mouth. Smoky finish.*	£8.90	GRA ADN	(B)
DRY CREEK BARREL FERMENTED CHARDONNAY, DRY CREEK VINEYARD 1993 California	*Elegant, spicy bouquet. Dry, full-bodied; frisky acidity. Integrated oak and long, creamy finish.*	£9.20	GRA WIN	(B)
VOSS CHARDONNAY, VOSS VINEYARDS 1992 California	*Butterscotch and tasty oak on nose. Essence of biscuit, honey and citrus. Clean, interesting finish.*	£9.60	GRA TH WR BU WIN	(B)
FETZER BARREL SELECT CHARDONNAY, FETZER 1993 California	*Honey and sweet baked apples on nose. Toasty and emollient in mouth.*	£9.90	GRA DIR WIN	(B)
CLOS DU VAL CHARDONNAY CARNEROS, CLOS DU VAL 1993 California	*Melon and papaya nose. Passionfruit, kiwi and ripe banana. Solid backbone of fresh oakiness.*	£10.50	DBY HOL CWI MD DD HDL NAD	(S)
VITA NOVA CHARDONNAY, CLENDENEN & LINDQUIST 1993 California	*Honeyed and big. Exciting and encouraging. Good, traditional style. Savoury and crisp with adequate oak.*	£11.00	M&V	(S)

CALERA CHARDONNAY, CALERA WINE CO 1993 California	*Rounded, full flavour. Sensitive use of oak. Honey flavours. Good vitality in finish.*	£11.20	MWW CPW WIN OD MRF	(B)
SWANSON CARNEROS CHARDONNAY, SWANSON VINEYARDS 1992 California	*Melon, papaya and avocado aromas. Lemon, lime, hazelnut and oaky vanilla flavours.*	£11.30	DBY CEB DIR AV	(G)
SAINTSBURY CHARDONNAY, SAINTSBURY 1993 California	*Golden. Lusciously ripe melon, peach and mango. Soft, velvety, buttery, oak and fruit.*	£11.30	HA DBY ADN HHC CHF DIR	(G)
WENTE CHARDONNAY ESTATE RESERVE, WENTE BROTHERS 1993 California	*Hot vanilla on nose with perfumed marshmallow spiciness. Firm acid and appropriate oak.*	£11.50	HBJ	(B)
FETZER VINEYARDS RESERVE CHARDONNAY, FETZER 1993 California	*Buttery, fresh nose; apple, melon and nectarine hints. Beautifully made; zesty acidity and smooth oak.*	£11.60	GRA DIR OD WIN HVW	(G)
MARIMAR TORRES CHARDONNAY, MARIMAR TORRES 1992 California	*Honeyed nose with hints of apple and pineapple. Fresh fruit with enjoyable new oak.*	£11.80	JEF DBY CEB DIR HOU	(S)
ACACIA CHARDONNAY, ACACIA 1993 California	*Floral nose with good, clean fruit. Slightly herbaceous with lemon zip and soothing, caramelised oiliness.*	£12.00	BI	(S)
CRICHTON HALL CHARDONNAY, CRICHTON HALL 1992 California	*Herbaceous, Sauvignon nose. Palate has melon, mango and peach cooled by asparagus and coconut.*	£12.00	PAT HOL FUL	(G)

NORTH AMERICA • CALIFORNIA WHITE

ROBERT MONDAVI CHARDONNAY, ROBERT MONDAVI WINERY 1993 California	*Fresh, lemony nose. Ripe, delicious with almost lemonade sweetness. Good, chubby length.*	£12.40	ES MWW MZ TAN AV HDL	(B)
MORGAN CHARDONNAY, MORGAN 1993 California	*Light oak on nose. Palate has pineapple topped with vanilla. Lime peel and creamy oiliness.*	£12.50	BU BI	(B)
CHALK HILL CHARDONNAY, CHALK HILL 1992 California	*Lemon and lime peel on nose; hint of lemongrass. Spiciness in oak. Good, sweet fruit.*	£13.00	J&B	(S)
BERINGER PRIVATE RESERVE CHARDONNAY, BERINGER 1993 California	*Rich, fudge-like texture; mellowing coconut milk and warm toffee. Almondy bite. Zippy, citrus tones.*	£14.50	MTL BWC MWW CPW OD HDL	(G)
CLOS DU BOIS CALCAIRE, CLOS DU BOIS/THE WINE ALLIANCE 1993 California	*Gentle, honeyed nose. Lovely acidity; hint of ginger. Palate concentrated with good oak, acidity and balance.*	£14.80	GRA WIN	(B)
PETER MICHAEL WINERY CLOS DE CIEL CHARDONNAY, PETER MICHAEL WINERY 1992 California	*Good, deep, straw-like yellow. Gentle nose with hint of keen tropical fruits. Lazy but dignified oak.*	£16.30	L&W OD	(S)
KISTLER CHARDONNAY, KISTLER 1992 California	*Instant aroma of fresh, rich fruit overwhelms nose. Creamy oak balance. Honey and lemon in finish.*	£19.50	JN	(S)
CUVAISON CHARDONNAY RESERVE, CUVAISON WINERY 1990 California	*Excitable nose; hints of herbaceous green. Limes, lemons and pineapples. Creamy; honey sweetness.*	£19.50	GRA	(S)

NORTH AMERICA • CALIFORNIA WHITE

ROBERT MONDAVI CHARDONNAY RESERVE, ROBERT MONDAVI WINERY 1992 California	*Bright, lemony nose. Ripe, nutty fruit with a lanolin smoothness. Great oak. Firm, rounded finish.*	**£19.90**	ES MWW MZ	(S)
ERNEST & JULIO GALLO NORTHERN SONOMA ESTATE CHARDONNAY, 1992 California	*Palate offers honey, vanilla pod, lychee and melon. Shy of oak. Balanced, elegant.*	**£20.00**	E&J	(S)
CALERA CHARDONNAY MOUNT HARLAN, CALERA WINE CO 1993 California	*Figgy, green, delicious nose. Sweet malo and an overall fat sweetness. Well balanced acid.*	**£22.20**	GRA WIN	(S)

🍇

CALIFORNIA • OTHER WHITES

KINGS CANYON SAUVIGNON BLANC, HUGH RYMAN/ARCIERO WINERY 1994 California	*Herbaceous, earthy bouquet with zippy gooseberry fruit palate. Fresh and of good length. Rich character.*	**£4.00**	BU HHR TH WR	(S)
ROBERT MONDAVI WINERY, WOODBRIDGE SAUVIGNON BLANC 1993 California	*Subtle, floral and melon bouquet. Soft style with pleasing fruit and good, clean balance.*	**£6.00**	MZ HHC HDL	(B)
DRY CREEK CHENIN BLANC, DRY CREEK VINEYARD 1994 California	*Aromatic floral nose. Full fruit on palate. Ripe pears, apples and gooseberry. Lovely, long finish.*	**£6.70**	GRA DBY DIR WIN	(G)
BERINGER, FUMÉ BLANC, BERINGER 1993 California	*Classic Sauvignon, possessing a rich, smoky, oaky nose. Complex and fine.*	**£6.80**	MTL BWC MWW CPW AV OD HDL	(B)

NORTH AMERICA • CALIFORNIA SWEET WHITE

BONNY DOON CA' DEL SOLO MALVASIA BIANCA, BONNY DOON 1994 California	*Delicious, up-front, Muscatty nose. Complex mouthful with spicy, grape and lychee. Rounded texture.*	£7.60	DBY M&V TAN	**S**
CALLAWAY VINEYARDS, VIOGNIER, CALLAWAY VINEYARDS 1994 Temecula California	*Lively, rich and spicy nose. Weighty palate with citrus and juicy apricot flavours.*	£8.00	GRA	**B**
ROBERT MONDAVI WINERY, FUMÉ BLANC RESERVE, ROBERT MONDAVI WINERY 1993 California	*Full, smoky, rich nose with a touch of herbs following through onto palate. Integrated oak.*	£10.30	MWW MZ	**B**

CALIFORNIA • SWEET WHITE

MADRONA LATE HARVEST RIESLING, MADRONA 1993 California	*Pale, straw-coloured; raisiny bouquet. Pleasing, appley flavours.*	£4.40	HA ADN CHF	**S**
QUADY WINERY ESSENSIA ORANGE MUSCAT, QUADY WINERY 1994 California	*Lovely marmalade/ candied orange peel nose. Sweet marmalade and preserved orange flavours. Zippy acidity.*	£6.30	Widely available	**B**
QUADY WINERY ELYSIUM BLACK MUSCAT, QUADY WINERY 1994 California	*Beautiful, pure blackberry and bilberry. Vibrant and fresh. Clean fruit palate. Matches chocolate mousse excellently.*	£6.30	Widely available	**S**

Pinpoint who sells the wine you wish to buy by turning to the stockist codes. If you know the name of the wine you want to buy, use the alphabetical index. If price is your motivation, refer to the invaluable price guide index; red and white wines under £5, sparkling wines under £10 and champagne under £15. Happy hunting!

CALIFORNIA • ROSE

BLOSSOM HILL WHITE ZINFANDEL, BLOSSOM HILL California	*Rose petals and straw berry jam aromas. Sweet ripe fruit on palate. Lovely summer drinking.*	£3.90	MTL DBY PF	B
THE MONTEREY VINEYARD WHITE ZINFANDEL 1994 California	*Fresh, sweet peaches. Soft and rounded. It has intense fruit and good acidity.*	£4.80	SEA ABY CPW OD	B
SCHARFFENBERGER BRUT, SCHARFFENBERGER CELLARS 1987 California	*Rich, yeasty nose; well-balanced, rounded fruit palate. Good concentration with firm acids.*	£9.00	SKW	S **WINE OF THE YEAR**

CALIFORNIA • SPARKLING

CUVÉE NAPA BY MUMM BRUT, SEAGRAM CLASSIC WINE COMPANY California	*Rich, yeasty nose and clean, penetrating acid. Concentrated fruit on palate. Lean, powerful, elegant.*	£9.00	Widely available	B
CUVÉE NAPA BY MUMM ROSÉ, SEAGRAM CLASSIC WINE COMPANY California	*Excellent nose of peaches and tropical fruits. Some yeastiness. Good balance of fruit and acidity.*	£9.00	Widely available	B
ROEDERER ESTATE QUARTET, ROEDERER ESTATE California	*Medium mousse; yeasty nose; fresh and toasty. Nice balance of fruit and complexity.*	£13.00	MMD MWW ENO EVI	B

NORTH AMERICA • CANADA WHITE

TAITTINGER DOMAINE CARNEROS BRUT, TAITTINGER California	*Light, delicate nose; fairly well developed. Good middle flavours and balanced feel in mouth.*	£13.00	PF	B
J, JORDAN WINERY, 1988 California	*Pale, straw-coloured; yeasty greenness on nose. Good fruit and acid; plenty of flavour.*	£16.30	L&W	B
J SCHRAM, SCHRAMSBERG 1989 California	*Big, yeasty nose. Complex, balanced palate. Mouthfilling flavours; slightly hard finish.*	£19.10	L&W	B

CANADA • RED

HENRY OF PELHAM, BACO NOIR, HENRY OF PELHAM 1993 Ontario	*Rich, ripe nose, with fruit-filled aromas. Great palate, blackcurrant juices filling the mouth.*	£6.70	MWW MD EVI NAD	S
INNISKILLIN KLOSE VINEYARD CABERNET SAUVIGNON, INNISKILLIN WINES 1991 Niagara On The Lake	*Tantalizing nose; sweet berry fruits. Palate hints at Cabernet, with a velvety finish. Well balanced.*	£12.60	AV	S

CANADA • WHITE

HENRY OF PELHAM PROPRIETOR'S RESERVE CHARDONNAY, HENRY OF PELHAM 1993 Ontario	*Flowery nose with excellent balance and length on plate.*	£8.30	MD NAD	B

NORTH AMERICA • OREGON WHITE				
PAUL BOSC ESTATE CHARDONNAY, CHATEAU DES CHARMES 1993 Ontario	*Oaky nose with good lemony flavours. Creamy palate. Excellent fruit.*	**£8.40**	SG DBY	(S)
HENRY OF PELHAM BARREL FERMENTED CHARDONNAY, HENRY OF PELHAM 1993 Ontario	*Vanilla dominates nose; touch of pineapple and grapefruit. Not quite dry; sweet apple tones. Lemony acidity.*	**£10.40**	MD NAD	(S)
REIF ESTATE VIDAL ICEWINE, REIF ESTATE WINERY 1993 Niagara Penninsula	*A dessert wine. Citrus and honey with lemon acidity. Nice gulp.*	**£24.00**	MD NAD	(G)

OREGON • RED

FLYNN PINOT NOIR, FLYNN 1992 Oregon	*Sweet, ripe and alco- holic. Rich damson fruit and a touch of velvet. Lovely, creamy finish.*	**£10.00**	GRB	(B)
DOMAINE DROUHIN OREGON PINOT NOIR, DOMAINE DROUHIN OREGON 1992 Oregon	*Young, vibrant fruit. Classic Pinot. Ripe cher- ry/redcurrant. Savoury with gentle spice and subtle oak.*	**£17.00**	MZ CPW	(S)

OREGON • WHITE

ARGYLE RESERVE CHARDONNAY, THE DUNDEE WINE COMPANY 1992 Oregon	*Lively colour with soft, pineapple character and good length.*	**£9.60**	GRA TMW	(S)

WASHINGTON • BLENDS

SEMILLON CHARDONNAY, COLUMBIA WINERY, COLUMBIA WINERY 1993 Washington State	*Floral nose. Fresh, zippy grapefruit and lychee character. Pears and full oak.*	**£5.90**	FTH	(B)
HEDGES CELLARS RED MOUNTAIN RESERVE, HEDGES CELLARS 1991 Washington State	*Good, fruity nose, medium intensity. Cassis-filled palate with soft tannins. Plenty of depth.*	**£15.00**	WCR	(S)

PORTUGAL

A PART FROM SUCH UNIQUE PILLARS of vinous history as Port and Madeira, Portugal boasts one of the world's most interesting ranges of grape varieties. Sadly, until recently, conservative winemaking has done much to obscure their potential. A new generation of Portuguese producers and highly committed young Australians are together beginning to create exciting new styles unparalleled anywhere else in the world.

RED

TESCO DÃO, SOGRAPE, SOGRAPE 1991 Dão	*The colour of bricks, tangy, with full, dry fruit flavours and a beautiful, silky finish.*	£3.00	TO	(B)
J P TINTO, VINO DE MESA, J P VINHOS Pinhel Novo	*A very pleasant young wine. Light-coloured, with a flowery nose, simple fruits and a sweet spiciness. Clean and refreshing.*	£3.10	TH WR BU VW FUL	(S)
ALIANÇA BAIRRADA RESERVA, CAVES ALIANÇA 1991 Bairrada	*Full of character with a rich spiciness and a touch of caramel.*	£4.00	BP DBY DIR	(B)
JOSE SOUSA, JOSE MARIA DA FONSECA SUCCS, JOSE MARIA DA FONSECA SUCCS. 1990 Alentejo	*A classic, soft and mature wine with sweet fragrance and delicate, elegant style to the palate.*	£4.50	EH	(B)
QUINTA DO MANJAPÃO, QUINTA DO MANJAPÃO AGRICULTURAL SOCIETY 1992 Torres Vedras	*Robust, juicy wine, with mature depth and good length.*	£4.50	D&F	(B)

PORTUGAL • RED				
HERDADE DO ESPORÃO CABERNET SAUVIGNON, FINAGRA 1992 Alentejo	A gloriously dark, rich and succulent wine. Spicy and with a touch of vanilla to the palate. Good length.	£4.70	BU	(S)
LUIS PATO QUINTA DO RIBEIRINHO TINTO, LUÍS PATO 1992 Bairrada	Tannic, with firm fruit and lovely, peppery spice.	£5.20	WF ADN	(B)
QUINTA DE PANCAS CABERNET, PRODUCÃO DE VINHOS DE QUINTA LDA-PVQ 1992 Estremadura	Full-bodied, with a pronounced, spicy nose. Sweet fruit overcomes redcurrant acidity; soft wine with a long finish.	£5.50	RAV CWS SMF VW	(S)
D'AVILLEZ, JOSE MARIA DA FONSECA SUCCS. 1990 Alentejo	Fully-flavoured country wine, tannic, with a dominant herbal flavour.	£5.50	EH	(B)
TINTO VELHO, JOSE MARIA DA FONSECA, JOSE MARIA DA FONSECA SUCCS. 1988 Alentejo	Mature and supple. Rich nose and damson palate. Tannins have softened beautifully giving a delicious, well-balanced wine.	£5.60	EVI UBC NAD	(S)
TINTO DA ANFORA, J P VINHOS, J P VINHOS 1990 Alentejo	A ripe, berry nose; good mid palate with redcurrant and mint make a pleasant, drinkable wine.	£5.70	Widely available	(B)
ESPORÃO CAB SAUVIGNON, FINAGRA, FINAGRA 1991 Alentejo	Soft, easy drinking wine with sweet berries and milk chocolate tones.	£5.70	PLB TH WR BU	(B)
QUINTA DE CAMARATE, JOSE MARIA DA FONSECA SUCCS. 1989 Setúbal	Smokey, oak nose. A drier example with high acidity and some weight.	£5.70	Widely available	(B)

João Pato Tinto, Luis Pato 1992 Beiras	*Light, with strong red fruit and a dry finish.*	£5.90	WF ADN BU	(B)
Quinta de Pancas Cabernet, Producão de Vinhos de Quinta Lda-pvq 1991 Estremadura	*A big wine with lots of tannins that has excellent ageing potential.*	£5.90	WCR TH WR BU SAF	(B)
Alentejo Vinho do Monte, Sogrape 1991 Alentejo	*Typical Portuguese style with juicy fruits and structured tannins.*	£6.00	DBY SPR	(B)
J P Vinhos Quinta De Bacalhão, J P Vinhos 1990 Setúbal	*Peppery. Young Cabernet Sauvignon bouquet: sweet fruit, earthiness. Firm, jammy fruit. Perfect tannic presence.*	£6.00	EH JS	(B)
Garrafeira Te, Jose Maria da Fonseca Succs. 1988 Arrábida	*Fine colour and flavour with good length and complexity.*	£8.10	EH DBY VW G&M CHF EVI NAD	(S)
Reserva Especial, A A Ferreira, Ferreira 1986 Douro	*An old style wine with a large structure, chewy tannins and rough-hewn red fruit.*	£10.00	VDP OD	(B)
Quinta da Gaivosa, Domingos Alves de Sousa, Domingos Alves de Sousa 1992 Douro	*Dark wine with good framework. Oak on the palate and a distinct spiciness of chocolate to the length. Delicious.*	£11.00	D&F	(S)
Quinta de Foz, Quinta de Foz 1990 Beiras	*New wood to this well-rounded wine.*	£11.30	WCR U DN	(B)

SWEET WHITE

JOSE MARIA DA FONSECA SUCCS, MOSCATEL DO SETÚBAL 20 YEAR OLD Setúbal	Rich toffee and spice intermingled with ripe apricot and orange peel. Mature flavours and fine balance.	£14.20	EH MD NI EVI NAD	**B**

PORT

WAITROSE 10 YEAR'S OLD TAWNY, SMITH WOODHOUSE Douro	Cherry bronze colour, cashew nuts on the nose. Red fruits, toffee, eastern spices. Long finish.	£5.20	W MZ	**S**
TAWNY ROYAL OPORTO, ROYAL OPORTO WINE COMPANY Oporto	A sweet, brown tawny with a good equilibrium between fruit and toffee-like nose.	£5.40	PLB SMF	**B**
SAFEWAY VINTAGE CHARACTER PORT, CÁLEM, CÁLEM Oporto	A wonderful, spicy palate with a long, clear follow-through. Excellent ageing potential.	£6.30	SAF	**B**
SAINSBURY'S VINTAGE CHARACTER PORT, TAYLOR, FLADGATE & YEATMAN Oporto	Rich, full-bodied, mature. Well-balanced with nuances of chocolate and nuts. A sticky finish.	£6.50	JS	**S**
QUINTA DE LA ROSA FINEST RESERVE, QUINTA DE LA ROSA Oporto	A heady perfume of purple fruits – rich and ripe with a caramel undertone. Full-bodied, masculine.	£9.10	BTH CHF M&V RAE UBC	**S**

BIN 27, FONSECA GUIMARAENS Oporto	*A deep, inky colour. Spicy fruit cake with tones of blackcurrant. Heavy.*	£9.30	Widely available	(S)
QUINTA DE LA ROSA LBV, QUINTA DE LA ROSA 1990 Oporto	*A light wine reminiscent of wild cherry jam. Easy and supple with a fair length.*	£9.90	M&V	(B)
SAFEWAY 10 YEAR OLD TAWNY PORT, Oporto	*Clear, pale brick-red, with intense fruits. Sweetly balanced with soft tannins.*	£10.00	SAF	(S)
QUINTA DO NOVAL COLHEITA, QUINTA DO NOVAL 1976, 37.5CL Douro	*An elegant port of the 'pale-and-interesting' genre. A good balance between the different elements.*	£10.20	PRG VW	(B)
LATE BOTTLED VINTAGE, FONSECA GUIMARAENS, 1989 Oporto	*Rich, plum colour, with peppery perfume and taste of figs. Gutsy, firm finish.*	£10.80	MZ EVI	(B)
DOW'S CRUSTED PORT, DOW 1990 Douro	*An aromatic explosion of fruit and nuts. Firm and spicy with lingering sunkissed heat. Memorable.*	£11.00	Widely available	(G)
QUINTA DO CRASTO LBV, QUINTA DE CRASTO 1988 Oporto	*The nose has a toasted aroma. A well-structured port with stewed berry flavours.*	£12.00	ENO	(B)
QUINTA DA FOZ, A A CÁLEM, CÁLEM 1984 Oporto	*A good, silky texture and hidden depths to the nose. A soft and attractive port.*	£13.50	CHF DN	(B)

DOW'S 10 YEAR OLD TAWNY, DOW Douro	*Ruby colour. Lovely aroma of nuts, followed through with a full, nutty taste. Well made.*	£13.60	Widely available	(S)
QUINTA DO PORTO 10 YEAR OLD TAWNY, FERREIRA Douro	*Ruby colour with fresh, nutty nose. Exciting mixture of figs, mint, plum and bitter almonds.*	£13.70	BP TMW	(S)
QUINTA DA ERVAMOIRA 10 YEAR OLD TAWNY, ADRIANO RAMOS-PINTO Douro	*Cherry-bronze, silky liquid. Scent of damsons. Tastes powerfully of caramel and plum. Magnificent.*	£13.90	MMD HCK AV R EVI AMY TMW	(G)
QUINTA DO TUA, COCKBURN SMITHES & CIA LDA, COCKBURN 1987 Oporto	*Full and powerful with depth and substance. A complex length and a shimmering myriad of flavours.*	£14.00	JPH HV	(S)
TAYLOR'S 10 YEAR OLD TAWNY, TAYLOR, FLADGATE & YEATMAN Oporto	*A fiery, hot port with a clear, garnet colour, chocolatey tones and lots of fruit.*	£14.40	Widely available	(B)
QUINTA DO PANASCAL, FONSECA GUIMARAENS 1984 Oporto	*A deceptively strong initial impact on the nose. The palate has a lighter style.*	£14.50	L&W WR BU MZ	(B)
QUINTA DE LA ROSA VINTAGE PORT, QUINTA DE LA ROSA 1992 Oporto	*Dazzling garnet vintage. Smooth, intense spiciness. Contrast between initial sweetness and acidity. Dusky after-taste.*	£15.30	RAV M&V	(G)
QUINTA DO NOVAL VINTAGE PORT, QUINTA DO NOVAL 1982 Douro	*Very sweet and rich on the palate.*	£15.70	VWC ABY HOU VIL	(S)

QUINTA DO NOVAL VINTAGE PORT, QUINTA DO NOVAL 1982 Douro	*Raisin and plum aromas carry through to the palate creating a lovely depth. Surprisingly sharp finish.*	£16.30	Widely available	(S)
GOULD CAMPBELL VINTAGE PORT 1980, GOULD CAMPBELL Douro	*Deep, rubicund colour with touch of wood on nose. Generous flavours.*	£16.80	JEF TAN	(S)
DELAFORCE VINTAGE PORT, DELAFORCE 1985 Douro	*Medium weight, youthful with good, easy fruit, makes this an excellent quaffing port.*	£16.90	ES PF OD AV	(B)
WARRE'S CAVADINHA, WARRE 1982 Douro	*Nuances of fig and currant add to the balance of this stylish port. Fine tannins.*	£16.90	Widely available	(B)
GOULD CAMPBELL VINTAGE PORT 1983, Douro	*There is great potential for this port to develop its full softness.*	£17.00	JEF ES NI TAN AV WOI	(B)
QUARLES HARRIS VINTAGE PORT, QUARLES HARRIS 1980 Vila Nova de Gaia	*Dark scarlet. Berry aroma. Rich and ripe on the palate with herbal tones. Good backbone.*	£17.20	MD MWW DIR AMY NAD	(S)
GRAHAM'S MALVEDOS, W & J GRAHAM 1979 Douro	*A mature, open style with bags of powerful, but balanced, fruit.*	£17.30	Widely available	(B)
QUINTA DO SEIXO VINTAGE PORT, FERREIRA 1983 Douro	*Deep brick colour. New maturity with flavours softening into profound complexities of spice and fruit.*	£17.50	BP ENO HOU AMY TMW	(G)

Dow's Vintage Port, Dow 1980 Douro	*Deep, royal purple. A firm structure with ripe fruit and herbal strains. Elegant, soft finish.*	£18.00	Widely available	(S)
Warre's Vintage Port, Warre 1980 Douro	*A luscious liquid with long length. Stylish complexity comes out after a few minutes breathing.*	£18.50	Widely available	(S)
Quinta do Sagrado Single Quinta Port, Quinta do Sagrado 1988 Oporto	*Discreet and elegant with a ruby-red blush. Bouquet of sweet, young fruit. Slight woodiness.*	£18.50	LAU	(G)
Ferreira Duque de Bragança 20 Year Old Tawny, Ferreira Douro	*Attractive colour with good depth and flavours.*	£18.70	BP ENO NI TMW	(B)
Dow's Vintage Port, Dow 1985 Douro	*A mid-red colour with an oaky nose. Clean, clear and crisp. Interesting.*	£18.80	Widely available	(B)
Warre's Vintage Port, Warre 1983 Douro	*Soft with lots of balanced, ripe fruit. Complex, lingering qualities in the mouth.*	£19.10	Widely available	(S)
Fonseca Guimaraens, Fonseca Guimaraens 1976 Oporto	*Intense taste of nuts, figs, prunes, mint and a whisper of chocolate. Incredible opulence; fantastic length.*	£19.20	Widely available	(G)

Pinpoint who sells the wine you wish to buy by turning to the stockist codes. If you know the name of the wine you want to buy, use the alphabetical index. If price is your motivation, refer to the invaluable price guide index; red and white wines under £5, sparkling wines under £10 and champagne under £15. Happy hunting!

COCKBURN'S VINTAGE PORT, COCKBURN 1985 Douro	*Black tulip colour. Medium weight with wood, which sits comfortably on palate. Memorable.*	**£19.80**	VWC ES VW HV GSJ	(S)
COCKBURN'S VINTAGE PORT, COCKBURN 1991 Oporto	*A deep purple hue with a ripe, blueberry aroma which follows on to the palate.*	**£20.20**	JPH G&M HV	(B)
GRAHAM'S VINTAGE PORT, W&J GRAHAM 1985 Douro	*Deep, almost opaque morello cherry colour; smells of fresh tobacco leaves. Concentrated, ripe, powerful, intense.*	**£20.40**	Widely available	(G)
DOW'S VINTAGE PORT, DOW 1983 Douro	*Terracotta colour with a light structure. Soft fruit with a dusty, peppery note.*	**£20.60**	Widely available	(B)
FONSECA, FONSECA VINTAGE PORT 1985 Douro	*Deep, purply black colour. Young, spicy with mouth-watering qualities.*	**£20.90**	Widely available	(B)
QUINTA DO VESUVIO VINTAGE PORT, QUINTA DO VESUVIO 1989 Douro	*Full sweetness and a lightly smoky hint are found in this supple port.*	**£21.20**	JEF DIR	(B)
GOULD CAMPBELL VINTAGE PORT 1977, GOULD CAMPBELL 1977 Douro	*Excellent ruby colour and thick, viscous texture. Spicy mint flavours give it great impact.*	**£21.80**	JEF ES TAN WOI	(S)
GRAHAM'S VINTAGE PORT, W & J GRAHAM 1980 Douro	*A smell of damson jelly. Good ageing potential.*	**£22.00**	JEF DBY U BI VW G&M V&C	(B)

SMITH WOODHOUSE VINTAGE PORT, SMITH WOODHOUSE 1977 Douro	*Lovely, young colour, surprisingly light on the palate. Peppery aromas, fresh blackcurrant taste. Approachable.*	£24.00	JEF WR BU	(S)
TAYLOR'S VINTAGE PORT, TAYLOR, FLADGATE & YEATMAN 1985 Oporto	*Deep-coloured and full-bodied with peppery nose. Wonderful mixture of dark fruits. Juicy.*	£25.50	Widely available	(S)
QUINTA DO VESUVIO VINTAGE PORT, QUINTA DO VESUVIO 1990 Douro	*Incredible inky colour with heavy, dark chocolate smell. Full concentration of fruit and long finish.*	£25.80	Widely available	(S)
TAYLOR'S 20 YEAR OLD TAWNY, TAYLOR, FLADGATE & YEATMAN Oporto	*Pale and delicate with attractive colour. Good balance between different flavours.*	£25.80	Widely available	(S)
FONSECA GUIMARAENS, FONSECA 1967 Douro	*Good fruit balance in this sweet, nutty, easy-to-drink example.*	£26.00	VWC VW	(B)
WARRE'S VINTAGE PORT, WARRE 1977 Douro	*Garnet colour with fresh, spicy mint aromas. Figgy fruits with gentle tannins. Lively balance.*	£26.80	Widely available	(G)
GRAHAM'S VINTAGE PORT, W&J GRAHAM 1977 Douro	*A lovely, mouth-filling vintage port with lots of juicy fruits.*	£35.90	Widely available	(B)
QUINTA DO NOVAL COLHEITA 37.5CL, QUINTA DO NOVAL 1937 Douro	*A remarkable, old Port. Soft, long and sweet, with a silky finish.*	£77.50	PRG	(B)

MADEIRA

5 YEAR OLD DRY MADEIRA, D'OLIVEIRA, D'OLIVEIRA Madeira	*Beautiful nose of baked fruits, cashews and walnuts. Fresh orange, apricot fruit and gentle nuttiness.*	£8.90	MVN L&W G&M TAN	(B)
BLANDY'S 5 YEAR OLD BUAL, MADEIRA WINE COMPANY Madeira	*Clean, rich, honeyed fruit. Creamy walnuts and Christmas cake. Layered texture gives satisfying weight.*	£11.70	JEF BOO OD VIL	(B)
COSSART GORDON 5 YEAR OLD MALMSEY, COSSART GORDON Madeira	*Nose of crushed nuts and brown sugar. Rich, sweet fruit on palate; rounded finish.*	£12.00	Widely available	(B)
BLANDY'S 10 YEAR OLD MALMSEY, MADEIRA WINE COMPANY, Madeira	*Rich, molasses nose. Gorgeous flavours: powdered cheese, walnut, layers of milk chocolate. Fantastic length.*	£14.60	Widely available	(G)
BARBEITO CRISTAVAO COLOMBO 10 YEAR OLD MALMSEY, BARBEITO Madeira	*Well-made, modern Malmsey. Spicy nose and palate; silky texture. Rich, complex, prune flavour.*	£15.00	DN	(B)
HENRIQUES & HENRIQUES 10YR OLD SERCIAL Madeira	*Rich nose of coffee, caramel and nuts. Butterscotch palate. Hints of orange zest. Long finish.*	£15.40	VEX DBY CHF V&C TAN EVI	(S)
COSSART GORDON 10 YEAR OLD VERDELHO, COSSART GORDON Madeira	*Unctuous wine with pungent salted peanut nose, bronzed toffee and delicate walnut palate.*	£15.70	BU BOO TH WR BU DIR AV	(S)

COSSART GORDON 10 YEAR OLD MALMSEY, MADEIRA WINE COMPANY Madeira	*Marmalade and smoky aromas; exciting mix of prune, chocolate and raisins. Floral character. Good balance.*	£16.50	JEF DIR MRF WOI C NL	**B**
COSSART GORDON 15 YEAR OLD MALMSEY, MADEIRA WINE COMPANY Madeira	*Rich fig and chocolate aromas. Zesty acidity adds bite to the finish. Glorious length.*	£18.50	JEF	**B**
COSSART GORDON 15 YEAR MALMSEY, COSSART GORDON Madeira	*Chocolate and raisin aromas leap from this venerable wine. Subtle complexity; silky texture.*	£20.50	BU L&W WR BU ENO DIR	**B**
RUTHERFORD & MILES VERDELHO, RUTHERFORD & MIELS 1982 Madeira	*Marvellous nose of coffee and eclairs. Exotic flavours enhanced by a nutty/woody backbone.*	£25.70	BU MD FUL	**B**

SOUTH AFRICA

As the rest of the world cautiously acknowledges the extraordinary changes which have taken place in the 'new' South Africa, wine lovers have begun to notice similar changes in the style and quality of the stuff they are pouring out of South African wine bottles. The old 'cooked' style of reds is disappearing as, hopefully, is the tendency to make wine from unripe grapes.

RED

KWV CAPE CELLARS CABERNET SAUVIGNON, KWV 1992 Cape	Dry, earthy nose; robust, full-bodied and mature. Gentle, raisiny finish of impressive length.	£3.70	U GDS FUL	(B)
CHAMONIX CABERNET SAUVIGNON, CAPE CHAMONIX WINE FARM 1992 Franschhoek	Full, oaky flavour dominating ripe cassis. Good overall balance, well-defined tannic structure.	£3.90	CCW	(B)
TESCO ROBERTSON SHIRAZ/CABERNET, JOHN WORONTCHAK AT MADEBA Robertson	Well made. Clean, fruity blackberries and plums. Oak contributes vanilla sweetness and adds structure.	£4.00	TO	(S)
LIEVLAND CABERNET SAUVIGNON, LIEVLAND 1991 Stellenbosch	Good Cabernet nose, pronounced tannins on palate. Blackcurrant and mint flavours. Good depth.	£4.00	BWC	(B)
KWV ROUWKES DRIFT RUBY CABERNET/MERLOT, KWV 1992 Cape	Smooth, vanilla character with touch of pepper. An attractive greenness.	£4.00	NUR	(B)

SOUTH AFRICA • RED

STELLENZICHT CABERNET SAUVIGNON/MALBEC, STELLENZICHT 1993 Stellenbosch	*Classy. Ripe, full flavour. Smooth, mellow, and elegant. Young and simple; should mature nicely.*	£4.00	WST FUL	Ⓑ
STELLENZICHT CABERNET SAUVIGNON / SHIRAZ, STELLENZICHT 1993 Stellenbosch	*Fresh, lively nose. Straightforward, medium-bodied, youthful, juicy fruit and nice oak. Easy and stylish.*	£4.00	WST OD	Ⓑ
KWV CABERNET SAUVIGNON, KWV 1991 Cape	*Austere and intense. Well-developed, oaky character with blended tannins and fine length on finish.*	£4.40	Widely available	Ⓑ
AVONTUUR PINOTAGE, AVONTUUR 1994 Stellenbosch	*Strong, regional characteristics of concentrated, juicy fruit with smoke. Strong blackberry aromas mixed with oak.*	£4.40	AGM W	Ⓢ
FIRST RIVER CABERNET SAUVIGNON, EERSTERIVIER 1993 Stellenbosch	*Blackcurrant nose, still rather closed. Nice fruit and light tannins blended in New World style.*	£4.70	WSG	Ⓑ
STELLENVALE CABERNET SAUVIGNON/SHIRAZ, STELLENVALE 1990 Western Cape	*Slightly vegetal on nose, though mature. Broad and complex; good length and soft on finish.*	£4.80	PF	Ⓑ
KWV MOUNT PEARL SHIRAZ, KWV 1990 Cape	*Garnet red. Soft, jammy, developed nose. Sweet attack to palate; plum pudding character. Light drinking.*	£4.90	ECA ABY G&M VIL	Ⓑ
STELLENZICHT CABERNET SAUVIGNON BLOCK SERIES, STELLENZICHT 1993 Stellenbosch	*Fragrant, jammy nose with menthol and fruit. Luscious Merlot. Good extract. Powerful tannic structure.*	£5.00	WST W FUL OD	Ⓢ

STELLENZICHT MERLOT BLOCK SERIES, STELLENZICHT 1993 Stellenbosch	*Very pleasant, spicy, soft, toasted oak bouquet. Hot, sweet fruit and spicy oak on palate.*	**£5.00**	WST W OD	(B)
NEDERBURG CABERNET SAUVIGNON, NEDERBURG WINES 1991 Paarl	*Robust blackcurrant backed by firm tannins. Concentrated on palate.*	**£5.20**	Widely available	(B)
BELLINGHAM MERLOT, BELLINGHAM 1992 Franschhoek	*Ripe, red cherry. Creamy, vanilla, complex nose. Soft tannins. Austere finish, but lovely, juicy fruit.*	**£5.50**	EH	(B)
VREDENDAL CABARET, VREDENDAL CO-OP 1994 Olifants River	*Youthful purplish tinge. Delicious mouthfuls of juicy, black fruits with character and flair. Should develop.*	**£5.50**	RSS OD	(B)
LA MOTTE SCHOONE GEVEL MERLOT, LA MOTTE ESTATE 1993 Franschhoek	*Refined wine, good structure. Concentrated nose of black fruits. Full-bodied, soft tannins. Grippy raspberry.*	**£5.70**	RSS TO	(B)
FAIRVIEW SHIRAZ, CHARLES BACK FAIRVIEW 1992 Paarl	*Vivid ruby; red fruit aromas. Berries on palate; lovely weight and flavour.*	**£5.70**	CHN TO TAN	(B)
BON COURAGE SHIRAZ, BON COURAGE ESTATE 1993 Robertson	*Clean, lightish ruby; spice and berries bouquet. Perfume follows on to palate. Good length.*	**£5.70**	SAW DBY B	(S)
BACKSBERG KLEIN BABYLONSTOREN, BACKSBERG 1992 Paarl	*Clean nose. Ripe, black-currany bouquet. Intensified, fruit-filled palate. Good balance and great depth.*	**£5.90**	ECA DBY GDS HOU VIL	(B)

SOUTH AFRICA • RED				
CATHEDRAL CELLARS TRIPTYCH, KWV 1992 Cape	*Garnet rim. Delightful, spicy, earthy, berry fragrances. Light, firm tannins complement rich, ripe, minty blackcurrant.*	£6.00	ECA	(G)
FAIRVIEW MERLOT RESERVE, CHARLES BACK FAIRVIEW 1992 Paarl	*Ruby tinge, evolving slightly at rim. Soft, juicy, sweet oak and berry. Pleasing, old-style Claret.*	£6.00	CHN TO	(B)
SAXENBURG CABERNET SAUVIGNON, SAXENBURG 1992 Stellenbosch	*Interesting nose of wild fruits, herbaceous currant. Rich, chunky fruit on palate; powerful tannins.*	£6.00	ECA DBY G&M HVW	(B)
DIEU DONNÉ CABERNET SAUVIGNON, DIEU DONNÉ VINEYARDS 1993 Franschhoek	*Attractive, warm nose with a concentration of Bordeaux-style fruits. Makings of a truly delectable wine.*	£6.20	PAT FUL TAN	(B)
FAIRVIEW CABERNET FRANC / MERLOT RESERVE, CHARLES BACK FAIRVIEW 1992 Paarl	*Typically South African, with notes of rubber on nose. Generous fruit balanced against good acidity. Warm.*	£6.20	CHN ES FUL	(B)
FREDERICKSBURG CABERNET SAUVIGNON, FREDERICKSBURG 1990 Paarl	*Deep scarlet in colour. Rich, ripe berries on nose. Faint oakiness on the palate. Well balanced.*	£6.20	SAW RAV DBY CHF HV	(B)
FLEUR DU CAP MERLOT, BERGKELDER 1992 Coastal Region	*Concentrated blackberry nose. Elegant, black fruits with gentle background of soft tannins and balanced acidity.*	£6.30	MMD DBY	(B)
FAIRVIEW SHIRAZ RESERVE, CHARLES BACK FAIRVIEW 1993 Paarl	*Deep, black cherry; green, eucalyptus, wild flowers and berry bouquet. Ripe, sweet palate; chunky tannins.*	£6.60	CHN ADN HOL	(S)

SOUTH AFRICA • RED

FAIRVIEW CABERNET SAUVIGNON, FAIRVIEW 1993 Paarl	*Well-developed nose, filled with spicy, warm aromas. Cassis and pepper on palate. Elegant wine.*	£6.80	CHN W	(B)
GOEDE HOOP VINTAGE ROUGE, GOEDE HOOP WINE ESTATE 1990 Stellenbosch	*Rustic, burnt character, interspersed with juicy blackcurrants and cherries. Palate dominated by vegetal fruit.*	£6.80	BD	(S)
WILDEKRANS PINOTAGE, WILDEKRANS 1993 Walker Bay	*Concentrated, up-front, red berried fruit with lime. High acidity. Classy, but gluggable.*	£7.00	BI HOU	(B)
ZONNEBLOEM MERLOT, STELLENBOSCH, STELLENBOSCH FARMERS' WINERY 1992 Cape	*Hedonistic wine. Warm, oaky bouquet. Concentrated fruit palate, reminiscent of granny's summer pudding.*	£7.10	PGR	(B)
FLEUR DU CAP CABERNET SAUVIGNON, BERGKELDER 1989 Coastal Region	*Mature, enticing nose. Ripe, berry fruits invade the palate. Fully rounded, complex wine.*	£7.30	MMD DBY	(B)
VRIESENHOF KALLISTA, VRIESENHOF 1991 Stellenbosch	*Tinges of burnt wood and blackcurrants on the nose. Ripeness of summer fruits on palate. Good length.*	£7.50	FTH WR TAN	(B)
GRANGEHURST PINOTAGE, GRANGEHURST 1993 Stellenbosch	*Warm, smoky orangey nose; soft tinge of oak. Mulled wine spiciness. Concentrated, fleshy raspberry fruit.*	£7.80	BI	(B)
NEIL ELLIS VINEYARD SELECTION CABERNET SAUVIGNON, NEIL ELLIS 1993 Stellenbosch	*Attractive, clean, plum-my nose. Lively, palatable wine, with hints of Cabernet and mint. Good ageing potential.*	£8.10	FTH MTL DBY ADN HOU	(B)

SOUTH AFRICA • RED				
WARWICK FARM TRILOGY, WARWICK FARM 1991 Stellenbosch	*Distinguished, ripe cedar nose with meaty fruit. Succulent, juicy flavours balanced by smooth blended tannins.*	£9.00	RW TH WR BU NI	G
ALTO CABERNET SAUVIGNON, ALTO ESTATE 1988 Stellenbosch	*Cigar-box aromas. Chunky, chewy, lush fruit. Mature, ripe berry. Fleshy and full. Good acidity.*	£9.30	MMD DBY	S
GLEN CARLOU PINOT NOIR, GLEN CARLOU 1994 Paarl	*Sweet strawberry and plenty of soft oak. Easy-drinking, rounded style. Ripe, jammy, red fruit.*	£9.50	AUS	B
MEERLUST RUBICON, MEERLUST ESTATE 1989 Stellenbosch	*Warm, maturing nose of blackcurrants. Soft, ripe cassis. Approachable, luscious fruit, balanced by lively acidity.*	£10.00	MMD BOO DBY SEB HOL AV	G
MEERLUST CABERNET SAUVIGNON, MEERLUST ESTATE 1991 Stellenbosch	*Impressive, concentrated berry nose with spicy over-tones, although not tradi-tional Cabernet. Chunky, fleshy. Big on tannins.*	£10.00	MMD BOO DBY HOL CNL	B
CLARIDGE RED WELLINGTON, CLARIDGE 1991 Wellington	*Sweet, rich, berry nose, leaving no surprises on the palate with its rich, cassis flavours.*	£10.00	L&W BOO	S
GLEN CARLOU GRANDE CLASSIQUE RESERVE, GLEN CARLOU 1992 Paarl	*Concentrated, with much rich, ripe fruit and creamy vanilla oak. Fleshy berry; perfect tannic balance.*	£10.50	AUS	S
KANONKOP CABERNET SAUVIGNON, KANONKOP 1991 Stellenbosch	*Cabernet in Bordeaux style. Young, aggressive, but good. Rich, chewy, jammy fruit. Fine tan-nins.*	£10.60	RSS DBY OD CNL	S

SOUTH AFRICA • WHITE				
KANONKOP PAUL SAUER, KANONKOP 1991 Stellenbosch	*Restrained but hints at Bordeaux grapes. Hot, stewy flavours of bramble. Generous wood and meaty.*	£10.60	RSS JS OD	(S)
NEDERBURG PRIVATE BIN 161, NEDERBURG WINES 1988 Paarl	*Delicious mouthfuls of blackcurrants and redcurrants. Flavours of English September hedgerows. Ages well.*	£11.50	CAX	(B)

WHITE

DE WET CAPE BAY WHITE, DE WET CO-OP 1994 Worcester	*Soft, elegant nose of elderflowers and green apples. Very refreshing with zingy acidity. Lovely balance.*	£3.10	FTH	(B)
TABLE BAY EARLY RELEASE CHENIN BLANC, KYM MILNE 1995 Robertson	*Light and delicate with aromatic, tropical overtones. Juicy fruit, ripe with zippy acidity. Quaffable stuff.*	£3.50	VW	(S)
KWV ROUWKES DRIFT CHENIN BLANC, KWV 1994 Cape	*Fresh Cox apple aromas. Hints of honey and demerara sugar. Lovely, clean, fruit appeal.*	£3.60	NUR	(B)
STELLENZICHT CHARDONNAY, STELLENZICHT 1994 Stellenbosch	*Classical, tropical, toasty aromas. Smooth, elegant toffee/caramel and light, nutty oak.*	£4.00	WST W	(B)
NEETHLINGSHOF GEWÜRZTRAMINER, NEETHLINGSHOF 1994 Stellenbosch	*Lovely, clean and fresh exotic fruit, lightly spiced, with tangy citrus acidity on finish.*	£4.50	ECA DBY VW CPW G&M HOU	(B)

SOUTH AFRICA • WHITE

CAPE VIEW CHARDONNAY SUR LIE, KYM MILNE 1994 Stellenbosch	*Ripe, peachy, creamy nose; oak, peaches and cream, buttery palate. Crisp acidity and long finish.*	**£4.50**	VWC VW	**B**
AVONTUUR LE CHARDON, AVONTUUR 1992 Stellenbosch	*Soft, smoky aroma. Oak, pineapple and subtle lemon, melon and coconut flavours.*	**£4.99**	AGM BWC	**S**
BAY VIEW CHARDONNAY, LONGRIDGE 1992 Coastal Region	*Appealing, soft, spicy fruit with vanilla and pineapple. Good acidity holding it together in mouth.*	**£5.70**	LON DBY	**B**
WELTEVREDE GEWÜRZTRAMINER, WELTEVREDE 1994 Robertson	*Rich, ripe lychee, mango character. Runny honey and baked apple flavours abound. Softly textured.*	**£5.70**	HOH DBY VIL EVI	**B**
BON COURAGE CHARDONNAY, BON COURAGE ESTATE 1994 Robertson	*Pale green lemon; slightly dusty, creamy nose. Tangy and lively in mouth.*	**£6.10**	SAW DBY	**B**
KLEIN CONSTANTIA ESTATE CHARDONNAY, KLEIN CONSTANTIA ESTATE 1993 Constantia	*Oaky, toasty nose. Ripe tropical fruit in mouth; touches of pineapple and mango. Slight lemon peel finish.*	**£6.50**	DBY W U DIR AV	**B**
NEIL ELLIS ELGIN VINEYARD SELECTION SAUVIGNON BLANC, NEIL ELLIS 1994 Elgin	*Light, fruity nose with a hint of vanilla. Elegant palate with integrated lemon. Good length.*	**£6.90**	FTH MTL DBY HOU	**B**

Pinpoint who sells the wine you wish to buy by turning to the stockist codes. If you know the name of the wine you want to buy, use the alphabetical index. If price is your motivation, refer to the invaluable price guide index; red and white wines under £5, sparkling wines under £10 and champagne under £15. Happy hunting!

SOUTH AFRICA • SWEET WHITE

LA MOTTE FUMÉ BLANC, LA MOTTE ESTATE 1993 Franschhoek	*Grassy nose; appealing green quality with ripe, soft fruit flavours.*	£6.90	MMD	B
VILLIERA BLANC FUMÉ CRU MONRO, VILLIERA ESTATE 1994 Paarl	*Smoky, gooseberry nose. Vibrant and powerful wine with good fruit, acidity and length.*	£7.00	WR	B
HAMILTON RUSSELL CHARDONNAY 1994, HAMILTON RUSSELL VINEYARDS Walker Bay	*Strong new oak on nose; tinges of melon and avocado. Dry, moderate acidity, good, creamy fruit.*	£7.40	TAN AV	B
LOUISVALE CHARDONNAY, LOUISVALE FARMS 1993 Stellenbosch	*Very ripe, open nose with honey and tropical fruit. Dry, clean with good acidity. Finishes well.*	£8.70	WTR W HHC RD TRO	B
PLAISIR DE MERLE CHARDONNAY, STELLENBOSCH FARMERS' WINERY 1993 Paarl	*Subtle in mouth with touch of green fruit. Good acidity poking through with creamy finish.*	£10.00	CAX	B
GLEN CARLOU RESERVE CHARDONNAY, GLEN CARLOU 1993 Paarl	*Ripe, spicy oak with delicious, amorous fondue centre. Hottish finish. Exciting.*	£10.00	AUS OD	B

SWEET WHITE

BON COURAGE NOBLE LATE HARVEST, BON COURAGE ESTATE 1994 Robertson	*Immediate raisin nose following on to palate. Good acidity; very sweet, syrupy finish.*	£5.50	SAW DBY HVW	B

SPARKLING

SAINSBURY'S MADEBA BRUT, GRAHAM BECK Robertson	*Soft touch; good length and structure. Clean finish.*	£6.80	JS	(B)
TRADITION BRUT CARTE D'OR, CHARLES DE FÈRE, VILLIERA Paarl	*Good mousse; clean fruit and nice, crisp acidity. Hints of citrus fruits on the palate.*	£7.00	WST	(S)
KAAPSE VONKEL, SIMONSIG ESTATE 1992 Stellenbosch	*Lovely, warm, toasty nose; gorgeous, nutty character; good length and complexity. Long finish.*	£9.00	LAW	(S) WINE OF THE YEAR
PIERRE JOURDAN BLANC DE BLANC, CLOS CABRIERE, 1992 Franschhoek	*Pale lemon colour. Bready, clean, simple, young nose. Clean, simple, tight style.*	£11.00	AGR	(B)
PIERRE JOURDAN CUVÉE BELLE ROSE, CLOS CABRIERE 1992 Franschhoek	*Ripe cherries and good yeastiness. Soft summer fruits. Clean, dry finish.*	£13.20	AGR VW	(B)

FORTIFIED

KWV WHITE JERIPIGO, KWV 1979 Cape	*Complex aromas of caramel and toffee. Rich, raisin palate with honey and nuts. Warm, intense.*	£7.00	ECA W	(G)

SOUTH AMERICA

THE WINEMAKING REVOLUTION has only really taken effect in Chile over the last 15 years or so, following the arrival of outside investment and expertise, the introduction of modern equipment and the development of new wine regions. Today things are moving fast - as they are on the other side of the Andes in Argentina and even further north in Uruguay and Mexico.

ARGENTINA • RED

SANTA JULIA MALBEC OAK RESERVE, LA AGRICOLA 1992 Mendoza	Lovely, full-bodied plums; some tar intermingled with spice. Rich, smooth balance	£3.80	T&T	(B)
TRAPICHE CABERNET SAUVIGNON RESERVE, TRAPICHE 1992 Mendoza	Enticing liquorice and stewed fruit on nose. Sweet vanilla and American oak dimension.	£4.90	SG DBY	(S)
BODEGA NORTON MALBEC, BODEGA NORTON 1994 Mendoza	Interesting, dried fruit aroma and chocolaty palate. Firm tannins. Soft, easy-drinking wine.	£6.50	BOO BWC CPW AV HDL UBC	(B)
WEINERT CARRASCAL, BODEGA Y CAVAS DE WEINERT 1989 Mendoza	Juicy, ripe blackberry nose dominates. Layers of spice and leather; ripe tannins on palate.	£6.80	FVM SV HOL DIR R CNL	(S)
FOND DE CAVE CABERNET SAUVIGNON, MENDOZA RIVER 1992 Mendoza	Strong Cabernet fruit with reassuring, gripping tannins. Good balance with an enduring, thoughtful finish.	£7.00	SG	(S)

St Michael Trapiche Red, Trapiche 1991 Mendoza	*Concentrated, rich, sweet. Ripe with spice, burnt rubber tones, tobacco and vanilla.*	£7.00	M&S	**(G)**
Weinert Malbec, Bodega y Cavas de Weinert 1991 Mendoza	*Heady mixture of jammy plums, damsons and chocolate plus hefty tannins. Powerful and concentrated.*	£7.60	FVM SV HOL DIR NI HVW R	**(S)**
Catena Estate Cabernet Sauvignon, Catena Estate 1992 Mendoza	*Full, rich, classy wine with fine, balanced tannins and rich, dark, coherent fruit. Lasts wonderfully in mouth.*	£8.00	BI FUL	**(B)**
Luigi Bosca Syrah, Leoncio Arizu 1988 Mendoza	*Juicy, blackcurranty, with a brambly nose. Notes of tobacco and vanilla on the middle palate.*	£8.10	PAM BTH NI HVW NY	**(B)**
Trapiche Medalla Tinto, Trapiche 1993 Mendoza	*Plummy, with damson and dynamic tannins. Powerful, fresh and interesting.*	£9.00	SG	**(B)**
Weinert Cabernet Sauvignon, Bodega y Cavas de Weinert 1989 Mendoza	*Ripe on nose, reminiscent of port or sherry, continuing on palate. Good weight and acidity.*	£9.60	FVM SV HOL DIR HVW R CNL	**(B)**
Santa Florentina Cabernet Sauvignon, La Riojana 1994 La Rioja	*Cherry nose. Characteristic, well-made wine with ripe, jammy blackberry. Good concentration, pleasant style.*	£22.80	RIO	**(B)**

Pinpoint who sells the wine you wish to buy by turning to the stockist codes. If you know the name of the wine you want to buy, use the alphabetical index. If price is your motivation, refer to the invaluable price guide index; red and white wines under £5, sparkling wines under £10 and champagne under £15. Happy hunting!

ARGENTINA • WHITE

ETCHART TORRONTES, BODEGAS ETCHART S.A. 1994 Cafayate	*Fresh, grapey nose with tropical fruit. Sweet fruit on palate cut by a stab of acidity.*	£4.00	CWS TH WR BU U CAX UBC	**B**
SANTA JULIA CHARDONNAY, LA AGRICOLA 1995 Mendoza	*Aromatic, lifted aromas; creamy character on palate. Long finish.*	£4.00	T&T	**B**
CATENA ESTATE CHARDONNAY, CATENA ESTATE 1993 Mendoza	*Ripe, green fruit on nose. Oaky, creamy fruit flavours.*	£8.00	BI	**S**

BRAZIL • WHITE

AURORA EARLY RELEASE WHITE, AURORA 1994 Rio Grande Del Sur	*Attractive, leafy perfume. Light, clean and fresh. Fruit flavour develops in mouth.*	£4.00	EH	**B**

CHILE • RED

VALDEZARO CABERNET SAUVIGNON, CARTA VIEJA 1994 Maule	*Classic Claret nose with herbal overtones. Lovely, juicy, soft fruits on palate. Oaky, minty character.*	£3.00	FBG	**B**

CONO SUR CABERNET SAUVIGNON, CONO SUR 1993 Chimbarongo	*Herbaceous, leafy notes complemented by developed ripe berry. Complex, juicy flavours blending with powerful oak.*	£3.80	WST W FUL OD	**S**
JOSE CANEPA MERLOT, JOSE CANEPA Y CIA 1994 Rancagua	*Sweet, rich, concentrated blackcurrant. Soft, easy, ripe fruit, spicy on palate. Youthful, but long finish.*	£4.00	T&T	**B**
CARMEN CABERNET SAUVIGNON, CARMEN VINEYARDS 1993 Rapel	*Classic Claret nose of ripe cassis and eucalyptus. Full and rounded. Good length and complexity.*	£4.10	SG DBY OD	**B**
VIÑA SANTA RITA 120 CABERNET SAUVIGNON, VIÑA SANTA RITA 1992 Maipo	*Smooth, ripe fruits. Well-blended flavours. Overall balance of gluggable fruit.*	£4.40	GRA DBY DIR SHB	**B**
VIÑA SANTA RITA 120 PINOT NOIR, VIÑA SANTA RITA 1994 Casablanca/Maipo	*Soft, pleasing style of Pinot Noir. Persistent, concentrated cherry fruit. Silky smooth, ripe and rounded.*	£4.60	GRA DIR JS	**B**
UNDURRAGA CABERNET SAUVIGNON, UNDURRAGA 1992 Maipo	*Earthy notes and herbaceous tones. Jammy, sweet fruit and dominant vanilla oak. Youthful.*	£4.70	PLB DBY GDS AV	**B**
MONTES MERLOT & CABERNET, DISCOVER WINES 1992 Curico	*Delightful, lively garnet. Fresh peppery bouquet; mouthfuls of young, juicy, berry fruits. Fine structure and firm finish.*	£4.80	SV DBY HW VIL NY	**B**
UNDURRAGA MERLOT, UNDURRAGA 1994 Maipo	*Concentrated cherry on nose. Sweet fruit mid-palate with soft, grippy tannins.*	£4.90	PLB DBY GDS AV	**B**

CASILLERO DEL DIABLO CABERNET SAUVIGNON, CONCHA Y TORO S.A. 1992 Maipo	*Wonderful, ripe, succulent fruit on nose. Good, curranty Cabernet with minty, herbal overtones.*	£4.90	RWV RAV VW	(B)
ST MICHAEL MAIPO CABERNET SAUVIGNON RESERVE, CARMEN VINEYARDS 1993 Maipo	*Light black cherry robe and bouquet of wild berries. Delicate, colourful, soft, chewy flavours.*	£5.00	M&S	(B)
JOSE CANEPA PRIVATE RESERVE CABERNET SAUVIGNON, JOSE CANEPA Y CIA 1992 Maipo	*Rich blackcurrant; leathery/spicy overtones. Good complexity; some oak. Very well made.*	£5.00	T&T JS	(S)
VIÑA SANTA RITA RESERVA MERLOT, VIÑA SANTA RITA 1994 Maule	*Young, chunky wine showing dark chocolate and plums on nose. Sweet oak and berry finish.*	£5.10	GRA DBY DIROD WIN	(B)
VALDIVIESO BARREL FERMENTED MERLOT, VALDIVIESO 1993 Lontue	*Lovely, smoky nose; hints of cedary oak. Mellow, full-bodied style; rich, ripe, creamy berry fruit.*	£5.20	TLC WR BU THW	(S)
TORRES CABERNET SAUVIGNON, MIGUEL TORRES 1993 Curico	*Fresh, redcurrants and blackberries. Elegant, good finish.*	£5.20	Widely available	(B)
CARMEN RESERVE CABERNET SAUVIGNON, CARMEN VINEYARDS 1993 Maipo	*Sweet Ribena nose. Soft, luscious cherry against strong tannins and oak influence. Smooth and rich.*	£5.40	SG DBY OD	(B)
CARMEN RESERVE MERLOT, CARMEN VINEYARDS 1993 Rapel	*Creamy, plummy nose. Sweet, jammy fruit on palate. Soft oak, spicy fruit and discreet tannins.*	£5.40	SG DBY OD	(S)

SANTA CAROLINA SPECIAL RESERVE MERLOT, SANTA CAROLINA 1992 Maipo	*Delightfully fresh, youthful flavour of juicy fruits, with herbaceous hints. Good structure, soft tannins.*	£5.60	ECA DBY	**B**
SANTA CAROLINA PINOT NOIR, SANTA CAROLINA 1994 Maipo	*Lovely concentration of seductive strawberry and raspberry. Lively and exotic with vibrant jammy flavours.*	£5.60	ECA WR BU TH G&M	**B**
ECHEVERRIA CABERNET SAUVIGNON RESERVA, VIÑA ECHEVERRIA 1992 Molina	*Lively, fresh nose with tones of redcurrant and bramble. More dignified palate with touches of cedar and tobacco.*	£5.60	HOH MTL HCK HOL HVW WOI VIL	**B**
CALITERRA RESERVA CABERNET SAUVIGNON, VIÑA CALITERRA 1991 Curico	*Nose of hot, ripe, currant. Sweet plums. Cabernet and intense blackcurrant. Soft, tannic finish.*	£5.80	Widely available	**S**
HACIENDA SAN CARLOS CABERNET SAUVIGNON/ MALBEC, MIGUEL VIU MANENT 1994 Colchagua	*Big, thick colour. Delicious, chunky, sweet fruit. Simple, direct wine, well-balanced and long.*	£5.80	BD	**B**
CONO SUR CABERNET SAUVIGNON RESERVE, CONO SUR 1992 Chimbarongo	*Hot, minty nose with metallic overtones. Chewy, soft, ripe fruits and gentle Merlot flavours.*	£5.90	WST W FUL OD	**B**
CONO SUR PINOT NOIR SELECTION RESERVE, CONO SUR 1994 Chimbarongo	*Young, vibrant black cherry and a hint of undergrowth. Rounded and smooth. Silky extraction.*	£6.00	WST W FUL OD	**S**
CONO SUR PINOT NOIR SELECTION RESERVE, CONO SUR 1993 Chimbarongo	*Sweet oak and jammy raspberry on still youthful Pinot. Very smooth and silky. Warm spiciness.*	£6.00	WST OD	**B**

SOUTH AMERICA • CHILE RED

ERRAZURIZ DON MAXIMIANO RESERVA, ERRAZURIZ 1993 Aconcagua	*Rich, satisfying nose with hints of almond and vanilla pod. Good, berry palate with cedar, bark and tobacco.*	£6.80	HM DBY TO OD	(S)
ROWAN BROOK RESERVE CABERNET SAUVIGNON, JOSE CANEPA Y CIA LTDA 1993 Maipo	*Ripe, mulberry aromas. Rich, velvety, sweet fruit balanced by good acidity and oak-chip tannins.*	£7.00	A	(B)
WILLIAM FEVRE CABERNET SAUVIGNON MIRAMONTE DE SAN FERNANDO, WILLIAM FEVRE 1994 San Fernando	*Ripe, fresh, curranty, purply Cabernet with truffles and cedar on nose. Fresh berry fruit on the palate.*	£7.00	HBJ	(B)
MONTES ALPHA, DISCOVER WINES 1991 Curico	*Good, Bordeaux-style red with lush fruit and minimal but evident tannins. Vanilla and pepper on finish.*	£8.00	Widely available	(B)
DON MAXIMIANO SPECIAL RESERVE, ERRAZURIZ 1993 Aconcagua	*Mint, spice, young oak aromas. Delicious, rich, ripe blackcurrant balanced by big, peppery tannins.*	£8.50	HM FUL	(B)
SANTA RITA CASA REAL CABERNET SAUVIGNON, SANTA RITA 1993 Maipo	*Vibrant cherry aroma. Fruity middleweight with complex coffee and sweet cassis flavours. Good acidity.*	£9.60	GRA DIR WIN SAF	(S)
MAGNIFICUM CABERNET SAUVIGNON, JOSE CANEPA Y CIA LTDA 1990 Curico	*Distinctive nose of rich currants. Big, fat, luscious blackberry. Blended tannins and strong vanilla oak.*	£10.00	A	(S)
MAGNIFICUM CABERNET SAUVIGNON, JOSE CANEPA, JOSE CANEPA Y CIA 1993 Curico	*Lovely cassis and spice aromas with notes of violets. Rich and hot on palate with powerful, sweet berries. Excellent.*	£10.50	T&T	(S)

205

SOUTH AMERICA • CHILE WHITE

VIÑA SANTA RITA CASA REAL CABERNET SAUVIGNON, VIÑA SANTA RITA 1994 Maipo	*Dark berry, rich, plummy and concentrated. Dry with ripe tannins. Big, fat, creamy.*	£11.00	GRA DIR WIN	**B**

CHILE • WHITE

JOSE CANEPA Y CIA SAUVIGNON BLANC, JOSE CANEPA Y CIA 1994 Maipo	*Good fruit structure and lively balance. Some sweetness to fruit.*	£ 3.40	T&T SMF W	**B**
CALITERRA CHARDONNAY, VIÑA CALITERRA 1994 Curico	*Fresh, very clean aroma and a soft, rounded fruit palate.*	£ 4.10	Widely available	**S**
CALITERRA SAUVIGNON BLANC, VIÑA CALITERRA, 1995 Curico	*Lively, zingy wine with excellent, grapefruit character.*	£ 4.10	HBR BY CW STO BI MZ OD	**B**
JOSE CANEPA CHARDONNAY, JOSE CANEPA Y CIA 1994 Maipo	*Excellent, fruity bouquet with good length and concentration on palate.*	£ 4.20	NUR	**S**
DE MARTINO SAUVIGNON BLANC, SANTA INES 1995 Maipo	*Grassy, lime and grapefruit bouquet. Rich, ripe fruit palate with some sweetness.*	£ 4.40	MD MAY WA D	**S**
SANTA CAROLINA SAUVIGNON BLANC, SANTA CAROLINA 1995 Lontue	*Interesting, exotic, floral nose; slightly herbaceous. Some sweet fruit and hints of spice and alcohol.*	£ 4.50	ECA G&M OD	**B**

UNDURRAGA CHARDONNAY, UNDURRAGA 1994 Maipo	*Buttery, oaky nose; soft, oaky, tropical fruit salad on palate. Decent drinking.*	£4.85	PLB DBY AV	(S)
VILLARD ACONCAGUA SAUVIGNON BLANC, VILLARD FINE WINES 1994 Casablanca Valley	*Green nose; grassy and herbaceous. Clean, aggressive palate with fresh finish and good length.*	£5.00	Widely available	(B)
VIÑA SANTA RITA, RESERVA SAUVIGNON BLANC, VIÑA SANTA RITA 1994 Maule	*Clean, well-pronounced, grape flavours. Ripe character with good balance and complexity throughout.*	£5.00	GRA L&W MWW DIR WIN	(S)
JOSE CANEPA PRIVATE RESERVE CHARDONNAY, JOSE CANEPA Y CIA 1994 Rancagua	*Bright lemon; spicy oak on nose. Full, rich, fruit style. Good oak blending.*	£5.00	T&T	(B)
CALITERRA CASABLANCA ESTATE CHARDONNAY, VIÑA CALITERRA 1994 Casablanca	*Clean citrus, tropical fruit, lychee and ginger. Oily with grapefruit length. Tangy summer wine.*	£5.10	Widely available	(S)
CASABLANCA SAUVIGNON BLANC, WHITE LABEL, VINA CASABLANCA 1994 Curico	*Floral, clean and fresh wine. Good balance of fruit and acidity.*	£5.10	MOR BOO AN ENO OD HVW UBC	(S) WINE OF THE YEAR
VALDIVIESO BARREL FERMENTED CHARDONNAY, VALDIVIESO 1993 Lontue	*Green fruit on nose with hints of avocado and watermelon. Chunky middle palate.*	£5.20	W FUL	(B)
VIÑA SANTA RITA RESERVA CHARDONNAY, VIÑA SANTA RITA 1994 Maipo	*Peachy/lemony citric nose with light oak. Good acidity; clean, pleasant light finish.*	£5.30	Widely available	(B)

CALITERRA RESERVA CHARDONNAY, VIÑA CALITERRA 1994 Curico	*Fragrant, mature peach with sweet oak. Ripe, fat, chunky style. Fine oak; good balance.*	£5.70	HBR DBY BI FUL	B
VIÑA SANTA RITA MEDALLA REAL CHARDONNAY, VIÑA SANTA RITA 1994 Casablanca	*Fresh peach aroma. Clean, herbaceous Chardonnay. Slightly creamy; very well balanced.*	£6.60	GRA DBY DIR JS WIN	B
CASABLANCA VALLEY CHARDONNAY, VINA CASABLANCA 1994 Casablanca	*Lemon and grapefruit on nose, flattened slightly by vanilla oakiness. Asparagus and pesto.*	£6.60	MOR ADN OD HVW	S
VILLARD ACONCAGUA RESERVE CHARDONNAY, VILLARD FINE WINES 1993 Casablanca Valley	*Some botrytis character. Banana and vanilla pod. Light coconut smoothness.*	£6.70	BP DBY	B
SANTA MONICA CHARDONNAY, SANTA MONICA 1995 Rancagua	*Clean, fruit bouquet with sweet fruit palate; good depth and length.*	£6.70	HDL	B
CASA LAPOSTOLLE SELECTION CHARDONNAY, CASA LAPOSTOLLE 1994 Colchagua	*Peachy, nectarine and tropical fruit aromas. Caramelised fruit palate enlivened by citrus acidity. Integrated oak.*	£6.80	GRA OD WIN	S

MEXICO • RED

L A CETTO CABERNET SAUVIGNON, L A CETTO 1992 Baja California	*Perfumed nose. Sweet, ripe red fruits. Full-flavoured and chewy with high tannins.*	£4.60	ALS DBY VDV TAN R VIL	B

SOUTH AMERICA • MEXICO RED

PETITE SIRAH, L A CETTO, L A CETTO 1993 Baja California	*Clean nose following on to a smooth, rich palate. Plenty of fruit, with good acid/tannins.*	**£4.60**	Widely available	**G** WINE OF THE YEAR

SPAIN

DESPITE SOME OF THE MOST CONSERVATIVE attitudes in the wine world, Spain is quietly undergoing the early phases of a quiet revolution. Top class wines are beginning to emerge from previously underperforming regions, while new styles are being produced in traditional areas like Rioja. Much remains to be done, particularly with sparkling wines, but Spain has more to offer today's wine drinkers than ever before.

RED

SAINSBURY'S JUMILLA, AGAPITO, AGAPITO 1994 Jumilla	*Young bouquet with a touch of oak. Soft palate with tannin and acid. Good, well-structured fruit.*	**£3.50**	JS	**B**
ALBOR TINTO, DO RIOJA, CAMPO VIEJO, CAMPO VIEJO 1994 Rioja	*Good fruit and vanilla nose; quite light and lean.*	**£3.80**	Widely available	**B**
EL DRAGON TEMPRANILLO, BERBERANA, BERBERANA 1993 Rioja	*Fruity, with spice and cooked aromas; good structure with weight and depth. Will last well.*	**£3.90**	PLB SMF TO	**B**
FUENTE DEL RITMO BARREL AGED TEMPRANILLO BODEGAS CENTRO ESPAÑOLAS 1993 La Mancha	*Good colour, mid-ruby red; fruity wine with meaty, large finish.*	**£4.00**	TH W TH BU WR OD	**S**
RIOJA GLORIOSO, BODEGAS PALAÇIO, BODEGAS PALAÇIO 1991 Rioja	*Restrained nose of raspberry. Well balanced. Juicy, figgy flavours; slightly peppery, spicy character.*	**£4.30**	OHI HLV	**B**

VIÑA ALCORTA CRIANZA TEMPRANILLO, BODEGAS CAMPO VIEJO, BODEGAS Y BEBIDAS, 1992 Rioja	*Vanilla/oak nose; light; chewy, mature palate with some good fruit flavours.*	£4.30	BP BOO DBY	(B)
GRAN CALESA, COSTERS DEL SEGRE, RAIMAT, RAIMAT 1990 Costers Del Segre	*Typical wine from this region; firm fruit that finishes well and will last.*	£4.50	M&S	(S)
OAK AGED TEMPRANILLO RIOJA, BERBERANA, BERBERANA 1993 Rioja	*Cherry, raspberry and oak character. Flavours follow through from nose on to palate. Well balanced.*	£4.50	SAF BOO CWS DBY MD FUL VIL	(B)
LAGUNILLA RIOJA CRIANZA, LAGUNILLA 1988 Rioja	*Soft, oaky and cherry bouquet; savoury nose. Soft, ripe, fruit palate. Well-balanced; good finish.*	£4.50	WAV	(B)
LOS LLANOS RESERVA, BODEGAS LOS LLANOS S.A. 1990 Valdepeñas	*Some complexity to this wine; juicy, sweet fruit. Balanced, with a long finish.*	£4.50	MTL HCK DBY L&S HVW AMY UBC	(S)
NAVARRA AGRAMONT TINTO CRIANZA, BODEGAS PRINCIPE DE VIANA 1991 Navarra	*Good, delicate nose; slightly minty with soft, oak aromas. Well balanced; strong fruit and tannins.*	£4.60	TH WR BU OD L&S HVW	(S)
RIOJA TEMPRANILLO, MARQUÉS DE GRIÑON 1992 Rioja	*Spicy cinnamon. Oak aromas over red fruits; dry, toasty vanilla oak palate. Well-defined and restrained fruits.*	£4.60	MD AMY NAD	(B)
SANTARA CABERNET MERLOT, CONCA DE BARBERA, CONCAVINS/ HUGH RYMAN 1993 Conca de Barbera	*Young Cabernet nose; superb wine with excellent balance. Very clean with good tannins.*	£4.70	HAG HHR CWS CPW FUL	(S)

SPAIN • RED				
VALDEMAR VINO TINTO, DO RIOJA, MARTINEZ BUJANDA 1994 Rioja	*Soft, raspberry nose; very soft palate. Fruity and commercial, ready to drink this year.*	£4.70	TH DBY TH WR BU	B
RIOJA VIÑA AMEZOLA CRIANZA, BODEGAS AMEZOLA DE LA MORA 1990 Rioja	*Nice, fruity style; quite good spicy nose. Light fruit palate; finishes well.*	£4.90	BU TH WR BU R W UBC	B
VIÑA ALBALI VALDEPEÑAS GRAN RESERVA, BODEGAS FELIX SOLIS 1987 Valdepeñas	*Good fruit nose and palate, some chocolate. Reasonable length.*	£4.99	PEC SMF FUL	B
VALLFORMOSA PENEDES RESERVA, VALLFORMOSA 1987 Penedés	*Mature, elegant nose; tarry, weighty fruit.*	£5.20	FTH	B
BODEGAS CORRAL DON JACOBO CRIANZA, BODEGAS CORRAL 1990 Rioja	*Garnet-red; delicate, yet alcohol nose with balanced acidity. Stacks of tannin.*	£5.20	GRA WIN	B
DON JACOBO RIOJA CRIANZA, BODEGAS CORRAL, 1991 Rioja	*Raspberry nose; intense and oaky. Complex flavours with bags of cherries. Seductive yet structured.*	£5.20	GRA WIN	G
VIÑAS DE GAIN, RIOJA, COSECHEROS ALAVESES 1991 Rioja	*Spicy, mellow nose; full-bodied front palate with good structure. Tangy and creamy.*	£5.40	VTS BTH CNL	B
RAIMAT CABERNET SAUVIGNON, RAIMAT 1991 Penedes	*Nice, rich wine, full and complex. Stylish, smooth tannins.*	£5.60	PLB CWS DBY HVW GSJ	B

RAIMAT TEMPRANILLO, RAIMAT 1991 Penedés	Oaky, stylish wine with fruit; Very good start which finishes well. Good quality.	£5.60	PLB DBY TH WR BU U VW HVW GSJ	(S)
CONDE DE VALDEMAR CRIANZA, DO RIOJA, MARTINEZ BUJANDA 1992 Rioja	Ripe bouquet; pleasant, round feel. High acidity.	£5.60	TH MTL DBY CHF	(B)
GRAN SANGRE DE TORO, MIGUEL TORRES 1989 Penedés	Nice, oaky fruit. Rich, ripe, sweet palate with creaminess; wild strawberry aromas. Classic wine.	£5.80	Widely available	(G)
ENATE TEMPRANILLO/ CABERNET CRIANZA, VIÑEDOS Y CRIANZAS DEL ALTO ARAGON SA 1992 Somontano	Fresh and fruity nose; ripe, juicy palate. Good flesh and soft end.	£5.90	CWS HOU AV EVI	(S)
VIÑA ALBALI VALDEPEÑAS CABERNET SAUVIGNON, BODEGAS FELIX SOLIS 1991 Valdepeñas	Cool, creamy strawberries with a dash of coconut. Commercial, smooth oak and fruit character.	£5.99	PEC	(B)
ENATE CRIANZA, SOMONTANO, ENATE 1992 Somontano	Rich, plummy style; rather bitter cherry stone finish. Good viscosity.	£6.30	L&W MWW AV TMW	(B)
RIOJA FAUSTINO V, BODEGAS FAUSTINO MARTINEZ 1990 Rioja	Spicy, mature, oaky nose; good grip to palate; soft and round.	£6.40	Widely available	(B)
CASTILLO FUENTEMAYOR GRAN RESERVA, AGE 1985 Rioja	Clean, fruity nose with some spice; good balance, appealing fruit and grip.	£7.70	U	(B)

SPAIN • RED				
RIOJA CONDE DE SALCEDA FOURTH CRIANZA, VIÑA SALCEDA 1991 Rioja	*Soft, raspberry, black-currant and figgy bouquet; Spicy, balanced and quite long.*	£7.70	MVN ADN G&M TAN R	B
TORRES GRAN CORONAS, MIGUEL TORRES 1990 Penedés	*Pleasant, fruit nose and palate; good, sweet and friendly, with some tannin.*	£7.80	Widely available	B
MARQUES DE GRIÑON, DOMINIO DE VALDEPUSA, CABERNET SAUVIGNON, MARQUES DE GRIÑON 1991 Rioja	*Deep, red wine with robust spritzy fruit palate. Bitter oak character with quite concentrated flavours.*	£8.40	MD NAD	B
MARQUÉS DE GRIÑON DOMINIO DE VALDEPUSA CABERNET SAUVIGNON, VIÑEDOS Y BODEGAS DE MALPICA 1990	*Bitter, chocolate nose; palate has good fruit extract, bitter chocolate flavours continue on length.*	£8.40	PLB DBY MD NAD	S
VIÑA VALDUERO RESERVA, BODEGAS VALDUERO S.A. 1987 Ribera del Duero	*Youthful hue. Bright, light aromas; cherry following through onto palate. Good balance and length.*	£8.50	L&S UBC	B
ENATE RESERVA, SOMONTANO VIÑEDOS Y CRIANZAS DEL ALTO ARAGON S.A. 1992 Somontano	*Masses of oak on bouquet and powerful, oak palate. Fairly strong tannins with grip.*	£8.50	AV	B
OCHOA NAVARRA GRAN RESERVA, OCHOA 1986 Navarra	*Fresh, fruity, cherry bouquet; good flavour, quite sweet with some hard tannins.*	£8.70	DWS MTL HOL HOU	B
TEMPRANILLO COL. LECCIO, ALBERT I NOYA, ALBERT I NOYA 1993 Penedés	*Good colour with strong, rich, dark plum and cherry fruit nose; powerful, well-balanced fruit and subtle oak.*	£8.80	VR	S

SPAIN • RED				
RIOJA RESERVA, VIÑA ARDANZA, LA RIOJA ALTA S.A. 1987 Rioja	*Spicy oak and vanilla nose; big, cherry palate. Soft, creamy and ready with good length.*	£9.40	Widely available	(G)
CHIVITE 125 ANIVERSARIO GRAN RESERVA, BODEGAS JULIAN CHIVITE, 1988 Navarra	*Nice, bright colour with positive, spicy fruit. Well-made, commercial style.*	£9.50	BJC DBY HOL DIR OD WIN R	(B)
RIOJA RESERVA, VIÑA ARDANZA, LA RIOJA ALTA S.A. 1986 Rioja	*Warm, ripe, fruit nose; mellow with vanilla and bitter chestnut. Soft palate with decent structure.*	£10.00	Widely available	(B)
PALOS VIEJOS RIOJA, COSECHEROS ALAVESES 1990 Rioja	*Good, clean, fruit nose; strawberry fruit palate with attractive, ripened flavours. Terrific balance. Fine style of wine.*	£10.00	VTS	(B)
MARTINEZ BUJANDA RIOJA GARNACHA, MARTINEZ BUJUNDA 1987 Rioja	*Fresh, new oak nose; good balance on palate with some chewy oak.*	£10.60	JN TH WR BU HVW	(S)
RIOJA CONDE DE VALDEMAR GRAN RESERVA, MARTINEZ BUJANDA 1987 Rioja	*Oaky nose with some complexity; light palate, quite elegant.*	£10.60	DBY TH WR BU HVW	(B)
RIBERA DEL DUERO CRIANZA, BODEGAS RODERO S L 1992 Ribera del Duero	*Oaky nose with a hint of vanilla. Sweet and tannic wine.*	£10.70	WPL MTL	(B)
PESQUERA, RIBERA DEL DUERO, PESQUERA 1991 Ribera del Duero	*Deep hue in glass; pleasant fruit nose. Palate very dry with good fruit length.*	£11.90	BOO DBY DIR TAN OD HVW UBC	(B)

SPAIN • WHITE

MARTINEZ BUJANDA CABERNET SAUVIGNON, MARTINEZ BUJANDA 1989 Rioja	*Nice texture with a mature, oaky finish.*	**£12.60**	VEX MTL TH WR BU CHF EVI	(B)
TORRES BLACK LABEL, MIGUEL TORRES 1985 Penedés	*Smoky aromas. Smooth, soft, melted caramel but oaked on palate with warmth of alcohol.*	**£18.90**	Widely available	(B)

WHITE

SANTARA CHARDONNAY, CONCA DE BARBERA, CONCAVINS/HUGH RYMAN 1994 Conca de Barbera	*Fine, elegant, aromatic nose with full, fruity, sensual mouth. Creamy lanolin smoothness; fine fresh finish.*	**£4.00**	HAG HHR VW JS FUL	(B)
SAUVIGNON - LURTON, J & F LURTON 1994 Rueda	*Powerful nose, full of unusual fruity/goose-berry aromas. Round and well-balanced. Ripe fruit finish.*	**£4.40**	FCV OD	(B)
RAIMAT CHARDONNAY, RAIMAT 1994 Penedés	*Fresh fruit on palate with good, spritzy acidity. Light woodiness and some good, fruit flavours.*	**£5.40**	PLB DBY GSJ	(B)
CASTILLO DE MONJARDIN CHARDONNAY, BODEGAS CASTILLO DE MONJARDIN 1992 Navarra	*Nutty, gold colour. Green, toasty nose; citrus palate.*	**£5.60**	L&S WOI	(B)
MONOPOLE BARREL FERMENTED RIOJA, CVNE 1992 Rioja	*Zippy nose with intense greengage and tropical fruit aromas. Well-integrated, spicy vanilla oak.*	**£5.80**	Widely available	(B)

Wine	Description	Price	Codes	
CONDE DE VALDEMAR RIOJA BLANCO, MARTINEZ BUJANDA 1993 Rioja	*Deep colour; big aromas of rich, ripe fruit and fine oak. Ripe, oily and developed.*	£7.40	VEX MTL DBY	(S)
SOMONTANO ENATE CHARDONNAY, VIÑEDOS Y CRIANZA DEL ALTO ARAGON S.A. 1993 Somontano	*Biscuity, yeasty nose with shy, oak backbone. Good tropical fruit and nuttiness. Medium fruity finish.*	£8.50	MWW AV	(B)
VIÑA ARDANZA, LA RIOJA ALTA S.A. LA RIOJA ALTA 1989 Rioja	*Heavy wine in classic, old Rioja mould: clean, mellow fruit and pleasant oily texture.*	£9.90	Widely available	(B)
MARQUÉS DE ALELLA ALLIER, BODEGAS MARQUÉS DE ALELLA 1994 Alella	*Toasty, spritzy and fresh. Colour of Burgundian classics. Long, fruity middle palate with clean finish.*	£11.40	MOR TAN	(B)
CHIVITE NAVARRA COLECCION 125, BODEGAS JULIAN CHIVITE 1994 Navarra	*Fruit and oak with pineapple/Caribbean fruit nose. Smooth middle palate; lemongrass zestiness.*	£12.30	BJC DBY DIR WIN R	(S)

SWEET WHITE

Wine	Description	Price	Codes	
CASTILLO DE LIRIA MOSCATEL, GANDIA S.A. GANDIA Valencia	*Light, fresh, grapey style. Delightful, fragrant, refreshing with good, tangy acidity. Good aperitif*	£3.30	PLB SMF W FUL TAN	(B)
VICTORIA WINE MOSCATEL DE VALENCIA, Valencia	*Delicate, fresh, grapey nose. Lightly honeyed, aromatic and floral. Classy, long finish.*	£3.90	VWC	(B)

ROSE

GURPEGUI BERCEO ROSADO, GURPEGUI 1994 Rioja	*Light, strawberry, violet aromas. Sweet, easygoing fruit and nice, zesty acidity.*	£4.00	RWW	**B**

SPARKLING

TANNERS CAVA BRUT, Penedés	*Toasted, biscuity nose; crisp palate; good balance. Fresh, clean, attractive palate*	£6.50	TAN	**B**
CAVA CONDE DE CARALT BLANC DE BLANCS, CONDE DE CARALT Penedés	*Good mousse; fresh, clean, apple nose; large bubbles.*	£6.60	BP DBY OD	**B**

FORTIFIED

SAINSBURY'S MANZANILLA PASADA, BODEGAS DEL DUCADO, VINICOLA HIDALGO Jerez	*Clean, tangy, fresh nose. Hints of saltiness. Light and refreshing on palate. Soft on finish.*	£3.20	JS	**B**
SAINSBURY'S OLD OLOROSO , FRANCISCO GONZALEZ FERNANDEZ, MORGAN Jerez	*Hazelnut aromas, hints of orange. Refined, with a saltiness and good acidity balancing the sweet fruit.*	£3.40	JS	**S**

SAINSBURY'S AGED AMONTILLADO, BODEGAS DEL DUCADO Jerez	*Burnt sugar and floral aromas. Good, complex structure and balance. Lovely, nutty finish.*	£3.40	JS	**B**
TESCO SUPERIOR PALO CORTADO, SANCHEZ ROMATO Jerez	*Nutty, yeasty nose. Creamy vanilla. Hints of honey and toffee with clean backbone. Good concentration.*	£4.00	TO	**S**
MALT HOUSE VINTNERS GRAN CAPATAZ AMONTILLADO, GARVEY Jerez	*Fresh, lively nose. Lovely clean fruit, some sweetness balanced by good acidity.*	£4.20	MHV	**B**
SOMERFIELD AMONTILLADO SHERRY, PEREZ MEGIA Jerez	*Elegant, attractive nose, concentrated hazlenut aromas. Perfect combination of slight fruit acidity and cream on palate.*	£4.20	SMF	**B**
SOMERFIELD CREAM SHERRY, PEREZ MEGIA Jerez	*Sweet and nutty. Balance of rich caramel sweetnes with roasted nuts. Creamy finish.*	£4.20	SMF	**B**
WAITROSE SOLERA JEREZANA DRY OLOROSO, LUSTAU Jerez	*Lovely, yeasty, creamy nose. Full of rich fruit balanced by good acidity.*	£5.00	W	**S**
TESCO FINEST PALE AMONTILLADO, SANCHEZ ROMATE Jerez	*Excellent, nutty character on nose. Fresh and lively palate with an intense, dry finish. Good length.*	£5.00	TO	**B**
PANDO FINO, WILLIAMS & HUMBERT Jerez	*Beautiful, fresh nose: classy, elegant, tangy. Clean, fresh style. Attractive floral and citrus fruit.*	£6.30	EH DBY CHF MD V&C AMY CUM	**S**

DOMECQ LA INA, DOMECQ Jerez	*Fresh, tangy nose. Clean, tangy fruit on palate. Refreshing and uplifting. Fine length.*	£7.30	Widely available	**B**
DON NUÑO OLOROSO, LUSTAU, EMILIO LUSTAU Jerez	*Sweet, luscious style. A mélange of flavours: sultanas, marmalade and muscovado sugar. Unctuous richness.*	£8.40	DWS EVI	**B**
DON ZOILO MANZANILLA, DON ZOILO Jerez	*Powerful, yeasty nose; fresh and salty. Typical salty palate with good, tangy, zesty character.*	£8.70	DBY THMD WR BU VIL NAD	**B**
DON ZOILO OLOROSO, DON ZOILO Jerez	*Stylish 'oloroso'. Rich, soft caramel on nose. Ripe palate of dried fruits and roasted nuts.*	£8.90	Widely available	**S**
DON ZOILO AMONTILLADO, DON ZOILO Jerez	*Intense amontillado style. Full and richly flavoured with lots of nutty, burnt sugar characteristics.*	£8.90	Widely available	**B**
1796 RICH OLOROSO, JOHN HARVEY Jerez	*Mouthfilling, rich, nutty and raisin flavours. Hints of chocolate and coffee. Rich, sweet, concentrated fruit.*	£9.50	JPH GDS HV	**B**
GONZALEZ BYASS MATUSALEM, GONZALEZ BYASS Jerez	*Rich with wonderful, nutty, raisiny aromas. Explosive palate: raisins, dried fruits, crushed nuts and cream.*	£19.20	Widely available	**G**
AMONTILLADO DEL DUQUE, GONZALEZ BYASS Jerez	*Soft, with some saltiness. Incredibly rich concentration of flavour, but still quite dry. Wonderful weight.*	£19.30	Widely available	**S**

MATUSALEM OLD OLOROSO, GONZALEZ BYASS Jerez	*Intense caramel nose. Roasted almonds and maltesers on the palate. Concentrated flavours. Well balanced.*	**£19.40**	Widely available	(B)
APOSTOLES OLD OLOROSO, GONZALEZ BYASS Jerez	*Marmite nose. Top quality old 'oloroso'. Excellent weight of fruit. Dry and nutty balance.*	**£19.40**	IDV MTL DBY ADN PF AV OD	(S)

OTHER COUNTRIES

THIS YEAR'S CHALLENGE produced champions from some diverse parts of the world, however there have been some year on year upsets. Out go Cyprus, India, Israel, Lebanon – in rush French winemaking skills in the guise of Luxembourg and Morocco. Greece, traditionally known for its Retsina, still shows itself to be a fast developing, quality winemaking nation.

GREECE • BLEND

SEMELI WHITE, G & A KOKOTOS 1994 Attica	Soft, rounded wine, spicy and dry. Exotic fruit flavours and excellent, long finish of fruit.	£4.50	GWC	B
CO-OP OF SAMOS, SAMOS NECTAR 1985 Samos	Rich fruitcake and nutty flavours. Concentrated, sweet raisins cut by gentle acidity. Great length.	£7.30	GWC TAN	S
DOMAINE HATZIMICHALIS MERLOT D 1993 Atalanti	Sweet tea-leaf nose. Ripe fruit, boiled sweets and glycerine against background of soft tannins.	£17.50	GWC HOL	B

LUXEMBOURG • SPARKLING

CUVÉE DE L'ECUSSON, BERNARD MASSARD	Frothy, shy nose; creamy, off-dry palate. Very attractive commercial style.	£7.80	EP CEB MRF	B

MOROCCO • RED

RABBI JACOB, SINCOMAR, SINCOMAR PARLIER ET FERMAUD Rabat	*Dark, black cherry colouring with burnt eggy aroma. Big, round, soft style; sweet, full, palate*	£3.80	VER CWI BG	(B)

PERSONAL TASTING NOTES

PERSONAL TASTING NOTES

PERSONAL TASTING NOTES

PERSONAL TASTING NOTES

PERSONAL TASTING NOTES

PERSONAL TASTING NOTES

PERSONAL TASTING NOTES

PERSONAL TASTING NOTES

Tesco Mataro, Kingston Estate	£ 2.00	B
Les Vieux Cepages Grenache, Les Vignerons De Villeveyrac, Coltiva Il Rosso, Gruppo Coltiva 1994	£ 2.40	B
Asda Sicilian Rosso, Siv Spa	£ 2.70	B
Safeway Young Vatted Merlot, Russe 1994	£ 2.90	B
Calatrasi Safeway Sicilian Red, Calatrasi 1994	£ 2.90	B
Safeway Cabernet Sauvignon, Svischtou 1991	£ 3.00	B
Valdezaro Cabernet Sauvignon, Carta Vieja 1994	£ 3.00	B
Egri Csillagok Cabernet Sauvignon, Egri Csillagok 1994	£ 3.00	B
Carl Reh River Route Merlot, Carl Reh 1994	£ 3.00	B
Rovit Cabernet Sauvignon 1986	£ 3.00	B
Tesco Dão, Sogrape, Sogrape 1991	£ 3.00	B
Vinexport Merlot, Vinexport 1994	£ 3.00	B
Dealul Classic Pinot Noir, Dealul Mare 1990	£ 3.00	B
J P Tinto, Vino De Mesa, J P Vinhos	£ 3.10	S
Somerfield Claret, Louis Eschenauer	£ 3.20	B
La Vieille Ferme Reserve Rouge, Pierre Perrin 1992	£ 3.30	B
Pasqua Valpolicella 1993	£ 3.30	B
Gorchivka Vineyards Cabernet Sauvignon 1993	£ 3.40	B
Calvet Claret Yves Barry, Calvet 1994	£ 3.40	B
Ca'vit Trentino Principato Rosso Valdadige 1994	£ 3.40	B
Bulgarian Reserve Cabernet Oriachovitza 1990	£ 3.50	B
Special Reserve Cabernet Sauvignon, Lovico Suhindol 1990	£ 3.50	B
Uvica Merlot, Uvica 1994	£ 3.50	B
Somerfield Cabernet Sauvignon Del Veneto, Pasqua 1994	£ 3.50	B
Valea Meilor Pinot Noir 1990	£ 3.50	B
Sainsburys Jumilla, Agapito, 1994	£ 3.50	B
Brookhollow Red, Brookhollow	£ 3.50	B
Gamay/Syrah Vin De Pays Des Coteaux De L'Ardeche, Les Vignerons Ardechois 1994	£ 3.60	B
KWV Cape Cellars Cabernet Sauvignon, K W V 1992	£ 3.70	B
La Croix Rouge, La Croix 1994	£ 3.70	B
Chateau De Murviel, 1994	£ 3.70	S
Santa Julia Malbec Oak Reserve, La Agricola 1992	£ 3.80	B
Bucklow Hill Dry Red, Southcorp	£ 3.80	B
Cono Sur Cabernet Sauvignon, Cono Sur 1993	£ 3.80	S
Victoria Wine Claret, Calvet	£ 3.80	B
Piccini Rosso Toscano, Piccini 1994	£ 3.80	B
Rabbi Jacob, Sincomar Parlier Et Fermaud	£ 3.80	B
Albor Tinto, Do Rioja, Campo Viejo 1994	£ 3.80	B
Syrah Chais Cuxac, Val d'Orbieu 1993	£ 3.90	S
Cordevino Cabernet Merlot Tre Veneziela, Pasqua 1993	£ 3.90	S
Chamonix Cabernet Sauvignon, Cape Chamonix Wine Farm 1992	£ 3.90	B
Domaine Rochevue 1993	£ 3.90	B

El Dragon Tempranillo, Berberana 1993	£ 3.90	B
Angoves Tea Tree Estate Malbec, 1994	£ 4.00	B
Baden Pinot Noir 1991	£ 4.00	B
Jose Canepa Merlot, Jose Canepa Y Cia 1994	£ 4.00	B
Château Du Capitoul, 1993	£ 4.00	B
Domaine De Coudougne, Terroirs d'Occitanie 1992	£ 4.00	B
Domaine Bassac Syrah, Delhon Frères, 1994	£ 4.00	B
Le Cordon Red, Gabriel Meffre, 1994	£ 4.00	B
Lievland Cabernet Sauvignon 1991	£ 4.00	B
Chianti Villa Selva, Villa Selva 1994	£ 4.00	B
Alianca Bairrada Reserva, Caves Alianca 1991	£ 4.00	B
Tesco Robertson Shiraz/Cabernet, John Worontchak At Madeba	£ 4.00	S
KWV Rouwkes Drift Ruby Cabernet/Merlot, KWV 1992	£ 4.00	B
Stellenzicht Cabernet Sauvignon/Malbec, Stellenzicht 1993	£ 4.00	B
Stellenzicht Cabernet Sauvignon/Shiraz, Stellenzicht 1993	£ 4.00	B
Fuente Del Ritmo Barrel Aged Tempranillo, Bodegas Centro Españolas 1993	£ 4.00	S
Carmen Cabernet Sauvignon, Carmen Vineyards 1993	£ 4.10	B
Domaine De La Louveterie, 1993	£ 4.10	B
Giordano Barbera Del Piemonte, Giordano 1994	£ 4.10	B
Chianti Classico Montecchio, Montecchio 1990	£ 4.10	B
Merlot Chais Cuxac, Val D'orbieu, 1993	£ 4.20	B
Barone Di Turolifi Libecchio Rosso, Barone Di Turolifi 1992	£ 4.30	S
Rioja Glorioso, Bodegas Palaçio, 1991	£ 4.30	B
Vina Alcorta Crianza Tempranillo, Bodegas Campo Viejo, Bodegas Y Bebidas, 1992	£ 4.30	B
Co-op Australian Cabernet Sauvignon, Angoves 1992	£ 4.40	B
Viña Santa Rita 120 Cabernet Sauvignon, Viña Santa Rita 1992	£ 4.40	B
La Serre Cabernet Sauvignon, La Serre 1994	£ 4.40	B
Chais Baumiere Cabernet Sauvignon, Domaine De La Baume, 1993	£ 4.40	B
Chais Baumiere Syrah, Domaine De La Baume 1994	£ 4.40	B
Chais Baumiere Syrah, Domaine De La Baume 1993	£ 4.40	B
Domaine St Eulalie Minervois, Domaine St Eulalie 1992	£ 4.40	B
KWV Cabernet Sauvignon, KWV 1991	£ 4.40	B
Avontuur Pinotage, Avontuur 1994	£ 4.40	S
Penfolds Rawsons Retreat Ruby Cabernet/Cabernet Sauvignon/ Shiraz, Penfolds 1993	£ 4.50	B
Jacob's Creek Shiraz/Cabernet, Orlando Wines 1993	£4.50	B
Saint Chinian Siala, Maurel Vedeau, 1993	£ 4.50	B
Cantina Sociale Miglionico Montepulciano d'Abruzzo 1993	£ 4.50	B
Jose Sousa, Jose Maria Da Fonseca Succs, Jose Maria Da Fonseca Succs 1990	£ 4.50	B
Quinta do Manjapao, Quinta do Manjapao Agricultural Society 1992	£ 4.50	B
Gran Calesa, Costers Del Segre, Raimat, 1990	£ 4.50	S

Oak Aged Tempranillo Rioja, Berberana, 1993	£ 4.50	B
Lagunilla Rioja Crianza, Lagunilla 1988	£ 4.50	B
Los Llanos Reserva, Bodegas Los Llanos S.A., Bodegas Los Llanos S.A. 1990	£ 4.50	S
August Sebastiani Cabernet Franc, Sebastiani Vineyard 1993	£ 4.50	B
Viña Santa Rita 120 Pinot Noir, Viña Santa Rita 1994	£ 4.60	S
Clos l'Envege Côtes de Bergerac, Yves Pages et Associes 1993	£ 4.60	S
Syrah Domaine du Barres, Caroline de Beaulieu, 1993	£ 4.60	S
Trentino Cabernet Sauvignon, Ca'vit Trentino 1992	£ 4.60	B
Tedeschi Valpolicella Classico Superiore, Tedeschi 1991	£ 4.60	B
L A Cetto Cabernet Sauvignon, L A Cetto 1992	£ 4.60	B
Petite Sirah, L A Cetto, 1993	£ 4.60	B
Navarra Agramont Tinto Crianza, Bodegas Principe de Viana 1991	£ 4.60	S
Rioja Tempranillo, Marqués de Griñon, Marqués de Griñon 1992	£ 4.60	S
Undurraga Cabernet Sauvignon, Undurraga 1992	£ 4.70	B
Herdade do Esporao Cabernet Sauvignon, Finagra 1992	£ 4.70	B
First River Cabernet Sauvignon, Eersterivier 1993	£ 4.70	S
Santara Cabernet Merlot, Conca de Barbera, Concavins/Hugh Ryman 1993	£ 4.70	S
Valdemar Vino Tinto, Do Rioja, Martinez Bujanda 1994	£ 4.70	S
Montes Merlot & Cabernet, Discover Wines 1992	£ 4.80	B
Château St Martin Baracan, 1990	£ 4.80	B
Côtes Du Rhone Domaine St Etienne, M Coulcomb 1993	£ 4.80	B
Côtes Du Rhone Domaine Des Moulins, Georges Duboeuf 1994	£ 4.80	S
Stellenvale Cabernet Sauvignon/Shiraz 1990	£ 4.80	B
August Sebastiani Cabernet Sauvignon, Sebastiani Vineyard 1993	£ 4.80	B
Lindemans Bin 45 Cabernet Sauvignon 1993	£ 4.90	B
Casillero Del Diablo Cabernet Sauvignon, Concha Y Toro 1992	£ 4.90	B
Yvecourt Yvon Mau, 1993	£ 4.90	B
Côtes Du Rhone Cuvée Des Capucines, Domaine du Vieux Chene 1992	£ 4.90	B
Copertino Riserva, C S Copertino 1992	£ 4.90	B
KWV Mount Pearl Shiraz, KWV 1990	£ 4.90	B
Rioja Vina Amezola Crianza, Bodegas Amezola de La Mora, Bodegas Amezola De La Mora 1990	£ 4.90	B
Stratford Zinfandel, Stratford	£ 4.90	B
Trapiche Cabernet Sauvignon Reserve 1992	£ 4.90	S
Unduragga Merlot 1994	£ 4.90	B
Nanya Creek Shiraz, Angoves 1993	£ 5.00	B
Rosemount Shiraz/Cabernet Sauvignon, Rosemount 1994	£ 5.00	S
Angoves Nanya Creek Cabernet Sauvignon, Angoves 1993	£ 5.00	B
Angoves Ridgemount Estate Cabernet Sauvignon, Angoves 1992	£ 5.00	B
Tollana Black Label Cabernet Sauvignon, Tollana /Penfolds 1992	£ 5.00	S
Parrots Hill Shiraz, BRL Hardy Wine Co 1992	£ 5.00	B

REDS UNDER £5

Geoff Merrill Cabernet Sauvignon, Geoff Merrill 1990	£ 5.00	S
St Michael Maipo Cabernet Sauvignon Reserve, Carmen Vineyards 1993	£ 5.00	B
Jose Canepa Private Reserve Cabernet Sauvignon, Jose Canepa Y Cia 1992	£ 5.00	S
Collection Anniversaire Reserve Claret, Yvon Mau 1992	£ 5.00	B
M de Montesquieu Rouge, Vins et Domaines 1992	£ 5.00	B
Chateau Laplagnotte Bellevue 1990	£ 5.00	S
Sainsbury's Red Burgundy Pinot Noir, Rodet	£ 5.00	B
Côtes Du Rhone Domaine Dionysus, Gabriel Aligne 1994	£ 5.00	B
Geoff Merrill Cabernet Sauvignon Atesino Barrique Aged,	£ 5.00	B
Villa Pigna Rozzano, Villa Pigna 1992	£ 5.00	B
La Pieve Chianti Rufina Riserva 1985	£ 5.00	S
Stellenzicht Cabernet Sauvignon Block Series 1993	£ 5.00	S
Stellenzicht Merlot Block Series 1993	£ 5.00	B
South Bay Vineyards California Pinot Noir	£ 5.00	B
Vina Albali Valdepenas 1987	£ 5.00	B

Malt House Vintners Obermeister Liebfraumilch, Urbanberger	£ 2.60	B
Frascati Superiore, Cantina Del Bacco, 1994	£ 2.90	B
Tesco Sicilian Dry White, Pellegrino	£ 2.90	B
Ryman Chardonnay, Ryman 1993	£ 3.00	B
De Wet Cape Bay White, De Wet Co-op 1994	£ 3.10	B
Carl Reh Sainsbury Chardonnay, Carl Reh 1994	£ 3.20	B
Chardonnay Hincesti 1992	£ 3.30	B
Hugh Ryman/Penfolds Kirkwood Chardonnay 1994	£ 3.30	B
Jose Canepa Y Cia Sauvignon Blanc 1994	£ 3.40	B
Czech Pinot Blanc, Nick Butler & Mark Nairn, 1994	£ 3.50	B
Terret Chardonnay, J. & F. Lurton, 1994	£ 3.50	B
Vinum Bonum Chardonnay, Vinum Bonum 1993	£ 3.50	B
Concilio Atesino Chardonnay, Concilio 1994	£ 3.50	B
Table Bay Early Release Chenin Blanc, Kym Milne, 1995	£ 3.50	S
KMV Rouwkes Drift Chenin 1994	£ 3.60	B
Vin de Pays Des Côtes De Gascogne Domaine Planterieu, Grassa, 1994	£ 3.60	B
Nuragus Di Cagliari, Cantina Sociale Di Dolianova, 1994	£ 3.70	B
Bucklow Hill Dry White, Southcorp	£ 3.80	S
Vouvray Demi-sec, Château Vaudenuits, 1990	£ 3.80	B
St Ursula/Ryman Riesling, 1994	£ 3.80	B
Geoff Merrill Sainsbury's Chardonnay Delle Tre Venezie,	£ 3.80	B
I Frari Bianco Di Custoza, Santi, 1994	£ 3.80	B
Lindemans Cawarra Semillon Chardonnay, Lindemans 1994	£ 3.90	B
Danubiana St Ursula Dunavar Chardonnay, St Ursula 1994	£ 3.90	S
Etchart Torrontes, Bodegas Etchart S A 1994	£ 4.00	B
Santa Julia Chardonnay, La Agricola 1995	£ 4.00	B
Asda South Australia Chardonnay, Angoves 1993	£ 4.00	B
Penfolds Riesling 'bin 202', Penfolds 1994	£ 4.00	B
Sunnycliffe, Deakin Estate Colombard/Chardonnay, 1994	£ 4.00	B
Aurora Early Release White, Aurora 1994	£ 4.00	B
Chapel Down 'SL', 1993	£ 4.00	B
Barkham Manor Kerner, Barkham Manor Vineyard 1992	£ 4.00	B
Santa Lugana 1994	£ 4.00	B
Safeway Bordeaux Oak Aged, Cave de Landerrouat, 1994	£ 4.00	S
Fortant De France Chardonnay, Skalli Fortant De France 1994	£ 4.00	B
Domaine De La Hallosiere Chardonnay, Les Vignerons De La Noelle, 1994	£ 4.00	B
Sancerre Gue d'Argent, Domaine Serge Laloue 1993	£ 4.00	B
Château Miraval Vin Blanc, Château Miraval 1993	£ 4.00	B
Gabriel Meffre Galet Vineyards Chardonnay, 1994	£ 4.00	B
St Michael Rudesheimer Rosengarten, Franz Reh 1993	£ 4.00	B
Chapel Hill Barrique Aged Chardonnay, Balaton Boglar 1993	£ 4.00	B
Lenotti Bianco di Custoza, Lenotti 1994	£ 4.00	S

Stellenzicht Chardonnay, Stellenzicht 1994	£ 4.00	B
Santara Chardonnay, Conca de Barbera, Concavins/Hugh Ryman 1994	£ 4.00	B
Kings Canyon Sauvignon Blanc, H Ryman / Arciero Winery, 1994	£ 4.00	S
Caliterra Chardonnay, Viña Caliterra 1994	£ 4.10	S
Caliterra Sauvignon Blanc, Viña Caliterra, 1995	£ 4.10	B
Le Piat de Chardonnay Vdp, Piat Père Et Fils 1994	£ 4.10	B
Wynns Coonawarra Estate Riesling, Wynns 1994	£ 4.20	B
Katnook Estate , Red Cliffs Estate Colombard Chardonnay, 1992	£ 4.20	B
Jose Canepa Chardonnay, 1994	£ 4.20	S
Langenbach Wonnegau Auslese, Langenbach 1992	£ 4.20	S
St Michael Domaine Virginie Mandeville Chardonnay, 1994	£ 4.30	B
Chais Baumière Sauvignon Blanc, Domaine De La Baume, 1994	£ 4.30	B
De Martino Sauvignon Blanc, Santa Ines, 1995	£ 4.40	S
Domaine De La Baume Chais Baumiere Chardonnay 1994	£ 4.40	B
Chardonnay Del Piemonte, Araldica 1993	£ 4.40	B
Sauvignon - Lurton, J & F Lurton, 1994	£ 4.40	B
Marienberg Chardonnay, Marienberg 1993	£ 4.50	B
Penfolds Rawson's Retreat 'Bin 21' Semillon Chardonnay, 1994	£ 4.50	S
Santa Carolina Sauvignon Blanc, Santa Carolina 1995	£ 4.50	B
Chateau La Jalgue Cuvee Prestige, Ginestet, 1993	£ 4.50	B
Laperouse, Vin De Pays d'Oc Penfolds & Val d'Orbieu, 1994	£ 4.50	B
Domaine De La Baume Philippe De Baudin Chardonnay, 1993	£ 4.50	B
Sauvignon, Philippe De Baudin, Hardy's 1994	£ 4.50	B
Semeli White, G & A Kokotos, 1994	£ 4.50	B
Neethlingshof Gewürztraminer, Neethlingshof 1994	£ 4.50	B
Cape View Chardonnay Sur Lie, K Milne 1994	£ 4.50	B
Vdp d'Oc Chardonnay Boise, Maurel Vedeau 1994	£ 4.60	B
Villa Fontana, Fontana Candida, 1992	£ 4.60	B
Chardonnay, Domaine Virginie, 1994	£ 4.70	S
Glen Ellen Proprietor's Reserve Chardonnay, Glen Ellen 1993	£ 4.70	S
Shawsgate Muller Thurgan/Seyral 1993	£ 4.75	B
Soave Classico, Tedeschi, 1993	£ 4.80	B
Undurraga Chardonnay 1994	£ 4.85	S
Pinot Blanc, Domaine J Riefle, 1993	£ 4.90	B
Cortese Alasia, Araldica, 1994	£ 4.90	B
Thorncroft Dry 1992	£ 4.95	B
Avontuur Le Chardon, Avontuur 1992	£ 5.00	S
Tesco Clare Valley Riesling, Mitchell 1994	£ 5.00	P
Tollana Black Label Chardonnay, Penfolds 1993	£ 5.00	B
Penfolds Semillon Chardonnay, Penfolds 1994	£ 5.00	S
Villard Aconcagua Sauvignon Blanc, Villard Fine Wines 1994	£ 5.00	B
Viña Santa Rita, Reserva Sauvignon Blanc, Viña Santa Rita 1994	£ 5.00	S
Jose Canepa Private Reserve Chardonnay, Jose Canepa Y Cia 1994	£ 5.00	P

Tokay Pinot Gris Clos de Hoen, Cave Vinicole de Beblenheim, 1994	£ 5.00	B
Chateau Haut Mazieres Blanc, 1992	£ 5.00	B
Chateau Haut Mazieres Blanc, 1993	£ 5.00	B
St Michael Mandeville Viognier, Domaine Virginie, 1994	£ 5.00	S
Chapel Hill Barrique Chardonnay, Balaton Boglar 1994	£ 5.00	B
Lugana Cru Villa Flora, Zenato, 1994	£ 5.00	B
Corbans Cooks Chardonnay, Corbans 1994	£ 5.00	B
Montana Kaituna Hills Sauvignon Blanc, Montana 1994	£ 5.00	S
Stoney Brook Chardonnay, Stoney Brook Vineyards 1993	£ 5.00	B

Moscato d'Asti, Araldica, 1994	£ 3.70	B
Co-op Sparkling Liebfraumilch, Rudesheimer Weinkellerei, 1992	£ 4.20	B
Moscato Spumante 'Regional Classics' Santero	£ 4.50	B
Asda Asti, Capetta	£ 4.50	B
Borelli Asti, Fratelli Martini	£ 4.70	B
Il Grigio Spumante, Collavini, Casa Vinicola E Collavini	£ 4.70	B
Co-op Asti Spumante, Fratelli Martini	£ 4.80	B
Malt House Vintners Asti Spumante, Santero	£ 4.90	S
Asti Spumante, Sperone	£ 5.00	B
Seppelt Great Western Rosé, Seppelt & Sons	£ 5.30	B
Vouvray Brut, Didier Champalou	£ 6.00	B
Martini Brut Special Cuvée, Martini & Rossi	£ 6.50	S
Mondoro Asti, Barbero, 1994	£ 6.50	B
Tanners Cava Brut	£ 6.50	B
Cava Conde De Caralt Blanc De Blancs, Conde De Caralt	£ 6.60	B
Sainsbury"s Madeba Brut, Graham Beck	£ 6.80	B
Tradition Brut Carte d'Or, Charles De Fère, Villiera	£ 7.00	S
Seppelt Pinot Rosé, Seppelt	£ 7.10	B
Crémant De Bourgogne Brut, Denis Fouquerand, 1992	£ 7.30	S
Crémant De Bourgogne Blanc De Blancs, Denis Fouquerand,1992	£ 7.50	S
Champagne De Nauroy Black Label N V, De Nauroy	£ 7.50	S
Sparkling Vouvray Brut, Chateau Moncontour, 1992	£ 7.50	S
Cuvée De l'Ecusson, Bernard Massard	£ 7.80	B
Cuvée One Pinot Noir Chardonnay, Yalumba	£ 8.10	B
Taltarni Brut Tache, Taltarni	£ 8.20	B
Saumur Brut, Bouvet Ladubay	£ 8.20	B
Mayerling Brut Crémant d'Alsace, Cave De Turckheim	£ 8.30	B
Champagne Ellner, Marquis d'Estrand, Ellner	£ 8.50	B
Crémant De Loire Château Langlois	£ 8.50	B
Seppelt Sparkling Shiraz, Seppelt 1990	£ 8.60	S
Kaapse Vonkel, Simonsig Estate, 1992	£ 9.00	S
Scharffenberger Brut, Scharffenberger Cellars 1987	£ 9.00	S
Cuvée Napa By Mumm Brut	£ 9.00	B
Cuvée Napa By Mumm Rosé	£ 9.00	B
Lessini Durello, Fongaro, 1989	£ 9.30	B

Champagne De Nauroy Black Label N V, De Nauroy	£ 7.50	S
Champagne Ellner, Marquis d'Estrand, Ellner	£ 8.50	B
Champagne Medot Brut NV, Medot et Cie	£ 11.00	B
Andre Simon Champagne Brut, Marne et Champagne	£ 11.20	S
Prince William Champagne, Marne et Champagne	£ 11.80	S
Champagne Medot Brut Reserve NV, Medot et Cie	£ 12.00	B
Champagne Fleury, 1988	£ 12.30	B
Champagne De Clairveaux Brut, Marne et Champagne	£ 12.50	B
Champagne De Telmont Grande Reserve, De Telmont	£ 13.00	B
Champagne Bonnet Prestige, A. Bonnet	£ 13.00	B
Champagne Billiot Cuvee de Reserve Brut, H. Billiot	£ 13.10	S
Champagne Bonnet, Carte Blanche, F. Bonnet	£ 13.50	G
Averys Special Cuvée Champagne, Averys Of Bristol	£ 13.70	S
Champagne H. Blin & Cie	£ 13.90	B
Champagne Oeil De Perdrix, Leonce d'Alba	£ 14.00	B
Champagne Le Brun de Neuville Brut Rosé	£ 14.10	B
Champagne Bonnet Rosé, F. Bonnet	£ 14.20	G
Merchant Vintners' Baron de Beaupré Champagne, Ellner	£ 14.40	B
Champagne Cuvée Reserve Brut, Bouché Père et Fils	£ 14.60	B
Champagne Nicolas Feuillatte Reserve Particuliere Brut 1er Cru	£ 14.60	S
Waitrose Vintage Champagne, F. Bonnet, 1989	£ 14.80	S
Champagne Drappier, Cuvée Speciale, Drappier	£ 15.00	B
Champagne Le Brun De Neuville Cuvée Selection	£ 15.00	S
Champagne Herbert Beaufort	£ 15.00	B
Champagne Duchatel Blanc De Blancs Brut, Alain Thienot	£ 15.00	B
Champagne Jacquart Brut Selection	£ 15.00	S

Every wine in this guide has at least one stockist code beside its entry, identifying where the wine can be sourced. The list below translates the code into the company name, with a telephone number for you to make enquiries direct.

Where the stockists are stated as WIDELY AVAILABLE there are more than 10 outlets who stock this wine. In these cases you should be able to find your wine in most good wine retailers.

Every effort has been made to list all the stockists with their relevant wines. Should you encounter any problems with finding a wine listed in this guide, then please write to: The International WINE Challenge, Publishing House, 652 Victoria Road, South Ruislip, Middlesex, HA4 0SX.

Code	Company	Phone	Code	Company	Phone
A	Asda Stores Ltd	0113 2435435	AWC	Anthony Wine Cellars	0171 722 8576
ABY	Anthony Byrne Fine Wines Ltd	01487 814555	A&A	A & A Wines	01483 274666
ACH	Andrew Chapman Fine Wines	01235 531452	A&N	Army & Navy Store	0171 8341234
ADG	Adgestone Vineyard	01983 402503	B	Benedicts	01983 529596
ADN	Adnams Wine Merchants	01502 727220	BAB	Bablake Wines	01203 228272
AFI	Alfie Fiandaca Ltd	0181 951 1603	BAK	Barkham Manor Vineyard	01825 722103
AG	Amazing Grapes	0181 202 2631	BAS	Black Sea & Russian Wine Co	0171 499 1300
AGR	Agrimar	01959 540000	BBR	Berry Bros & Rudd Ltd	0171 396 9600
AHW	A H Wines	01935 850116	BBV	Breaky Bottom Vineyard	01273 476427
AK	Arriba Kettle & Co	01386 833024	BC	Booker Cash & Carry	01933 371000
ALI	Alivini	0181 880 2525	BEC	Beaconsfield Wine Cellars	01494 675545
ALL	Alliance Wine Co Ltd	01505 506060	BEF	Beaminster Fine Wines	01308 862350
ALS	Albion Wine Shippers	0171 242 0873	BEL	Bentalls of Kingston	0181 546 1001
ALV	A L Vose & Co Ltd	015395 33328	BEN	Bennetts Wine & Spirits Merchants	01386 840392
AMA	Amathus	0181 886 3787	BES	Bestway Cash & Carry	0181 453 1234
AMD	Amadio Import	0171 724 3480	BFI	Bedford Fine Wines Ltd	01234 721153
AMP	Amps Fine Wines	01832 273502	BGD	Bottle Green	0113 243 1691
AMW	Amey's Wines	01787 377144	BH	B H Wines	01228 576711
ANM	Andrew Mead Wines	01547 560268	BI	Bibendum Wine Ltd	0171 722 5577
ASH	Ashley Scott	01244 520655	BIF	Buongiorno Italia Foods (UK) Ltd	01942 604234
AUC	Australian Wine Centre	01753 544546	BIL	Billecart Salmon (UK)	01932 224758
AUL	Auldman Stewart	0181 871 5217	BIN	Bin 89 Wine Warehouse	0114 275 5889
AUS	Australian Wineries	01372 274065			
AV	Averys of Bristol	01275 811100			
AVA	Ava Wines	01247 465490			

BKW	Berkeley Wines	01925 444555	
BLN	Belloni	0171 704 8812	
BLS	Balls Brothers Ltd	0171 739 6466	
BN	Bin Ends	01709 367771	
BNK	The Bottleneck	01843 861095	
BOD	Bodegas Direct	01243 773474	
BOO	Booths of Stockport	0161 432 3309	
BOS	Boschendal Estate Wines		
		0171 703 3568	
BSE	The Barrel Selection Agencies		
		01383 872238	
BTH	Booths	01772 251701	
BU	Bottoms Up	01707 328244	
BUC	Buckingham Vintners	01753 521336	
BUD	Budgens	0181 961 4600	
BUM	Bumblebee Wholefoods	0171 607 1936	
BUT	The Butlers Wine Cellar	01273 698724	
BVL	David Burns Vintners Ltd		
		01202 823411	
BWC	Berkmann Wine Cellars Ltd/Le Nez		
	Rouge	0171 609 4711	
BWI	Bute Wines	01700 502730	
BWL	Berkeley Wines Ltd	0181 683 0494	
BWS	The Barnes Wine Shop	0181 878 8643	
BYV	Byron Vintners	01159 704682	
B&B	Bottle & Basket	0181 341 7018	
CAG	Castang Wine Shippers	01503 220359	
CAP	Cape Province Wines	01784 451860	
CAR	C A Rookes Wine Merchants		
		01789 297777	
CAS	Castel Courtioux	01963 371095	
CAV	Cavendish House	01242 521300	
CAX	Caxton Tower	0181 758 4500	
CC	Chiswick Cellar	081 994 7989	
CD	Camisa Delicatessen	0171 437 7610	
CDE	Cote D'Or Wines	0181 998 0144	
CDM	Caves de la Madeleine	0171 736 6145	
CEB	Croque en Bouche	01684 565612	
CEN	Centurion Vintners	01453 763223	
CFT	Clifton Cellars	0117 973 0287	
CGW	The Cote Green Wine Company		
		0161 426 0155	
CHF	Chippendale Fine Wines		
		01943 850633	
CHH	Charles Hennings	01798 872485	
CHL	Chateau Lascombes	0181 661 0155	
CKB	Cockburn & Campbell	0181 874 0142	
CLP	Clapham Cellars	0171 978 5601	
CLS	Clissold Wines	0171 254 5269	
CNL	Connolly's (Wine Merchants) Ltd		
		0121 236 9269	
COE	Coe of Ilford Ltd	0181 551 4966	
COK	Corkscrew Wines	01228 43033	
COM	Compagnie du Vin	01334 840376	
CPW	Christopher Piper Wines Ltd		
		01404 814139	
CRL	The Wine Centre/Charles Steevenson		
	Wines	01822 615985	
CRM	Cravens	0171 723 0252	
CRS	Cooperative Retail Services		
		0161 832 8152	
CS	County Stores (Somerset)		
		01823 272235	
CT	Charles Taylor Wines	01372 728330	
CTH	Charterhouse Wine Co	01775 630680	
CTL	Continental Wine & Food Ltd		
		01484 538333	
CUM	Cumbrian Cellar	01768 863664	
CVR	The Celtic Vintner Limited		
		01792 206661	
CVW	Chiltern Valley Wines	01491 638330	
CVP	Patrice Calvet	01730 816044	
CVY	Chanctonbury Vineyard	01903 892721	
CVZ	Casa Vinicola Zonin	01737 351630	
CWI	(Pigs n' Piglets)	01558 650671	
CWL	Charles Wells Ltd	01234 272766	
CWM	Cornwall Wine Merchants Ltd		
		01209 715765	
CWS	The Co-operative Wholesale Society		
		0161 827 5925	
CWW	Classic Wine & Spirits	01244 288444	
C&A	Chennell & Armstrong Ltd/Griersons		
		01904 647991	
C&B	Corney & Barrow Ltd	0171 251 4051	
C&H	Cairns & Hickey	01132 6737465	
D	Davisons Wine Merchants		
		0181 681 3222	
3D	3D Wines	01205 820745	
DAM	Damis Agencies	01235 512278	
DBS	Denbies Wine Estate	01306 876616	
DBW	David Baker Wines	01656 650732	
DBY	D Byrne & Co	01200 23152	
DD	Domaine Direct	0171 837 1142	

DEL	Delicatessen Shop NW3	0171 435 7315
DIO	Dionysus	0181 874 2739
DIR	Direct Wine Shipments	01232 238700
DIT	Ditchling Wines	01444 239497
DN	Deinhard	0171 208 2520
DUW	Duncairn Wine Stores	01232 238700
DVC	De Ville & Co	0171 200 1801
DVI	Dartmouth Vintners	01803 832602
DVY	Davy & Co Ltd	0171 407 9670
DWI	Dedicated Wine Importers	
		01865 400330
DWS	Freixenet	01707 265532
D'A	D'Arcys	01412 264309
D&D	D&D Wines	01565 650952
EBA	Ben Ellis & Associates Ltd	
		01737 842160
ECA	Edward Cavendish & Sons Ltd	
		01794 516102
ECK	Eckington Wines	01246 433213
EE	Eaton Elliot Wine Merchant	
		01625 582354
ELV	El Vino	0171 353 5384
EM	Ebury Mathiot Wines	0171 708 0088
EMV	East Mersea Vineyard	01733 270318
ENO	Enotria Wines Cellars	0181 961 4411
EOO	Everton's of Ombersley	0116 2542702
EOR	Ellis of Richmond	0181 943 4033
EP	Eldridge Pope & Co plc	01305 251251
ES	Edward Sheldon	01608 661409
ET	Elliot & Tatham (Fine Wines)	
		0171 351 4008
ETV	Eton Vintners	01753 790197
EUR	Europa Stores Ltd	0181 845 1255
EVI	Evingtons Wine Merchants	
		0116 2542702
EW	Eldergate Wines	01908 607885
EWC	English Wine Centre	01323 870532
EWD	Euro World Wines	0141 649 3735
EWG	European Wine Growers	01524 701516
EX	Exmouth Wines	0171 278 8457
FAL	Falcon Vintners	0171 388 7055
FAR	Farr Vintners Ltd	0171 828 1960
FBG	Food Brands Wine Agencies	
		0171 978 5300
FDL	Findlater Mackie Todd & Co Ltd	
		0181 543 7528
FEN	Fenwick Ltd	0191 232 5100
FFR	F W Francis & Co	01483 502590
FFW	Farthinghoe Fine Wine & Food	
		01295 710018
FLM	Ferrers le Mesurier	01832 732660
FNZ	Fine Wines of New Zealand Ltd	
		0171 482 0093
FOZ	Fozard Wines UK	01625 528900
FRI	Friarwood Ltd	0171 736 2628
FRV	The Four Vintners	0171 739 7335
FS	Francis Stickney Fine Wines	
		0181 201 9096
FSW	Frank E Stainton	01539 731886
FTH	Forth Wines Ltd	01577 863668
FUL	Fuller Smith & Turner	0181 996 2000
FVM	FVM International	01453 860881
FW	FWW Wines (UK)	0181 786 8161
FWF	French Wine Farmers Ltd	
		0171 486 4811
FWM	Fields Wine Merchants	0171 589 5753
F&M	Fortnum & Mason	0171 734 8040
G	Gateway Foodmarkets	0117 9359359
GA	Guy Anderson Wines	01252 711196
GAR	Garland Wines	01372 275247
GBA	Georges Barbier	0181 852 5801
GDS	Garrards Wine Merchants	
		01900 823592
GEL	Gelston Castle Fine Wines	
		01556 503012
GER	Gerry's Wines & Spirits	0171 734 2053
GH	Goedhuis & Co Ltd	0171 793 7900
GHL	George Hill Ltd of Loughborough	
		01509 212717
GI	Grape Ideas	01865 791313
GMV	GM Vintners	01872 79680
GNW	The Great Northern Wine Co	
		0113 2461200
GON	Gauntleys of Nottingham	
		0115 941 7973
GRB	Granby Wines	01582 767910
GRI	Griersons	0181 459 8011
GRO	Grog Blossom	0171 794 7808
GRP	G R Pickard	01484 428526
GRT	Great Western Wine Company	
		01225 448428
GS	Gerald Seel	01925 819695
GSH	The Grape Shop	0171 924 3638
GSJ	Grants of St James's	0181 878 3777

GTA	Grand Terroir Associes	0171 584 9274
GWC	Greek Wine Centre	0181 888 0139
GWI	General WIne Company	01428 722201
GWM	Guildford Wine Market	01483 575933
G&J	G & J Greenall	01925 650111
G&M	Gordon & Macphail	01343 545111
HA	Haughton Agencies	01502 724488
HAD	Hadleigh Wine Cellars	01473 280275
HAE	Halewood International	0151 480 8800
HAG	The Hanwood Group	01455 556161
HAL	Hall Batson & Co	01603 415115
HAM	Hampden Wine Co	01844 201641
HAR	Harrods Ltd	0171 730 1234
HBJ	Heyman Barwell Jones	0171 730 0324
HBV	High Breck Vintners	01420 562218
HC	The Haslemere Cellar	01428 645081
HCK	Pierre Henck Wines	01902 751022
HD	Hollywood & Donnelly	01232 799335
HDL	Alexander Hadleigh	01489 885959
HDR	HDRA	01203 303517
HHC	Haynes Hanson & Clark	01711259 0102
HHR	H & H Ryman	01455 559384
HLV	Halves Ltd	01584 877866
HN	Harvey Nichols	0171 235 5000
HOH	House of Hallgarten	01582 22538
HOL	Holland Park Wine Co	0171 221 9614
HOT	House of Townend	01482 326891
HOU	Hoult's Wine Merchants	01484 510700
HR	Howard Ripley	0181 360 8904
HRV	Harrison Vintners	0171 236 7716
HS	Hilbre Scatchard Ltd	0151 236 6468
HSL	Hanslope Wines	01908 510262
HST	Heath Street Wine Co	0171 435 6845
HV	Hidden Spring Vineyard	01435 812640
HV	John Harvey & Sons	0117 927 5000
HVW	Helen Verdcourt	01628 25577
HW	Hedley Wright & Co	01279 506512
HWL	Howells of Bristol	01454 294085
HWM	Harvest Wine Group	01734 344290
HWW	High Weald Winery	01622 850637
H&D	Hicks & Don	01258 456040
H&H	Hector & Honorez Wines Ltd	
		01480 861444
IH	Ian G. Howe	01636 704366
IRV	Irvine Robertson Wines Ltd	
		0131 553 3521
IVY	Ivy Wines	01243 370280

IWS	International Wine Services	
		01494 680857
JAG	J A Glass	01592 651850
JAR	John Armit Wines	0171 727 6846
JAV	John Arkell Vintners	01793 823026
JCK	J C Karn	01242 513265
JEF	John E Fells & Sons Ltd	
		0181 749 3661
JEH	J E Hogg	0131 556 4025
JFD	York House Wines	01273 735891
JFE	James Fearon Wines Ltd	01248 370200
JFR	John Frazier Ltd	0121 704 3415
JMC	James E McCabe	01762 333102
JN	James Nicholson Wine Merchant	
		01396 830091
JOB	Jeroboams	0171 823 5623
JOH	John Liddington Ltd	01788 573751
JS	J Sainsbury Plc	0171 921 6420
JSN	John Sarson & Son	0116 289 1010
JUS	Just-in-Case	01489 892969
JWL	J W Lees and Co	01616 432487
J&B	Justerini & Brooks Ltd	0171 493 8721
KEL	John Kelly	01937 842965
KF	Kiwi Fruits	0171 930 4587
KOU	Kourtakis	01734 712629
KS	Kwiksave	01745 887111
LAH	Lamberhurst Vineyards	01892 890286
LAV	Les Amis du Vin	0181 451 0981
LAY	Laytons Wine Merchants Ltd	
		0171 388 5081
LCC	Landmark Cash & Carry Ltd	
		0181 863 5511
LEA	Lea & Sandeman Ltd	0171 376 4767
LES	C R S Ltd - Leos	0161 832 8152
LKN	Luckins	01371 872839
LLS	Lolonis Winery	0171 437 1428
LOL	Louis Latour Ltd	0171 409 7276
LON	Longridge Wines	0181 543 2211
LR	CLR	01372 468571
LS	Laurence Smith & Son	0131 667 3327
LTW	Littlewoods Organisation plc	
		0151 235 2222
LU	Luigi's Delicatessen	0171 352 7739
LUK	Lorch Schilling UK	01502 501159
LUV	Luvians/The Bottle Shop	01334 654820
LV	La Vigneronne	0171 589 6113
LW	Lurgashall Winery	01428 707292

LWE	London Wine Emporium Ltd	
		0171 587 1302
LWL	The Wine Business	0171 351 6856
LYN	Lyndhurst Wines	01703 282237
L&S	Laymont & Shaw Ltd	01872 70545
L&W	Lay & Wheeler Ltd	01206 764446
M6	M6 Cash & Carry (Blackburn) Ltd	
		01254 582290
MAK	Makro Self Service Wholesalers Ltd	
		0161 707 1585
MAR	Marco's Wines	0181 871 4944
MAY	F & E May Ltd	0171 405 6249
MBL	Marybelle UK	01892 525733
MCC	MCC Vintners	0141 647 4774
MCO	Malcolm Cowen Ltd	0181 965 1937
MD	Michael Druitt	0171 703 3568
MER	Harvey Mercer	01423 869089
MFL	Murrayfield Wines	0131 539 7718
MG	Matthew Gloag & Son	01738 621101
MHC	Manor House Wine Merchants	
		01446 775591
MHV	Malt House Vintners	01933 371000
MHW	Mill Hill Wines	0181 959 6754
MIT	Mitchells of Lancaster (Brewers) Ltd	
		01524 63773
MJW	Michael Jobling Wines	0191 261 5298
MK	McKinley Vintners	0181 671 7219
MLG	Milligans of Leeds	0113 266 8761
MM	Michael Menzel Wines	0114 268 3557
MMW	Maurice Mason Wine Services Ltd	
		0181 841 8732
MOK	Middlemas of Kelso	01573 224471
MON	Mondial Wines	0181 335 3455
MOR	Moreno Wine Importers	0171 723 6897
MPA	Marketplace	01225 783007
MRF	Mark Reynier Fine Wines Ltd	
		0171 978 5601
MRN	Wm Morrison Supermarkets	
		01924 821234
MRS	Morrisons	01274 494166
MRT	Martinez Fine Wine	01943 603241
MS	Malpas Stallard	01905 23127
MST	Manstree Vineyard	01392 832218
MTL	Mitchells Wine Merchants Ltd	
		0114 274 5587
MVN	The Merchant Vintners	
	Co Ltd	01482 329443

MW	Menai Wines	01248 681568
MWL	Manwood Wines Ltd	01565 654781
MWS	Midhurst Wine Shippers	01730 812222
MWW	Majestic Wine Warehouses	
		01923 816999
MYL	Myliko International	0120 439 2222
MYS	Mayor Sworder & Co Ltd	
		0171 735 0385
MZ	Mentzendorff & Co	0171 415 3200
M&C	Moet & Chandon	0171 235 9411
M&S	Marks & Spencer plc	0171 268 8580
M&V	Morris & Verdin Ltd	071 357 8866
NAD	Nadder Wines	01722 325418
NBV	Nutbourne Manor Vineyard	
		0171 627 3800
ND	Neville Dennis Wines	01782 615616
NET	Nethergate Wines	01787-277244
NI	Nobody Inn	01647 252394
NIC	Nicolas UK Ltd	0171 436 9338
NRW	Noble Rot Wine Warehouse Ltd	
		01527 575606
NSV	Northbrook Springs Vineyard	
		01489 892659
NUR	Nurdin & Peacock Ltd	0181 946 9111
NUM	Vinum Austria	01234 822718
NVN	Nevins	01744 24841
NY	Noel Young Wines	01223 844744
N&P	Nickolls & Perks Ltd	01384 394518
OAT	Oatley Vineyard	01278 671340
OBC	The Old Butcher's Wine Cellar	
		01628 810606
OCL	Olga Catering Ltd	0181 205 3669
OD	Oddbins Ltd	0181 944 4400
OHI	Oakhouse Wine Co	01584 810850
OPW	Old Parsonage Wines	01684 310124
ORG	The Organic Wine Co Ltd	
		01494 446557
OWS	Olsen Wine Shippers	0171 610 2829
OXB	Oxberry Wine Co	01725 518771
P	Parfrements	01203 503646
PAG	Pagendam Pratt & Partners Ltd	
		01937 844711
PAM	Pampas UK Ltd	01707 393015
PAT	Patriarche UK Ltd	0171 381 4016
PAV	Pavilion Wine Co	0171 628 8224
PCE	Pacific Coasters Enterprises Ltd	
		01329 285013

PEC	Pechiney UK Ltd	01753 522800
PEP	Peppercorn Wholefoods	0171 4311251
PEY	Philip Eyres Wine Merchant	
		01494 433823
PF	Percy Fox & Co Ltd	01279 633691
PGR	Patrick Grubb Selections	01869 340229
PHI	Philglas & Swiggot	0171 924 4494
PIC	Le Picoleur	0171 402 6920
PIM	Pimlico Dozen Ltd	0171 834 3647
PLA	Playford Ros Ltd	01845 526777
PLE	Peter Lehmann Wines (UK) Ltd	
		01227 731353
PMR	Premier Wine Warehouse	
		0181 866 7888
PO	Peter Osborne	01491 612311
POM	Pomona Wines	01634 235658
PON	Le Pont de la Tour	0171 403 2403
POP	The Pipe of Port	01702 614606
POR	Portland Wine Company	
		0161 962 8752
PST	Penistone Court Wine Cellars	
		01226 766037
PTR	Peter Green & Co	0131 229 5925
PUG	Pugsons of Buxton	01298 77696
PV	Prestige Vintners	01264 335586
P&R	Peckham & Rye	0141 3344312
QR	Quellyn Roberts Wine Merchants	
		01244 310455
R	R S Wines	01179 631780
RAC	Rackham's Dept Store	0121 236 3333
RAE	Raeburn Fine Wines	0131 332 5166
RAM	The Ramsbottom Victuallers Co Ltd	
		01706 825070
RAV	Ravensbourne Wine	0181 692 9655
RB	Richard Banks & Co	01225 310125
RBS	Roberson Wine Merchant	
		0171 371 2121
RD	Reid Wines (1992) Ltd	01761 452645
RDW	Rodney Densem Wines	01270 623665
REM	Remy & Associates	01491 410777
REN	Renvic Wines	01763 852470
RES	La Reserve	0171 978 5601
REY	Raymond Reynolds Ltd	01663 747040
RH	Rodney Hogg Wines	01933 317420
RHE	Rheinberg Kellerai	
RHV	Richard Harvey Wines	01929 480352
RIC	Richard Granger (Personal Wine	

	Merchant)	0191 281 5000
RIV	Riverside Wines	01823 324412
RM	Robert Mendelsohn	0181 455 9895
RML	Richard Mallinson	01256 770397
ROB	T M Robertson & Son	0131 229 4522
ROD	Rodney Densem Wines	01270 623665
ROI	Robin Oxford Int'l	01844 213822
ROV	Rouvinez Vins	01494 673615
RR	Robert Rolls	0171 248 8382
RTW	The Rose Tree Wine Co	01242 583732
RUI	Ruinart UK	0171 416 0592
RW	Richards Walford	01780 460451
RWI	Real Wine Co	01926 470094
RWC	Rioja Wine Corp Ltd	01824 703407
RWV	Rawlings Voigt Ltd	0171 403 9269
RWW	Richmond Wine Warehouse	
		0181 948 4196
R&I	Russell & McIver Ltd	0171 735 0385
S	S Wines	0171 351 1990
SAC	Le Sac a Vin	0171 381 6930
SAF	Safeway Stores plc	0181 848 8744
SAL	S A Wines	01732 780110
SAS	Sherston Wine Company (St Albans)	
		01727 858841
SAV	Sava Centre	01734 778000
SB	Sainsbury Brothers	01392 460481
SD	Scatchard Ltd	0151 236 6468
SEA	House of Seagram	0171 200 1801
SEB	Sebastopol Wines	01235 850471
SEL	Selfridges	0171 629 1234
SG	Stevens Garnier	01865 791313
SHA	Shawsgate Vineyard	01728 724060
SHB	Shaws of Beaumaris	01248 810328
SHG	Wine Shop on the Green	
		01437 766864
SHJ	S. H. Jones & Co Ltd	01295 251177
SHR	Sharpham Vineyards	01803 732203
SK	Seckford Wines	01206 262681
SKA	Skalli Fortant de France	0171 610 2898
SMF	Somerfield	0117 935 9359
SMV	St Martins Vintners	01273 777744
SOB	Stones of Belgravia	0171 2351621
SOH	Soho Wine Supply	0171 636 8490
SOM	Sommelier Wine Co	01481 721677
SP	St Paul's Wine Co	0121 378 1280
SPR	Spar Landmark Ltd	0181 863 5511
SSM	Stewarts Supermarkets	01232 704434

STA	Staple Vineyards	01304 812571
STB	Stokes Brothers (UK) Ltd	01303 252178
SU	Susser Ltd	0181 455 4336
SUM	Summerlee Wines Ltd	0181 997 7889
SV	Smedley Vintners	01462 768214
SW	Schuler Wine Ltd	01800 890 330
SWS	Stratford's Wine Shippers & Merchants	01628 810606
S&D	Saltmarsh & Druce	01993 703721
S&J	Simpkin & James	0116 262 3132
S&W	Superfood & Wines	0181 290 0077
TAN	Tanners Wines Ltd	01743 232400
TBW	Talbot Wines	0121 744 5775
TDS	Thresher Drink Stores	01707 328244
TDV	Todd Vintners	01795 532206
TF	Est Chevalier et Chateau de Chambert	0171 813 3482
TH	Thresher Wine Shops	01707 328244
THO	Thorncroft Vineyard	01732 372406
THP	Thos Peatling	01284 755948
TMW	The Moffat Wine Shop	01683 220554
TO	Tesco Stores plc	01992 632222
TOJ	Tony Jeffries Wines	01604 22375
TOS	Trumps of Sidmouth	01395 512446
TP	Terry Platt Wine Merchant	01492 592971
TPW	Topsham Wines	01392 874501
TRO	Trout Wines	01264 781472
TW	Thames Wine Sellers	0171 928 8253
TWC	The Wine Cellar	01329 822733
T&T	Thierry's Wine Services	01794 515500
T&W	T & W Wines	01842 765646
U	Unwins Wine Merchants	01322 272711
UBC	Ubiquitous Chip	0141 334 5007
UWM	United Wine Merchants Ltd	01232 231231
VAU	Vaux Breweries Ltd	0191 567 6277
VD	Vins Direct	01534 482322
VDP	Vinhos de Portugal (UK) Ltd	01865 791315
VDV	Vin du Van	01233 758 727
VER	Vinceremos Wines & Spirits Ltd	0113 243 1691
VEX	Vinexports Ltd	01886 812555
VIC	Vica Wines	01273 477132
VIL	Village Wines	01322 558772
VIW	Vintage Wines	0115 947 6565
VLW	Villeneuve Wines Ltd	01721 722500
VR	Vintage Roots	01734 401222
VT	The Vine Trail	0117 942 3946
VTH	Vintage House	0171 4372592
VTS	Vinites UK	0171 924 4974
VW	Victoria Wine	01483 715066
VWC	Victoria Wine Cellars	01483 715066
V&C	Valvona & Crolla Ltd	0131 556 6066
W	Waitrose Ltd	01344 424680
WAC	Waters of Coventry Ltd	01926 888889
WAV	Waverley Vintners Ltd	01738 629621
WAW	Waterloo Wine Co Ltd	0171 403 7967
WBK	W H Brakspear	01491 573636
WBR	Wadebridge Wines	01208 812692
WCA	The Wine Case	0181 297 2656
WCE	Winecellars	0181 871 3979
WCR	Greenalls Cellars	01925 444555
WCH	Winchcombe Wine Merchants	01242 604313
WCO	Coburns of Leese Wine Emporium	0131 346 1113
WDW	Windrush Wines Ltd	01451 860680
WEP	Welshpool Wine Company	01938 553243
WES	Wessex Wines	01308 427177
WF	Wine Finds	01584 875582
WFB	Mildara Blass	0181 947 4312
WG	Wines Galore	0181 858 6014
WGT	Four Vintners	0171 353 7733
WGW	Woodgate Wines	01229 885 637
WH	The Wine House	0181 669 6661
WHC	Whiclar & Gordon Wines Ltd	01372 745000
WHO	Wholefoods of Newport	01239 820773
WIA	Whighams of Ayr Ltd	01292 267000
WIC	Wickham & Co Ltd	01237 473292
WIL	Willoughby's of Manchester	0161 834 6850
WIM	Wimbledon Wine Cellar	0181 540 9979
WIN	The Winery	0171 286 6475
WIW	Women in Wine	0171 582 4319
WKV	Wyken Vineyard	01359 250240
WMK	Winemark Wine Merchant	01232 746274
WOA	Wallaces of Ayr Ltd	01292 262330
WOC	Whitesides of Clitheroe Ltd	01200 22281

WOI	Wines of Interest	01473 215752	WSG	Walter S. Siegel Ltd	01256 701101
WON	Weavers of Nottingham	0115 958 0922	WST	Western Wines	01746 789411
WOO	Wooldings Vineyard	01256 895200	WSO	Wine Society	01438 741177
WOT	Wootton Vineyard	01749 890359	WSV	Wineservice	0181 876 2095
WOW	Wines Of Westhorpe	01283 820285	WSW	Westcliffe Wines	01202 294670
WPL	Wine Portfolio	0171 352 7670	WTL	Whittalls Wines	01922 36161
WR	Wine Rack	01707 328244	WTP	W T Palmer	01865 247123
WRK	Wine Raks	01224 311460	WTR	The Wine Treasury Ltd	0171 730 6774
WRO	Wroxeter Roman Vineyard		WW	Wine World	01923 264718
		01743 350967	WWG	Wigglesworth Wines	01435 813740
WRT	Winerite Ltd	0113 283 7651	WWI	Woodhouse Wines	01258 452141
WRW	The Wright Wine Co	01756 700886	WWN	Wine Winners	01978 364821
WS	Wine Source	01225 783007	WWT	Whitebridge Wines	01785 817229
WSA	Wineshare	01306 742164	YAP	Yapp Brothers	01747 860423
WSC	The Wine Schoppen	0114 236 5684	ZON	Zonin	01737 351630

NOTES ON STOCKISTS

INDEX

INDEX

INDEX

INDEX